The
Future
Academic
Community

THE FUTURE
ACADEMIC
COMMUNITY

CONTINUITY
AND CHANGE

EDITED BY JOHN CAFFREY

AMERICAN COUNCIL ON EDUCATION, WASHINGTON, D.C.

© 1969 by American Council on Education
1785 Massachusetts Avenue, N.W.
Washington, D.C. 20036
Library of Congress Catalog Card No. 72-85883
SBN 8268-1296-1
Printed in the United States of America

CONTRIBUTING AUTHORS

LOUIS T. BENEZET, President, Claremont Graduate School and University Center

MURRAY H. BLOCK, President, Borough of Manhattan Community College

ROBERT BOGUSLAW, Professor of Sociology, Washington University

HOWARD R. BOWEN, President, University of Iowa

GLENN E. BROOKS, Associate Professor of Political Science, Colorado College

HARRY S. BROUDY, Professor of Philosophy of Education, College of Education, University of Illinois

JOHN CAFFREY, Director, Commission on Administrative Affairs, American Council on Education

DOUGLASS CATER, Professor of Public Affairs, Princeton University; formerly Special Assistant to President Lyndon B. Johnson

ROBERT D. CLARK, President, San Jose State College

M. K. CURRY, JR., President, Bishop College

BERTRAM H. DAVIS, General Secretary, American Association of University Professors

BERTRAND DE JOUVENEL, Economist and Writer; Professor, Paris Faculty of Law and Economics

ALBERT W. DENT, President, Dillard University

CONSTANTINOS A. DOXIADIS, President, Doxiadis Associates, and President, Athens Center of Ekistics

LLOYD H. ELLIOTT, President, George Washington University

ALVIN C. EURICH, President, Academy for Educational Development, Inc.

JAMES FARMER, Former Director, Congress of Racial Equality (CORE); Assistant Secretary, U.S. Department of Health, Education, and Welfare (1969–)

JOHN W. GARDNER, Chairman, Urban Coalition; Consultant, Carnegie Corporation of New York; Germeshausen Professor, Massachusetts Institute of Technology

LINCOLN GORDON, President, Johns Hopkins University

FERREL HEADY, President, University of New Mexico

JOSEPH M. HENDRICKS, Dean of Men, Mercer University

THEODORE M. HESBURGH, C.S.C., President, University of Notre Dame

H. THOMAS JAMES, Dean, School of Education, Stanford University

ROBERT JOHNSTON, Executive Director, United States Student Press Association

ROBERT H. KROEPSCH, Executive Director, Western Interstate Commission for Higher Education

HUGH W. LANE, President, National Scholarship Service and Fund for Negro Students

JOHN W. LEDERLE, President, University of Massachusetts

C. PETER MAGRATH, Dean, College of Arts and Sciences, University of Nebraska; formerly Professor of Political Science, Brown University, and Chairman, Advisory Committee on Student Conduct, Brown University, November 1966–May 1967

MARTIN MEYERSON, President, State University of New York at Buffalo

MALCOLM MOOS, President, University of Minnesota

KERMIT C. MORRISSEY, President, Community College of Allegheny County, Pennsylvania

FRANKLIN D. MURPHY, Chairman of the Board, Times Mirror Company

FRANKLIN PATTERSON, President, Hampshire College

MARTHA PETERSON, President, Barnard College

SAMUEL D. PROCTOR, Professor of Education, Rutgers—The State University; formerly University Dean for Special Projects, University of Wisconsin

ALICE M. RIVLIN, Senior Fellow, The Brookings Institution; formerly Assistant Secretary for Planning and Evaluation, Department of Health, Education, and Welfare

CLARENCE SCHEPS, Executive Vice-President, Tulane University

EDWARD SCHWARTZ, President (1967–68), United States National Student Association; graduate student, Brandeis University

WILLIAM H. SEWELL, Professor of Sociology (formerly Chancellor), University of Wisconsin, Madison; Visiting Scholar, 1968–69, Russell Sage Foundation

ALLAN P. SINDLER, Chairman, Department of Government, Cornell University; Chairman, Commission on the Interdependence of University Regulations and Local, State, and Federal Law, Cornell University, May–November 1967

JOSEPH E. SLATER, President, The Salk Institute

GRESHAM M. SYKES, Director, Administration of Justice Program, College of Law, University of Denver

THEODORE WALLER, President, Grolier Educational Corporation

JOSEPH WHALEY, Graduate of Antioch College; Peace Corps Trainee

LOGAN WILSON, President, American Council on Education

FOREWORD

THE PUBLISHED PROCEEDINGS of educational meetings usually attract attention from relatively few readers and contribute little of significance to the literature of the field concerned. I like to think that the papers presented at the American Council on Education's annual meetings are in the main exceptions to this rule.

My prediction is that the latest in our series, here issued under the title *The Future Academic Community: Continuity and Change,* will find an important place for itself. The subject calls for serious attention now: the shape of things ahead for us depends in no small measure on what we think and do *now* about the structure and function of the academic community. Our 1968 annual meeting was, I have been told repeatedly, one of the liveliest the Council has ever held. In my judgment, the intellectual excitement of those discussions is successfully conveyed in the printed pages of this book, presenting, as it does, contributions of authors from diverse backgrounds and with differing points of view. There is no substitute for the printed word, furthermore, in reaching a much larger group than the sixteen hundred persons who attended the Denver meeting during early October 1968.

Beginning with the papers of the 1964 annual meeting, the Council has published in hardback format a series that includes *Emerging Patterns in American Higher Education* (1965), *The College and the Student* (1966), *Improving College Teaching* (1967), and *Whose Goals for American Higher Education?* (1968), each edited by a member of the Council's executive or program staff. At the time of publication, the Council distributes without charge about 1,500 of the new title to member institutions and associations. In addition, more than 21,000 copies have been purchased. This demand is gratifying in its indication that these books have been and are still being widely read. Also pleasing is the frequency of reference to these volumes in text and footnotes of books and articles about higher education.

Although the five books deal with problems and issues of American higher education during the 1960s, my guess is that they will continue to be read and studied after the current decade has ended. In the years ahead the nature of the challenges that higher education will be called upon to meet will be enlightened by the substance of the papers and discussions made available in these volumes.

LOGAN WILSON, *President*
American Council on Education

PREFACE

CONCERN WITH THE FUTURE is not peculiar to this age, but in this decade there has been increasing interest in studying the future and in developing new techniques of speculation or, as Bertrand de Jouvenel's provocative essays are entitled, *The Art of Conjecture*. In the past two years, many conferences have been held on futures in general and on the future of higher education in particular. The Carnegie Commission on the Future Financing of Higher Education has undertaken a broad program of research into requirements and has already published a much-discussed report.

Among works of general speculation, one may cite *The Year 2000* (Herman Kahn and Anthony J. Wiener); the special summer 1967 issue of *Daedalus*, "Toward the Year 2000"; *Educational Requirements for the 1970s* (Stanley Elam and William P. McLure); *Agenda for the Nation* (Kermit Gordon); *Environment and Change: The Next Fifty Years* (William R. Ewald, Jr.); *Designing Education for the Future* (Edgar L. Morphet and Charles O. Ryan, 3 volumes); and *Campus 1980* (Alvin C. Eurich)—a list by no means complete.

The theme of the American Council on Education's Fifty-first Annual Meeting, in 1968, also the title of this volume, stemmed naturally from the theme of the Council's Fiftieth Annual Meeting, materials from which were published with the title *Whose Goals for Higher Education?* (Charles G. Dobbins and Calvin B. T. Lee).

In planning the 1968 Annual Meeting, the Council asked three presidents (Louis T. Benezet, Howard R. Bowen, and Lloyd H. Elliott), a student (Edward Schwartz), three professors (C. Peter Magrath, Allan P. Sindler, and Bertrand de Jouvenel), and the head of one of the Council's associated members (Alvin C. Eurich) to prepare background papers for discussion by the participants. Thirty-one men and women agreed to serve as members and chairmen of panels to react to the prepared papers; of these, there were eighteen administrators, five faculty members, two students, and six persons from noncollegiate agencies or organizations. All papers and commentaries, with revisions made subsequent to the Annual Meeting, are included in this volume.

The 1968 Annual Meeting benefited from the contribution of a number of speakers from outside the usual boundaries of the academic community.

Constantinos Doxiadis' "Cities in Crisis and the University" and Franklin Murphy's "Some Reflections on Structure" are based on their keynote speeches at the opening general session. James Farmer's "To Be Black and American" is based on his speech at the luncheon session on the first day. John Gardner's "The University and the Cities," presented as the address at the annual banquet, is reprinted here as it appeared in the Winter 1969 issue of *Educational Record*. The titles of most commentaries and speeches are phrases which I selected directly from the text itself.

As the person primarily responsible for organizing the materials for the 1968 meeting, and for the American Council on Education, I wish to thank all those who wrote or spoke the essays in this volume. Members of the Council's Board of Directors and of its Commission on Administrative Affairs made many valuable suggestions. The entire professional staff of the Council gave freely of their time and thoughts in planning the program upon which *The Future Academic Community* is based.

Special thanks are due to those who helped me with the "Predictions for the 1970s" study, especially to the thousands who patiently filled out the questionnaires. Logan Wilson, who suggested the study, generously gave of his aid and counsel. The staff of our Office of Research, especially Alexander W. Astin, Mrs. Janet Liechty, and Robert Panos, provided much appreciated planning and statistical services.

Mrs. Sybil Welden prepared most of the drafts of these essays, and of many revisions, and earned my further gratitude by rendering substantive assistance in planning and organizing the program, beyond the call of usual secretarial duties. Vesta Wine prepared accurate transcripts of several speeches. Appreciation is expressed to Laura Kent for editorial assistance with the commentaries. Olive Mills, of the Council's Publications Division, provided invaluable editorial services for the remainder of the materials and deserves special thanks for her thoroughness and ingenuity in the preparation of all manuscripts for both preliminary and final publication.

JOHN CAFFREY, *Director*
Commission on Administrative Affairs

CONTENTS

I wonder that a soothsayer doesn't laugh
whenever he sees another soothsayer.

Cato, according to Cicero,
De divinatione

JOHN CAFFREY

The Future Academic Community: ?

ALTHOUGH AN IRONIC QUESTION MARK trails the title above, by intention there is no question mark in the title of this volume. Though there are some uncertainties and disagreements about what the future will and should bring, as evidenced in a later paper in this set, there is no serious question that the academic community has a future. There is no easy linguistic device which permits one to attach a question mark unambiguously to a single word, and I will leave it to the reader, as a projective test, to guess which word I have in mind.

Louis Benezet, who deals in his paper with the conference subtitle, explores some of the implications of the notion that the best way to preserve the continuity of valued things and systems is to provide the means for their continuing change. On this point there is a very apt statement by a Japanese architect, Kenzo Tange:

> Tradition itself cannot constitute a creative force. It always has a decadent tendency to promote formalization and repetition. What is needed to direct it into creative channels is a fresh energy which repudiates dead forms and prevents living ones from becoming static. In one sense, for a tradition to live it must constantly be destroyed. At the same time, destruction by itself clearly cannot create new cultural forms. There must be some other force which restrains destructive energy and prevents it from reducing all about it to havoc. The dialectical synthesis of tradition and anti-tradition is the structure of true creativeness.[1]

Creativeness in resolving and even in harnessing the eternal tensions between tradition and anti-tradition, between continuity and change, is not

[1] Tange, "Tradition and Creation in Japanese Architecture," *Katsura* (New Haven, Conn.: Yale University Press, 1960), p. 35.

1

the sole responsibility of any one component of the academic community. As we have witnessed in recent years, these tensions stem both from conflicts between or among these segments and from pressures applied by the nonacademic community—the outsiders.

In some academic circles, one hears voiced a serious uncertainty about the very existence of "a" community, about the meaning of the word "community" itself, and about definitions of and qualifications for membership. Before we can meaningfully ask what "the" academic community must do to ensure, shape, and manage its future, to survive and prosper in spite of fearful pressures and crises, and to continue to merit the support by individuals and agencies to the extent of billions of dollars annually, we could well examine the components of "the" community and their several roles and stakes in a *common* future.

The Core Community Structure

In attempting to draw the not always solid line which separates the insiders from the outsiders, some questions may be more useful than their answers. For example, one simple approach to naming and defining the members of the family is to ask which ones of them could be excluded from the list of insiders without substantially altering the nature or purposes which colleges and universities serve. At the head of the insiders' list one unhesitatingly places the faculty. (A persistent tale in the academic folklore pictures an indignant faculty member, in a discussion of governance, saying sternly, "Sir, the faculty *is* the university!") Second, but not in importance, comes the student body, without which a faculty may exist but not as an institution properly called a college or a university.

In operational terms, these two segments constitute the inner core of the academic community. Exponents of the "free university" (or college) may insist that groups of students can teach themselves, but this is hedging. Sooner or later, someone moves to head the class, and ultimately, by any other name smelling just as sweet, a faculty emerges, as indeed it did historically. The major formal difference is simply professionalism.

Touching the inner core are the administrators and technicians. One may argue that until the nineteenth century the college administrator was simply a principal officer of the faculty, and both faculty and students at times appear to believe that administration is even now a dispensable function. But this is not the year 1800, and the complexity of today's management problems and of the systems devised to solve them, has created a new profession—one of the few important ones, by the way, for which little or no formal training is available. Academic man may regard the academic manager as a necessary evil, but now and in the future he *is* necessary. Together with the administrator, one must include the host of technical and quasi-professional specialists required to operate laboratories, observatories, reactors, libraries, and computer centers, to manage university hospitals, presses, and heating plants, to monitor research and construction contracts, to maintain buildings and grounds, to pay bills and salaries, to raise money, to deal with the public and its government, to schedule football games and buses, to produce television programs, to keep vital records, to housekeep conferences and workshops, to fill out Federal questionnaires, and to put out fires—to name but a partial list.

Also tied to the inner core are the governing boards, whose operational participation is often minimal and periodic, but who bear the undeniable, real, legal burdens of trusteeship. It may be argued that it is unfortunate, or even a legal fiction of no consequence, that our colleges and universities are public corporations—but they are. No one person owns an accredited academic institution, not even a trustee *qua* individual citizen. Nor, in fact, mystical though the concept may seem, do the trustees "own" the institution. Under the charters of both public and private institutions, the trustees, as a group, are responsible to those who granted the charter to see that its purposes are fulfilled. The institution and its property are managed *in trust* in the public interest. Someone must bear this responsibility, and it is impractical to locate it in the public at large. Some may not like this system, but the corporation is a legal, political, and economic creation which is integral in the structure of our present world. Granting the present legal necessity to perform the function of trusteeship in the public interest, one may argue that trustees ought to be chosen in different ways, or that they should represent other constituencies, or that they should do or have as little to say as possible, but the function exists, it is vital, and I suspect that the system which makes the function necessary will be with us for a while—certainly for the foreseeable future.

Within each of these four components of the academic community, there are, of course, some differences—graduate and undergraduate students, tenured faculty and teaching assistants, presidents and bursars. But students have more in common among themselves than they have with faculty, and so on. And, to anticipate a major point, I maintain that these four family members have more in common—or should have—among themselves than they have, in their aggregate, with any other major social institution. No matter what the division of labor, or of responsibility or authority, and regardless of the fights for power, rights, or freedoms by any community member, each one has a stake in the future of the whole community. If this does not survive, in whatever form, then the stake each member has in the interests of his own group becomes meaningless. If any of the four leaves it to the others to ensure or design the future of the whole community or neglects his own responsibility, the whole community will suffer. In my view, such suffering is what we are experiencing now on so many campuses, where we are paying the price in dissension, destruction, or violence for not having thought clearly in the past about the present which was its future.

The structure of the academic community and of many of its institutions is changing, whether we like it or not. Any structure which works is acceptable to a pragmatist. The model of the corporation dominates the scene, but to those who understand its potentials it still is or can be an amazingly flexible and adaptable invention, as witness the great variety of forms it takes, even within the academic system. If in the future we decide to change the model, human ingenuity is the only obstacle. One structure which has occurred to me is that of the five schools of Philosophy of Ancient Greece. One could assign the faculty to The Academy of Plato or to The Lyceum of Aristotle, the students to The Garden, with Epicurus, the governing boards to The Tub, with Antisthenes and his Cynics, and put the administrators out on The Porch with Zeno and his Stoics.

Interdependency of Interests

Regardless of structure or model or hierarchy or modes of governance, these four essential members of the academic community exist because their basic functions exist: To teach, to learn, to serve the teacher and the learner, and to guard the public interest. Putting aside every debate or quibble about *how* these basic functions are best served, the primary responsibility of both present and future academic communities is to understand their community of interest and to assert with unwavering aggressiveness their determination to forge and manage the future, insofar as possible, without serious detriment to any other member of the family. If this community forgets itself and its common stake and destiny, there are powers outside that community who will be only too glad to step in and manage for us.

John W. Gardner has tried to imagine how historians of the future might regard the collapse of this century's civilization. Gardner observes:

> Men can tolerate extraordinary hardship if they think it is an unalterable part of life's travail. But an administered frustration—unsanctioned by religion or custom or deeply rooted values—is more than the spirit can bear. So increasingly men rage at their institutions. All kinds of men rage at all kinds of institutions, here and around the world. Most of them have no clear vision of the kind of world they want to build; they only know that they don't want the kind of world they have.

Looking backward from the twenty-third century, Gardner's envisioned historians make some quotable comments about our times:

> They observed that men came to demand more and more of their institutions—and with greater intransigence. And they noted that the demands for instant performance led to instant disillusionment, for while aspirations leaped ahead, human institutions remained sluggish—less sluggish, to be sure, than at any previous time in history, but still inadequately responsive to human need. . . . Many institutions were designed to obstruct change rather than facilitate it. . . . The institutions were, after all, designed by human beings, and most men most of the time do not want the institutions *in which they themselves have a vested interest* to change. Professors were often cited as an interesting example of this tendency, because they clearly favored innovation in other parts of the society but steadfastly refused to make universities into flexible, adaptive, self-renewing institutions.
>
> . . . They pointed out that 20th century institutions were caught in a savage crossfire between uncritical lovers and unloving critics. On the one side, those who loved their institutions tended to smother them in an embrace of death, loving their rigidities more than their promise, shielding them from life-giving criticism. On the other side, there arose a breed of critics without love, skilled in demolition but untutored in the arts by which human institutions are nurtured and strengthened and made to flourish.

Gardner then concluded his remarks [2] on an almost wistful note but one which, again, seems appropriate to the subject of these papers:

> In short, men must be discriminating appraisers of their society, knowing coolly and precisely what it is about society that thwarts or limits them and therefore needs modification. And so must they be discriminating protectors of their institutions, preserving those features that

[2] Extracts from an address delivered at the spring commencement, Cornell University, 1968. Italics in the original.

nourish and strengthen them and make them more free. To fit themselves for such tasks, they must be sufficiently serious to study their institutions, sufficiently dedicated to become expert in the art of modifying them.

In a community rent internally by pressures for change and squeezed externally by demands for "efficiency," cost-benefit analyses, or simple conformity, it is easy for members to engage in scapegoating. But no one of the four constituencies of the core I have named so far can abrogate its responsibility. If the trustees fail to appoint good men to presidencies and other principal offices, or to approve the changes which must be made and which by law or charter they must approve, or to help in every way to provide the financial support which progress requires; or if the administrators fail to lead and mediate among the powers, external and internal, which harass and sometimes seek to rend the community they serve, or to apply the technology of change to every relevant aspect of their responsibility, or to provide the leadership which furthers wise decisions by all members of the academic community; or if the students neglect their primary responsibility for their own welfare, or their role as learners, or the fact that—even though others may forget it—the academic institution exists primarily for their benefit; or if the faculty forget that without students they are merely scholars, or that change cannot be made without their consent if the essential continuities are to be preserved, or that their responsibility for achievement of the fundamental goal of student learning is at least as great as that of students—if any of these fail, the whole community may not only suffer pain but death. Though the forces of circumstance play their part in shaping the future, one of the sources of man's progress is his unwillingness to cease his struggle to shape that future as much as he can. As Samuel Johnson said, "The future is purchased by the present."

The Present as Prologue

To talk about "the" academic community is not sufficient to create or preserve it. It does not necessarily follow that the existence of common goals and interests creates a community. Presumably, all men desire to live and all nations to survive, and yet members of the world community have not relinquished their right to push mankind toward mutual destruction in war. Residents of our great cities presumably have more in common with each other than with residents of cities in foreign lands, and yet we are torn by strife among neighbors. If, as some partisans maintain, the academic community is a myth, then we had jolly well better *create* that community and turn myth into reality. Militant students, for example, appear to want very much to be truly admitted and recognized as members of this community, and they have pushed beyond the maxim, "If you can't lick 'em, join 'em" to the principle, "If you can't join 'em, wreck 'em." One might paraphrase an honorable old maxim, "If you see that change is inevitable, relax and enjoy yourself." But change is not always relaxing or enjoyable, and so it may be well to consider the possibility that the best response to inevitability is to use the dynamics of change as means to promote benefits to ends common among the members of the academic community.

The sad thing is that so much of the dissension among the presumptive members of the academic community is about means, not ends. Presumably, most members of all sectors want to preserve and enhance what is good, including useful tradition, in higher education. There is an additional complication when the members of the academic community attempt, together or severally, to choose among alternative futures on the basis solely of their own sectional interest. In partisan debate, there is an easy temptation to assume that the confronting parties are monolithic or homogeneous—that all administrators have the same opinion or interest, that all students agree on goals or tactics of protest, that all faculty members are interested in nothing but their own research, that all trustees care only about investments or budgets. In conflict situations, literal or figurative, there is not only a natural tendency for a group to want to close its own ranks but also to perceive other groups as having all the characteristics of their most active, threatening, or adamant minorities.

One may, for example, turn to the writings of Carl Davidson, leading ideologue of Students for a Democratic Society, and note his reference to "the institutions and society we are trying to destroy" and to "the duty of a revolutionary not only to be intolerant of but to actually suppress the anti-democratic activities of the dominant order" and falsely conclude that such neo-Fascist doctrines are typical of all student leaders—or even of all of SDS. When Davidson says of the universities that "Since they are without legitimacy in our eyes, they are without rights," we may be misled into closing our minds to what less extreme student leaders, those in the majority, are saying. (See the paper by Edward Schwartz in this volume.)

Each of the four inner circle components I have named so far not only appears to the other three to be homogeneous but also appears at times to feel that it and it alone stands at the ramparts guarding the realm. The trustees see themselves as wardens of the public interest intervening from on high, with the unquestionable legal authority granted to most governing boards in institutional charters, to demand order. Militant students, some of them, appear to feel that only if they are the dominant faction in the academic community, however broadly or narrowly viewed, can the institution be saved from itself. The faculty, as professional inheritor of the role played by parents, even among the most primitive peoples, sees itself as the critical mass in the academic community. Granted that students can slow an institution down or bring it to a halt, nothing essential about the character of the academic community can be changed unless the faculty consents. And the administrator sees himself as somehow above all factions, impartial, responsible for the *whole* institution, charged with seemingly impossible tasks of balancing forces from within and pressures from without. No one of these four groups can alone "save" them all, build a healthier and more creative community, or determine our future choices.

The often-quoted words of Abraham Lincoln, from his annual message to Congress in December 1862, bear repeating in this context:

> The dogmas of the quiet past are inadequate to the stormy present. The occasion is piled high with difficulty, and we must rise with the occasion. As our case is new, so we must think anew and act anew. We must disenthrall ourselves, and then we shall save our country.

For "country" read "academic community." And for "we" read "all of us—faculty, students, administrators, trustee." As Lincoln went on to say, "No personal significance or insignificance can spare one or another of us. . . . We—even we here—hold the power and bear the responsibility." When Lincoln says, "We cannot escape history," I understand him to mean more than that we cannot change it: we cannot escape having to deal with its consequences. The future cannot be escaped either, and the four principals must somehow manage together to turn need into power to master the future for the common good of the community, to turn hope into viable plans, and to turn the demands for participation into bonds which both preserve and advance higher education. The academic community will exist and serve its historic purpose only if the glossy concept can be translated into constructive patterns of action.

In what John Milton called "the never-ending flight of future days," we shall have to deal with other concepts and components of this abstract entity, the academic community. In one sense, all institutions of higher education, and all of the more than seven hundred voluntary associations of individuals and institutions in higher education, are part of the academic community.

Outside the firm line which can be drawn around the four primary constituents of our community are the groups which may sometimes feel that they are members but which might fail to pass some of the tests of essentiality: the alumni, the parents, the local (geographical) community. Each has a different stake in the vitality of the academic community, which in turn has a stake in their support and good will. One cannot expect the larger public, the outsiders, to comprehend the intricacies of internal struggles to make important changes in higher education while at the same time preserving vital continuities.

Comments from the Past

Crisis is nothing new to higher education. Facing a world which looked at that time as grim as ours today, Edmund E. Day, at his inauguration as president of Cornell University in 1937, in a different but not irrelevant context, made these timely remarks:

> Force is in the field, armed, aggressive, and arrogant. War in some quarters has become so natural a phase of government action that it no longer has to be declared. The outlook for peace-loving peoples is in certain respects most ominous. The life of the university is inevitably affected by this world situation. . . . As a people we are afflicted at times with attacks of unwarranted impatience. Even our leaders sometimes succumb. All through our political and economic life are evidences of the virus of immediacy. . . . Our universities, like our social institutions, suffer at times from too great outside insistence upon quick practical results.

If what President Day said thirty-one years ago sounds as if it had been written today, hearken to Frederick A. P. Barnard, speaking at his inauguration at Columbia College (now University) one hundred and four years ago:

> Within the past twenty or thirty years, our long-tested and successful system of collegiate instruction has . . . been so persistently decried and so seriously menaced as to fill the friends of sound education throughout the country with alarm and to compel them to discuss the whole theory and practice of our higher education with anxious earnestness and by the light of first principles.

For a criticism of the rigidity of response currently criticized by some who strive for changes, it is hard to improve on Henry P. Tappan, an early president of the University of Michigan, speaking one hundred and eighteen years ago:

> We set about putting up the same kind of buildings; we create the same number of professors to teach the same things on the same principles; we get together a few books and some philosophical apparatus; and then we have the same annual commencements, with orations and poems, and the conferring of degrees; and we get under the same pressure of debt and make the same appeals to the public to get us out of it.

Controversy over student codes of conduct and who should make and administer them has been with us for some time. Even Charles William Eliot, speaking at his inauguration at Harvard in 1869, remarked on the matter:

> The petty discipline of colleges attracts altogether too much attention from both friends and foes. It is to be remembered that the rules concerning decorum, however necessary to maintain the high standard of manners and conduct which characterizes this college, are nevertheless justly described as petty.

Many of our internal problems are almost ours alone, and many of our institutions are busy wrestling with them, though sometimes not using all the help which may be available. In this volume, C. Peter Magrath and Allan Sindler describe what happens when faculty, students, and administrators try to work together to improve internal governance. It becomes evident from both papers that the very process of co-participation may be even more valuable than the products of the work—and hence may have to be repeated periodically. Edward Schwartz and Lloyd Elliott examine the problems of changing internal structures and of the applicability of the concepts and practices of political democracy to the academic community. Even if the principle of "One man, one vote" were acceptable to all members of the academic community (and one doubts that it is), the size and complexity of our institutions demand division of labor and high specialization in performance. In addition to searching for ways to improve participation in governance, we are struggling slowly to apply relevant new technology to do what must be done and do it efficiently and well. Alvin Eurich's paper examines some practical ideas which may help in managing the future with improved control and better aim.

In addition to the strains within the academic community—arising from struggles for new modes of governance, for revision of the curriculum and of instructional methods, for the rights and freedoms of faculty and students, for the principle of responsible self-regulation to replace *in loco parentis*, or simply for parking spaces—we are beset with social, political, and economic forces and pressures from outside the community. As Howard Bowen's paper points out, we face severe financial problems now, and they may worsen in the next decade. Pressure from disadvantaged and minority groups, long denied a fair share of the values of higher education, are mounting from without and echoed from within our colleges and universities. Legislative committees of the states demand efficiency, parents and civic groups and editorialists demand that we make students behave differently, business and industry demand that we meet their manpower needs, labor demands a voice in academia, Federal and state funding agencies demand that we make our accounting systems accountable, and the pressures of war and social upheaval create enormous demands on our ingenuity in solving unprecedented problems of research and development. As one college president said recently, "I am so *sick* of the word 'demand'!" But demands must sometimes be acknowledged, and cannot always be waved off. We will not even be able to refute unreasonable or inappropriate ones unless we define and exploit the resources of common strength in common causes and enterprises.

Queries

The alternatives which must be considered now, and the choices which will help determine the future, are of concern to the whole academic community, not just to those few charged with special responsibility for planning. Future-oriented thinking is policy-making. Planning never ends. Only the questions change.
· What are the most pressing needs of higher education in the next decade?
· What resources will be needed to meet these needs, and how will they be found and allocated?
· What national, human goals are relevant to the character of higher education in the next decade?
· What must be the nature of the physical environment of tomorrow's campus?
· What kind of student population—and general citizenry—must higher education serve in the next decade?

- What will be the impact of new technologies which can even now be predicted?
- Of all the factors that determine the character of higher education, which are beyond practical control by the academic community—and which can be controlled?
- What techniques are now available or needed to help educational leaders interpret and manage future developments in higher education?
- What current studies devoted to the future are relevant to the future of the academic community?
- What substantive issues, with foreseeable impacts and effects, must be faced aggressively now, while there are still alternative courses of action?
- What is the optimum contribution that each member of the academic community can make to envisioning and shaping the common future?
- What new approaches to policy-making and planning can be developed within the academic community in order to include both the thinking and the best energies of all concerned?
- What new organizational concepts and structures might be developed to ensure more coherent and creative future-making?

As De Jouvenel points out,[3] we cannot yet or ever touch the future which is being molded now. Yet, as far as the academic community is concerned, Benjamin Franklin's remark about hanging together or hanging separately has never been more apt. The desire for change is better expressed in common future-making than in disputing who is in and who is out—or how far. The future academic community will not be built or preserved by any one of its members alone.

In a community which does not readily permit its leaders—or anyone else—to try to set its future unilaterally, one of the functions of leadership is to try to forecast the probable consequences of aspirations, policies, and plans. It is important that as much as possible of what the future brings be the product of intention. All of us who have a stake in the future of higher education must think carefully what we really want, for, within reasonable limits, we shall probably have—and have to live with—many products of our wishing.

[3] Bertrand de Jouvenel, *The Art of Conjecture* (New York: Basic Books, 1966).

PART 1

PROBLEMS . . .

The university cannot survive as an arena where gladiatorial groups fight to the death, where violent pressures toward reform and unyielding resistance to reform produce either upheaval or paralysis, or both. And it must be recognized that a university is very easy to disrupt. It is held together neither by steel cables nor enforceable laws. All that holds it together normally are good will, tolerance, and a common respect both for reason and for reasonableness. When extremists set about it, these binding threads can be all too readily snapped, unless many courageously make the effort to sustain, protect, and advance the institution in which they have a share and a stake.

From "The University's Integrity and the University Man,"
an address by Robert F. Goheen to new students
at Princeton University, September 22, 1968

Nothing destroyeth authority so much as the unequal and untimely
interchange of power pressed too far and relaxed too much.

Francis Bacon, *Of Empire*

LOUIS T. BENEZET

Continuity and Change: The Need for Both

UNDERTAKING TO WRITE about change and continuity in higher education
ought properly to qualify as hazardous duty. The situation is moving so
fast that description is difficult, analysis virtually impossible.

Reactions of the public to the current college scene are agitated and
diffuse. To be sure, the attention is mainly centered on student uprisings.
Stroll down a campus walk when the students are not demonstrating—
they do still study—and the college, with its tradition of quiet removal,
appears much the same. But other changes are at work within the large,
quiet buildings, changes as momentous and disturbing in their way as
are the traumatic events of student activism.

Seen from the outside some of the most evident changes are:

· New construction continuously going on throughout the academic
  plant.
· Continual ebb and flow of faculty members, both in their professional
  duties and in job turnover.
· Decrease in all-campus functions except for major athletic events,
  commencement, and special convocations.
· Decrease in organized student social life such as proms, official week-
  ends, and the like.
· Increase in news stories of financial crises in both public and private
  institutions as well as in state higher education systems.
· Eclipse of the president as a leadership figure except during campus
  crises.
· Increase in public attention to the impact of national events upon
  higher education, and vice versa.

15

A visitor from Mars would conclude that higher education must be some new social phenomenon to be causing such a stir. For the large majority of Americans, he would be right. Since 1940 the population of the United States has increased by 50 percent; its college enrollment has quintupled. That hard fact alone cannot explain all the disturbances that are going on. On the other hand, both the causes and the effects of such enormous change-by-growth are part of the social dynamics that in the middle third of the twentieth century have brought our nation from adolescence to the strengths and the self-doubting complaints of middle age.

The American university has been trying to keep its head in the midst of mounting stress. Its heritage from British and European antecedents left it too narrow a base from which to absorb all the impacts upon a structure now called on to provide near-universal opportunity for higher education. The ancient university was a world unto itself, ruled by its own guilds and choosing its few inhabitants with utmost reserve. The universe of knowledge which it had been created to preserve was in the main inert, responsive to the scholar's bidding. The products of scholarship did not at once return to make demands upon the scholars. The students at Bologna in the twelfth century may have organized in order to employ professors, but they did so to improve procedures rather than to determine what was to be taught.

Today the universe surrounding the college is live and demanding, permitting no separation of space or time between the outside urgencies of what is going on and the call upon the scholar to take heed.

It seems that time and events have caught up with higher education in America. The situation has been described by Robert Heilbroner in *The Future as History,* in which he notes that America with her gospel of optimism and power to make history has come, during the late twentieth century, to realize that history has placed its own demands upon her. What we will do henceforth will be determined in fair measure by what history expects of us. T. S. Eliot earlier expressed the idea in *Murder in the Cathedral* in a line of Thomas Becket: "Only the fool, fixed in his folly, may think he can turn the wheel on which he turns."

The notion of the university as something that governs its own present and determines its own future dies hard. So long as the university could enroll the select few and serve the restricted aims to perpetuate scholarship and to preserve gentility, self-determination was possible. Now, higher education has passed into the public domain. It has done so not only through its mass enrollments but also through its conscription by government to serve a widening range of national purposes: national defense, the knowledge industry, and, most recently, the equalization of opportunity.

Still the university seeks to keep some continuity with the past if only because knowledge denied history remains no more than a record of current experience. The university seeks to hold on to its institutional roots even while feeling its leaves and branches torn by the winds of change that are blowing. Just as knowledge denied history becomes less than knowledge, a university denied its heritage as an institution becomes less than a university. It might as well become a cluster of data-vending machines. And its chances of adding perspective—not to say wisdom—are gone.

Elements Changed and Elements Unchanged

In preparation for this discussion of change and continuity in higher education, I sent letters to a number of educators, chosen from among administrators, organization directors, and senior professors.[1] They were asked to give their opinions concerning what has remained the most unchanged and what is most changed. The question was proposed in open form; no blanks, check-scales, or leading phrases were provided. Answers therefore were entirely individual and free from suggestion. The educators represented a full range of institutional and geographic backgrounds.

Perhaps the most noteworthy element in the answers was their tendency to confirm Heilbroner's thesis that it has become less pertinent to talk about what we are doing to history and more important to discover what is happening to us. Tolstoy, in *War and Peace*, wrote that wars are carried out, not as planned by generals, but as the outcome of the mass will of a people. Higher education has been slow to admit that it is not in sole possession of its destiny. We have been schooled on catalogue prose that describes a list of educational aims and then assures its clientele that these aims are regularly accomplished by the faculty, having first been laid down by the administration and approved by the board of trustees. Meanwhile, the supporting evidence of such accomplishment remains thin.

The educators who responded to the question about change and continuity in higher education over roughly the past thirty years concurred most closely on four principal changes and two points of continuity. Of

---

[1] The respondents are listed at the end of this paper.

these, four would have to be called unplanned and only two reflect even
a measure of institutional planning.

Principal Areas of Change

SYSTEMATIZATION OF HIGHER EDUCATION

Structurally the greatest change since before World War II is the
national growth from a congeries of autonomous institutions scattered
about the land to great state and regional systems of higher education.
The private institution, to be sure, has not yet become immersed in public systems. But it has joined consortia of both private and public institutions wherever it found either gain or defensive strength in doing so.
Raymond Moore, in a study made for the U.S. Office of Education,
identified over fifteen hundred different instances of consortia, with
continual crossings of private and public institution lines.

One particularly encouraging change is the trend toward separate collegiate units, either autonomous or semiautonomous, within one university or college cluster. The avowed aim is to combat depersonalization of
the educational experience. Whether or not the cluster system grows
further will depend in part on the question of its economic viability
versus the cost of the undivided large institution.

Over half the states now have systems of higher education that are, in
varying degrees, formal. State systems inevitably have limited the power
of individual colleges and universities to plan for themselves; no state is
rich enough to support the ambitions of each individual institution. Thus,
the growing practice is to make central decisions concerning how far each
institution shall go in the spread of its fields and the growth of its advanced degree programs. State planning indeed is hardly new; the first
planned system assigning missions to the different institutions was laid
down in Oregon in 1931. What has changed is the degree to which the
workings of the system are carried out by a central administration with
power to act, including the power to have the last voice before the appropriations committee of the state legislature.

INFUSIONS OF FEDERAL MONIES

One of the principal unplanned changes involved in the systematization of higher education is the emergence of the national university. Today's national university is not what George Washington had in mind
when he proposed it. It may be either publicly or privately controlled.

What it constitutes is a subsidized wealth of resources for research and training which only massive infusions of Federal grant money could have made possible. Seventy-eight universities in fiscal year 1966 each received more than $10 million of Federal subsidy. As William Friday observes, "They engage in production and management activity unheard of a quarter century ago."

Federal subsidies for research and other forms of public service have helped eliminate whatever frugality the university had inherited from its ecclesiastical ancestry. A professor on a Federal grant suddenly realizes that he is entitled to his own full-time secretary. For years he had been getting along on one-sixth of a departmental typist. His abandonment of all former prudence about submitting material for typing, Xeroxing, etc., is but one small element in the escalation of the costs of higher education during the past decade. We call it the price of the knowledge explosion and examine it no further; why should we if the public will pay? Unfortunately for the private institution without the Federal grant, the parent must pay. It may be only the parent's ignorance of the precise uses of his undergraduate tuition dollar that has kept him from rebellion against fees that have risen three and four times as fast as the national price index for other goods and services. Only medical and hospital costs have risen faster.

The Federal government's involvement in developing the national university has thus brought a new standard of expenditure in higher education. It has also widened the gap between the university and the college. The college, by and large, has not been taken up by the national knowledge industry. Therefore the difference between university salaries and college salaries has increased by a factor of two or three since the beginning of the post-Sputnik decade. The concentration of Federal monies in a few universities is compounded by the choices of large philanthropic foundations, which cannot help being influenced by so much attention paid to these institutions as the safest recipients for teaching and research grants.

More recently the entry of government agencies into funding new college programs of educational opportunity at the school and college levels gives some promise toward redressing the balance, since colleges as well as universities can participate.

There is little question, however, that the massive Federal impact upon university financing has, by its very dynamism, worsened the college financial situation. The Higher Education Facilities Act of 1963, which makes available one-third grants for academic buildings for institutions small or large, private or public, has—needless to say—spurred building construction on hundreds of campuses. But the grant requires that the other two-thirds of the funds be raised from college resources, and it further requires that enrollments be expanded to justify the new construction. Colleges thus find themselves scrambling to raise extra capital funds, taking emphasis away from the raising of current funds. The buildings, once realized, must be maintained; the additional students must be educated. Many colleges have taken advantage of title III of the program, which provides for low-interest loans for the balance of the building cost, with a resulting added load for interest payments on a non-revenue-producing building.

The Higher Education Acts have permitted a broad improvement of educational facilities that would not otherwise have been possible within the decade. But the added strain such crash programs have brought to colleges of limited financial resource has plunged them into financing programs that many are simply not capable of maintaining. Hence, with all the good it has brought, the Federal intervention into higher education has meant for a sizable proportion of higher education a worsening of its already serious financial predicament.

PROFESSIONALIZATION OF THE FACULTY

Socially, the greatest change that has taken place on the American campus is the professionalization of the faculty.

The emergence of the professor as a professional relates closely to his marketability in the national knowledge industry, for it was only a question of time before the technological revolution would come to the scholar. The dramatically higher status available to the faculty specialist has spread out from those fields, such as nuclear physics, where it was a direct reward for services rendered, to those fields of less direct utility yet comparable ambition. The 1966 American Council survey of quality in graduate education put the capstone on a column of rewards for the professor who concentrates efforts upon developing his particular subject matter and who equates academic excellence in his students with the degree of specialization they achieve.

The pattern of faculty activity both inside and outside the institution has changed accordingly. The original faculty corporation *was* the university. It is now quite unstable, composed of mobile professors whose employment depends on regional or national conditions in their field, rather than on an organic relationship to their institution and even less on the relationship to their administrative heads. The product is a harder-working man, a more sophisticated, knowledgeable person, and often, despite his outer loyalties, a devoted teacher. The difference in his teaching is that his devotion is mainly expended on his apprentices, as the system requires him to put first in priority and interest the reproduction of his own scholarly kind.

With such powerful changes at work strengthening the professor as a specialist, it has become more difficult to promote faculty responsibility for institutional educational policy. The specialist professor may become a teaching prima donna, answerable to no one for his whims of student grading. To the iron convention that the teacher is not to be visited in class has been added, by implication, the rule that his methods of evaluation are not to be questioned.

Granting the wealth of improvement in academic standards, the professor's bent toward his special discipline to the exclusion of other obligations is worrisome to administrators who remember different times. Sharvy Umbeck was moved to see as a "symptom of the erosion of the profession . . . the failure of the group to develop a code of ethics for the teacher."

Two important books published in the first part of 1968—*The Higher Learning in America: A Reassessment*[2] by Paul Woodring, and *The Academic Revolution*[3] by Jencks and Riesman—make the point that, whereas faculty devaluation of undergraduate teaching, particularly of courses in liberal education, has been a major factor in student disaffection, students tend to blame the administration and not the professors for their feelings of alienation. A report of the American Association of University Professors this year blames an insistence of administrators upon greater faculty research output for the lowered faculty attention to teaching—a remarkable revelation indeed.

But regardless of which way the finger should point, it seems that campus events of spring 1968 may force through a basic reconsideration of instructional posture by American institutions, small and large.

CHANGES IN STUDENT ATTITUDES

Of all the changes in the institutional scene from pre-World War II until now, the most dynamic change is the attitude of college students. Thanks to the growth of a social psychology of the college campus

[2] New York: McGraw-Hill Book Co.
[3] Garden City, N.Y.: Doubleday & Co.

during the past decade, we have some check on the games that news magazines like to play with slogans for college generations. At no time has it been possible to discover more than 15 percent of any student body who typified the slogan behavior: "silent generation," "beats," "radical Right," "New Left." Never before in our college history, however, have the actions of a few leaders carried so many with them. Impartial observers of ongoing behavior tell us that the leaders of student activism in the late 1960s are some of the most intellectually capable and socially responsive students in the institutions involved.

It is useless to try to separate current student activism from the behavior of youth throughout the nation and, indeed, throughout the Western world. Somehow the present generation of youth has reacted more sharply than any in recent decades to the contrasts between human precept and human performance. Too many decades of war have cheapened human life. The ultimate expression was reported some time ago when a crowd of junior high school pupils paraded down the street with megaphones and cards reading, "We Protest Against The Evil In The World."

It is by now redundant to say that youth's revolt is avowedly against the establishment and that students wishing to punch something see their university as a most convenient symbol of the establishment. One should remember that such generalized resentment has been countered by positive signs during the past five to seven years: enthusiasm for the Peace Corps and the Vista programs; volunteer service centers for tutoring dropouts, visiting handicapped persons, and like activities; and, in 1968, the enlistment in campaigns for presidential candidates believed to represent social idealism in some form or other. Somehow the greatest relief to middle-aged observers has come from the young activist whose enthusiasm for a candidate miraculously moved him to shave off his beard and put on shoes.

Beneath these manifestations the thoughtful educator has been moved by the dead-seriousness and sincerity that students exhibit about their desire to connect education with important human values. The obstreperous clamor of students to gain a part in campus governance may be understood and perhaps accommodated—assuredly we face further trouble if it is flatly rejected—provided it points toward a new meeting place of student, professor, and administrator in the cause of a genuinely liberating educational experience. In that spirit contributors to this essay were in agreement that increased student educational concern is the best sign among the changes that have come in our time. This expression of concern does not include desires simply to embarrass and disrupt the institution.

The channel of student activism has deepened during the past five years. In general, the rise of demonstrations paralleled the post-Sputnik era and the academic press for excellence. During the first third of the decade demonstrations typically were set off by some incident of administrative will or by opposition to parietal rules. The second phase was political, marked by growing resentment to the Vietnam war or to racial injustice. The latest phase has escalated into outright demands for Student Power in the governance of the institution. In Students for a Democratic Society, we have an openly revolutionary student movement on a national scale.

The involvement of students in college governance has had a thin, clear line of history among a few institutions, notably Antioch. Why the demands for more community-government systems like Antioch's did not spread much earlier may be a question for social historians. On two undergraduate campuses in the past, I urged students often and rather vainly to initiate educational policy committees and to meet with faculty on substantive matters of the curriculum. Now demands to participate are everywhere about our heads.

Whether the higher education community can absorb the sudden thrust and turn it into a long-range series of plans for sharing responsibility may be a test for our maturity. There is evidence that the alternative may be worse than chronic annoyance by hecklers. Students of the New Left have announced intentions to disrupt university administrations from coast to coast. Most administrators are not yet quite so suggestible as some of their alumni, who have been telling them for years that this sort of thing was afoot, under orders from Moscow carried by certain professors of economics and government. The New Left movement, if it is a movement, shows little Marxism. With some exceptions,[4] the philosophy to which it seems to adhere is a sort of classic anarchy. Just over one hundred years ago, in *Fathers and Sons*, Turgenev portrayed

---

[4] One exception might or might not be the statement of National Student Association president Edward Schwartz: "I want to transform at least one mass institution, where people are at present emasculated, atomized, separated, and frozen, into a community environment in which the relationships between people are considered seriously and the reactions of the community to the outside are taken seriously." (In *Fordham* magazine, March 1968.)

it faithfully in the debate between Pavel Petrovich, the faded aristocrat, and Bazarov, the young medical student:

> "We decided not to undertake anything," repeated Bazarov grimly. . . .
> "But to confine yourself to abuse?"
> "To confine ourselves to abuse. . . ."

Pavel explodes in impatience:

> "In old days young men had to study; they didn't want to be called dunces so they had to work hard whether they liked it or not. But now they need only say 'Everything in the world is foolery!' and the trick's done. Young men are delighted. And to be sure, they were simply geese before and now they have suddenly turned nihilists."
> ". . . I shall be quite ready to agree with you," Bazarov added, getting up, "when you bring forward a single institution in our present mode of life, in family or social life, which does not call for complete and unqualified destruction."

Things That Have Not Changed

METHODS OF TEACHING

Chief among the things that have not changed in the American college are the methods of teaching liberal education.

One of the educators responding to the survey has had the unusual experience of serving on curriculum committees as professor and dean at the same college for over forty years. The testimony of Julian Ross speaks for liberal arts colleges everywhere:

> Though the liberal arts curriculum has passed through a cycle of changes, such as the rise and decline of general education courses, it is now very similar to what it was in 1925. Both then and now it included requirements in foreign language, laboratory science, a series of distribution courses, and a thirty hour major.

The technology of teaching and learning, having nodded briefly to programed texts and teaching machines during the past fifteen years, now may indeed be changed by the computer. There seems little doubt that the computer represents changes in kind as well as degree for higher education. Other technological items, notably video tapes, seem to be moving toward the enrichment of study resources and will probably find greatest use in the library alongside the micro-reading devices that have been in use for forty years.

Except for what the computer may bring, it is generally agreed, the Ph.D. professor, teaching his field mainly with voice and chalk in a lecture hall or within his classroom of twenty to thirty students, will continue to be the modal experience in undergraduate education. Whatever new things the professor with his timeless teaching method can be inspired to undertake, thereon hang all the law and the prophets of future change.

THE MISSION AND THE STUDENTS

Behind the image of the unchanging classroom professor is another principal element of continuity, the mission of higher education: to bring about maximum intellectual growth among as large a proportion of our youth as we can muster the resource, energy, and ingenuity to accomplish. Concerning the teaching mission, one educator quoted from Meredith Wilson's address at the 1966 American Council on Education meeting:

> We have improved the speed, the comfort, and the security on almost every other road. But for the road from ignorance to knowledge we have little more help to offer than was available after man first mastered the art of writing.[5]

Has the student changed so much? So long as we continue to enroll largely the eighteen-year-old graduate of a four-year high school, it seems likely that basic change will be small even though the precollege experiences he has had, whether real or vicarious from television, have by now so expanded that he has become both more teachable and harder to impress. Today's student seems to take his economic future for granted. He is, on the other hand, more deeply impressed with the need to improve society. He shows, in the words of respondent Robert Goheen, "The paradoxical blend of introverted concern for self and altruistic concern for others." Yet, on the whole, Meredith Wilson may be correct in saying of all students, "They have not in fact changed . . . in the perception that their hour is the most important and most critical in history."

Throughout the brief discussions presented by educators for this survey, the recurring note of hope is that the American belief in progress through maximum educational opportunity will endure. If it is an illu-

---

[5] Wilson, "Teach Me, and I Will Hold My Tongue," *Improving College Teaching,* ed. Calvin B. T. Lee (Washington: American Council on Education, 1967), p. 8.

sion, "the impossible dream," then it is the kind of illusion—"remythologizing," theologians call it—that a nation needs.

At the current writing, colleges and universities are being given little chance to recant on the general conception that higher education in America should stand as a maximum opening to opportunity. The main thrust of Federal agencies as well as of the major foundations is taking that direction. The expressed belief in maximum educational opportunity has not been a spontaneous outpouring by virtuous congressmen and educators, so much as a partial answer to the urgent demands of America's poor, especially within the inner cities. These demands upon the college are now being carried on by militant ethnic groups, notably groups— such as the Black Student Union—already within the institutions.

The large-scale involvement of colleges and universities in education for the economically deprived could be a passing phenomenon. Sociologically, the world of the residential campus has remained remarkably homogeneous. Edward Sanders and Hans Palmer five years ago discovered that the socioeconomic pattern of students at the University of California was almost exactly the same as that of students in Stanford, Occidental, and Pomona.[6] If residential institutions, like organisms, practice homeostasis, it could be only a matter of time before they revert to a preoccupation with their traditional clienteles.

On the other hand, the changes in the wind could be longer-lasting. If they persist, they could bring a set of new dynamics to residential undergraduate education: dynamics comparable to the days of the postwar GI boom, but of longer duration. If it can be called more than a cliché to say that students educate each other more than the professors educate them, we may experience, in the invasion of the campus by new ethnic and economic groups, some major new energies for higher education. Even the curriculum might in time be affected.

Entropy or Synergism

When Ortega y Gasset wrote his dirge for Western society, *The Revolt of the Masses*,[7] he nevertheless ended hoping that the degradation he saw about him might be reversed by new energies marshaling themselves for a nationalization of Europe. By way of analogy, a new synergism for the

---

[6] *The Financial Barrier to Higher Education in California* (Claremont, Calif.: Pomona College, 1965).
[7] New York: W. W. Norton & Co., 1932.

American college might spring from the broadening of its clientele to include a full proportion of youth from all levels of society.

Since World War I thoughtful men have been haunted by predictions that time is running out for Western civilization. To the voices of Spengler, Ortega, and Toynbee is now added the clamor of students of the New Left. Far from proposing Utopian solutions, they appear to be calling upon institutions to get on with the disintegration. Doomsday preachers seize with Calvinistic joy upon the second law of thermodynamics, the gradual dissipation of energy which is called "entropy." They cite it as proof that Western society must decay. In like manner, a hundred years ago Darwin and Spencer were used to prove that future society must inevitably grow better and better.

We who for our sins have been charged with administering America's colleges and universities have too much immediately in front of us to spend time deciding by some cosmic analogy whether we shall be doomed or saved. In the next decade we must decide, for example, whether or not the phenomenon of the privately controlled institution is to be preserved and built into future higher education systems. It cannot be done through the individual will of each institution. In dozens of projections of future costs and funding prospects, *no evidence has appeared to show that private colleges can survive the escalating costs without public support of some sort.* Only a relative handful will so manage by their own luck and resources, and most of these are so heavily subsidized by government grants as to be quasi-public already.

The so-called "happy" diversity of higher education in America is rapidly growing unhappy. It will become downright miserable if, under the continued pressure of present economic forces, that diversity comes to mean a hardened division among the excellent, the mediocre, and the intolerably weak. Diversity is not good if it euphemizes the present regional derbies of colleges of unfairly matched strengths, struggling for the same competitive goals.

What can help us, instead, is a planned diversity in which a varying set of educational missions, clienteles, and public-private forms of control would be worked out. In the tradition of our country, it is to be hoped that this would be done on a state-wide rather than on a Federal basis.

An entire new order of public understanding is needed. The intense visibility of the campus during the current student uprisings has the public confused and disheartened. Once again college youth are said to be going to the dogs, while professors and administrators are derided as being incapable of putting their own house in order. They are said to be showing not only impracticality but cowardice.

The public understanding we need will have to start with an understanding among ourselves of the social contract of the institution. All parties to that contract should be witness to it at the outset of the college year. Before the social contract can be signed there should be long and searching talk. The greatest and the most damaging negative change that has come to higher education is a growing conclusion, arrived at by default, that *institution* is a meaningless or, at best, a superfluous word. After Robert Hutchins had entertained for a week at Santa Barbara a group of student leaders of the New Left, he is reported to have told them that he could perceive in their extended comments not one affirmative idea of what a university ought to be. Unhappily, at the same time, the professionalization of faculty into disciplinary cadres and away from the academic community has contributed to our failures to muster institutional strength.

Against these genuine worries about destructive change, the trauma of events such as happened on the Columbia, Howard, Stanford, and many other campuses in the spring of 1968 just may have shocked us enough so that there will be next year a stronger impulse to counsel together. If we surrender to the nihilist trends, transient though they may turn out to be, we may immobilize our institutions at the very time when we ought to be adding to their motive power.

There is, I am certain, an underlying wish on the part of students, faculty, and the public for institutions of higher learning to have stature and direction. Most of us agree that strong institutions are needed. They will be needed in the next century—as much as they have been needed in preceding centuries—if there is to be human purpose as well as content in learning. That is the continuity we should seek, throughout all the change that must and will come.

List of Respondents to a Letter of Query

Looking over the years you have spent actively in higher education, what elements seem to you the most unchanged? What elements, on the other hand, seem to have changed the most and, perhaps, to point toward continuing change?

Jacques Barzun, University Professor, Columbia University
Arthur H. Brayfield, Executive Officer, American Psychological Association
James S. Coles, Director, Research Corporation

William Friday, President, University of North Carolina
Edmund J. Gleazer, Jr., Executive Director, American Association of Junior Colleges
Robert F. Goheen, President, Princeton University
J. Glenn Gray, Professor, Colorado College
Eldon Johnson, Vice-President of the University, University of Illinois
Morris T. Keeton, Academic Vice-President, Antioch College
Charles P. McCurdy, Jr., Executive Secretary, Association of American Universities
John F. Morse, Director, Commission on Federal Relations, American Council on Education
Emil M. Mrak, Chancellor, University of California, Davis
Theodore Newcomb, Professor, University of Michigan
Julian L. Ross, Professor, Allegheny College
Richard H. Sullivan, President, Association of American Colleges
Sharvy G. Umbeck, President, Knox College
Logan Wilson, President, American Council on Education
O. Meredith Wilson, Director, Center for Advanced Study in the Behavioral Sciences

Continuity and Change: The Need for Both

HARRY S. BROUDY, FERREL HEADY,
SAMUEL D. PROCTOR, KERMIT C. MORRISSEY,
ALBERT W. DENT

One Continuity, Indispensable

HARRY S. BROUDY

AFTER EXAMINING the instances of continuity and change reported by Dr. Benezet's respondents, I have come to feel that only in one area is continuity indispensable: in the primary role of the university itself. Traditionally, this role is to develop and disseminate knowledge (the content of the various intellectual disciplines) and wisdom (the import of this content for whatever version of the good life a given epoch professes).

All else—curriculum, teaching, organization, administration, research —should be changed as required to enable the university to be faithful to its function. It is as unwise to make these instruments, whose virtue is their adaptability, a matter of tradition as it is to elasticize the central role of the academic community to accommodate social pressures. Yet these inversions have occurred, and it looks as if we may have changed and continued the wrong things.

One example is the systematization of higher education—with its attendant overbureaucratization and overcentralization—insofar as it was brought about by the inability of the institution to curb ambitions that are but remotely related to the basic role of the university.

The professionalization of the faculty and the increase of expenditures for academic requisites and prerequisites—welcome and beneficial as they have been—have also on occasion become ends in themselves. And one of the accessories before, during, or after the fact is the belief that it is simply not cricket to attribute to a colleague any motive other than the desire to advance and disseminate knowledge.

To be sure, numerous articles on the subject have been written, but so long as the indictments are anonymous (as this one is), the academic community regards the undoubted benefits derived from the largesse of the government and the foundations as more than ample justification for such vague evils as they may entail. Unfortunately, while academicians and administrators were complacently condoning in fact what they were deploring in principle, students and the public were losing faith in the loyalty of the university to its primary mission, and so still another establishment lost its credibility.

The difficulty is not, I believe, that academics acted from impure motives, but that they necessarily acted from mixed motives. The new academic affluence passed almost insensibly from being a pleasant adjunct to professional life to a necessity—a symbol of success. It was but a short step to the conviction that without private secretaries, luxurious offices, expensive equipment, and large staffs, no decent scholarly work could be done. Recognition, visibility, expansion of facilities and staff, and grantsmanship were transformed into ends in themselves.

That a project, a conference, a symposium, another volume of readings, another overseas enterprise does in fact contribute to knowledge is not enough to warrant its being supported by a university, unless this is its *primary* objective and most conspicuous outcome. The development of knowledge and wisdom may properly be regarded as a secondary outcome by a business corporation or the Department of Defense, but not by the university.

The university, when confronted by student uprisings and seizures, will find it difficult to invoke the supremacy of knowledge if it does not go into court with clean hands. But in at least four spots they are not quite clean.

1. The alliance between the university and the military and industrial establishments has not been watched carefully enough to prevent contamination of the university's loyalty to its central mission.

2. Not all institutions, and certainly not all individuals, have had their research and scholarly potentials adjudicated on merit alone. As a result, the search for knowledge and its effectiveness have been hampered. Of course, one can make a good case for pouring money into institutions where talent is already concentrated, and thus concentrate the talent even further and make it more advisable to pour in even more money,

and so on. However, this kind of reasoning falls more naturally on the ear when it comes from the Department of Defense and General Motors than when it comes from the university.

3. Specialism and the consequent professionalization are natural and desirable concomitants of the growth of knowledge. But specialism, if used to excuse the university from its responsibility for wisdom as well as for knowledge, betokens a betrayal of at least half of its central role. A student who persisted in asking where in the modern university he might study the good life would finally be dispatched to the psychiatric clinic. The departmental structure of the university is fine for the development and dissemination of knowledge, but not for wisdom. Wisdom, being concerned with the import that knowledge has for the great social and personal problems, entails interdisciplinary thinking.

4. The student and the university now spend the bulk of their time and energies in the mechanics of imparting information and developing conceptual and technical skills: that is, on didactics that can be done more efficiently by programed computer-aided instruction. Hence there is little time left, save at *Kaffeeklatsches* and teach-ins, for the kind of personal-encounter teaching involved in the exploration of value. This situation is inexcusable, and the shriek of students at the irrelevance of some of their departmental courses is understandable, albeit misguided. The students are wrong in believing (*a*) that departmentalized courses are the proper place for value education, and (*b*) that the department courses in the basic disciplines are unnecessary; they seem so only after one has mastered them. The faculty does not share their second error, but it is guilty of the first.

I share Dr. Benezet's feeling that the destiny of a university is not entirely in its own hands or even in the hands of the academic community. The changing conditions of the larger community exert enormous pressures on all social institutions; it is not necessary that the university ignore these demands, and it is impossible to transcend them by claims to intellectual and moral superiority. Yet the more complex the social order, the greater the interdependence and the pressures, the more the viability of the whole system demands that each institution be loyal to its primary function, the reason for its being. Given this loyalty, we can be free and creative in our changes. Without this continuity, there is no criterion for change, as we live from one predicament to another, from crisis to crisis, so that in time even crisis loses its meaning and its occasional value as a stimulus to growth.

Accent on Change

FERREL HEADY

MY COMMENTS are directed to two issues faced by most large institutions of higher education. An appropriate response to each contains elements of both continuity and change. These issues are: (1) a revitalization of the teaching mission as it concerns the liberal education of undergraduates, and (2) a redefinition of the role of the university as an agent of social change in the larger community.

In the first case, my view is that we have not yet put enough stress on the necessity for change. In the second, my concern is that we not allow the desire for change to result in a break in continuity that would so drastically alter the nature of our institutions as to weaken them as instruments of higher education.

The two elements that have not changed in American colleges and universities, according to President Benezet, are, first, the mission of the university to bring about maximum intellectual growth among our youth, and, second, the methods of providing a liberal education. At the same time, he points out the dynamic change in the attitude of college students toward activism on and off the campus, the main target for student disaffection on campus being the alleged downgrading of undergraduate teaching and the resultant depersonalization and stagnation of liberal education.

The extent of this disaffection may be exaggerated, and ways of measuring it are certainly unreliable. But the problem indeed exists, and improvement can come only through conscious and sustained effort. I doubt that there is a villain in the piece, played either by the professor who loves his research grant more than his students or by the administrator who insists on promoting on the basis of publications rather than teaching. There is not even a student hero who is more responsive to good teaching and able to identify poor teaching. The explanation is more complex, and so is the remedy. Several facts of university life during the last twenty-five years have combined to dilute and subordinate undergraduate teaching. Some of these are by themselves highly commendable: the rising proportion of college-eligible youth actually attending college; advances in the status, prestige, and recognition of the academic profession; the deeper involvement of the faculty member in the local, national, and international setting; and the expanding support from the Federal government for a wide range of research and service activities.

Nevertheless, if the victim is the undergraduate student, it is high time that he be rescued and that the rescue operation be a joint one, with the students themselves taking part, along with faculty members, university administrators, and government officials. I can only suggest some of the possible courses of action. No single response will be sufficient, and any combination of responses must suit local needs.

The most potent incentive that a college or university can offer to encourage teaching excellence is through its system of recognition for the achievements of faculty members: decisions on initial appointments, promotions, salary increments, and tenure. The fault lies not in what our faculty handbooks say about the importance of good teaching, but in what our actions say about it when such decisions are made. Too often competence in teaching becomes incidental rather than pivotal. The reason is usually not that teaching is deliberately downgraded, but that there is a tendency to give weight to what seems more easily measured, such as published research, or to what seems more attractive to competing institutions, such as reputation as a productive (published) research scholar. If we are to improve on this front, we must devise different and better ways of ranking teaching performance, including fuller and more systematic utilization of student judgment than either our faculty members or our students are accustomed to. Achieving this goal will take more adjustments by professors than by students, but achieve it we must.

There are other ways to tackle the problem: by encouraging curricular innovation and new teaching techniques, and at the same time initiating organizational arrangements and supporting services within the university that will make these possible; by maintaining a faculty-student ratio that does not force either additional overcrowding or the turning over of more of the task of undergraduate instruction to graduate assistants; by further utilizing honors programs, the cluster concept, residential colleges, and other devices for humanizing the multiuniversity; and by seeking out noncategorical support from the Federal government and private foundations that can be used to reward teaching excellence as well as excellence in research.

Most of these measures put the accent on change rather than on continuity, and they cannot be realized unless we prove that our colleges and universities are not the conservative, status-quo-oriented institutions that our detractors contend, and that even our supporters frequently suspect they are.

On the question of the role of the university as an agent of social change, I take it for granted that the university has an obligation to serve the public and that the issue is how, rather than whether, the university should be at the service of society.

I agree with President Benezet that "time and events have caught up with higher education in America" and that "higher education has passed into the public domain." Equally important is his reminder that "a university denied its heritage as an institution becomes less than a university." In my opinion, this is the danger posed by the argument for change based on the proposition that the university as an institution has a direct responsibility for shaping society, that it "has an obligation to identify social wrongs and take an aggressive lead in rectifying them," that it "must be engaged, activist, reformist," to use the language of the 1966–67 *Annual Report* of the Carnegie Foundation for the Advancement of Teaching.

The important distinction here is that the institution must preserve its corporate neutrality on current social issues, rather than taking an institutional position that is binding on all members of the university community. This position was reaffirmed recently by a joint student-faculty committee at Antioch College, which concluded "that Antioch College shall not take an institutional stand on the war in Vietnam and that we remind ourselves that the only proper institutional stands for the College are on issues scrupulously defined as educational." As one reason for this stand, the committee cited the intent "to free individual advocacy from any shadow of institutional orthodoxy."

In urging continuity in this basic respect, I do not argue against a change in attitude that encourages segments of the university complex —whether they be individuals or groups among faculty members or students, research or service centers, quasi-autonomous units or agencies, or other parts of the university—from being involved in and actively identified with social action programs, as long as this is not made a condition for university affiliation in good standing. The movement should be toward the kind of urban-grant university that has been proposed by Clark Kerr, to bring the resources of higher education to bear on the immense problems of our metropolitan centers, rather than to make universities the agents of any controlling political elite, either on or off campus, however laudable the objectives of that elite may seem to be. The end product of such a trend would be institutions that are no longer universities, because such institutions would soon become the defenders, not the neutral critics, of the society that surrounds them.

A Sign of Commitment

SAMUEL D. PROCTOR

MANY OF THE PAPERS on continuity and change deal with student power and faculty participation in the governance of academic institutions. I judge that one of the truly significant changes is the presence of increasing numbers of black students and faculty on major campuses all over the country. They are not only present but also have vocalized their feelings about their role in the university community. Indeed, with race and war as two extremely explosive topics on every campus, the black student is very aware of his pivotal role. In a few words, I would like to raise some questions about this development.

First, are the universities willing to go the distance necessary to make up for the deficits that many black students suffer at the time of college admission? Obviously, unless some real effort is made to correct these deficits, it is no social gain to admit scores of black students and then expose them to insensitive and resentful teachers who demand performance equal to that of more privileged students. I speak largely of mathematics and natural science, for in social science and the humanities the deficit is more manageable. It is just as obvious that if the admissions standards remain as they are at the more prestigious schools and if changes in black readiness take place at the same pace, it will be a hopelessly long time before blacks reach 10–12 percent of the major university population.

It is not debatable that the destiny of America's black community rests heavily on the volume, competence, and speed of the universities' production of black technicians, scientists, interpreters, managers, and producers of every sort. What has happened in football and tennis must happen in biochemistry and engineering; what has happened in baseball and track must happen in sales and jurisprudence.

The nation is aroused—though not fully awake—to the massive problems of the black poor. But to give the real lift out of a century-deep pit of poverty, the best efforts of government and industry will still require an accelerated production rate of a black intellectual elite with deep social compassion. We cannot have much longer simply a scattering of privileged or fortunate blacks moving to the top. The ornamental appearance of such blacks inspires distrust, fragments the black community, and encourages the use of anarchistic strategies for change. It must become fairly obvious to a rapidly growing number of young blacks that real endeavor will pay off and that the pay-off is fastest when one pursues the goals of education that result in pay-off for everyone else.

Again, can the universities find the financial aid, prepare the environment for something more than just a dozen or so inconspicuous blacks, sensitize faculty and students whose social conditioning is inadequate to cope with an assertive black population, and line up department heads to do those honest things that help to bridge the gap between success in a less demanding situation and in a far more demanding one?

Next, are we prepared to change our views about education and to see it as something more than a rehearsal for life in suburban America at $18,000 a year? The affluent white majority imposes on poor whites and minorities an educational package that is sealed and delivered to those who plan to be joiners of the suburbanites. This point is perhaps overstated for emphasis, but change in education means revising the curriculum for those who plan to live and work closer to human need in America and abroad. The black student can easily tell when his education is provincial, when the extramural activities are not for him, and when he is frozen out. Similarly, he can tell when the gestures of hospitality are empty and when they are sincere. He looks for a sign of commitment and that sign is when the liveliness of concern in and out of class centers on the critical issues of the times rather than on the effete busy work that is required for credits and degrees but is useless otherwise.

Thus, change to broaden and to add variety to the university population goes further than resolving to recruit blacks. It means offering hospitality in the physical facilities and providing intellectual relevance in the curriculum. In fact, not black students alone, but the whole university population this year is making irrelevance in the classroom their new target.

None of these needed changes have to do with watering down anything. They have to do with a world falling apart while expensive institutions take in each other's laundry. The fact is that a serious approach to the literature of the angry revolutionaries, or a study of the aged poor, the rural drop-out, the Spanish-speaking minorities, and the solo parent, live and breathing, may constitute a far more rewarding semester than much of what passes for "college."

The explosion is more likely to occur first in teacher education, a field in which students will not wait to get to the action, in which theory is getting harder and harder to "for instance," and in which the total pressure to be where the action is bubbles with resentment against lectures on learning theory.

The public schools are in trouble everywhere. And black people are causing much of the trouble because their children are not *learning*. And uneducated children make problem adults. This process can be improved by a teacher education program that gets close enough to urban kids, hard-core kids, to find the threshold of their learning readiness and build from there.

A university that is remote from that challenge says in another way that it is an uncaring and detached patch of real estate that students from deprived backgrounds should shun. Happily, more and more universities are fortunate in having leaders who have worked through these issues and are ready to be boldly inclusive.

The Tired Animosities

KERMIT C. MORRISSEY

AMERICAN INSTITUTIONS of higher education are in the center of several upheavals—some of them threatening, some promising, and some so ambiguous that they defy both guess and hope. The effects of the increased infusion of Federal funds into higher education for the past fifteen years are reasonably clear, however, inasmuch as the new monies have contributed to faculty professionalism, and, by extension, to some unspecified measure of student dissatisfaction with college teaching. Moreover, universities have consented to the resulting imbalance between graduate and undergraduate effort and to a fiscal choice that has more often enriched the wealthy and deprived the poor within the same institutions.

With this extensive experience in Federal relations, it should be possible to maintain continuity in American higher education while introducing an essential change in financial support. Continuity in this context would include the "happy" diversity of American colleges and universities, and the change in financial support would be shaped by the fundamental concerns of the affected institutions.

The financial squeeze on higher education and the need for rapid development of professional manpower have led to a series of spasmodic, "knee-jerk" responses from the Federal government, each response intended to solve a specific problem. Every Federal response has, in fact, contributed to the instability of institutions selected to train professional manpower or to diversify collegiate opportunity.

American colleges and universities have greatly expanded their service capacity to accommodate a rising demand from several levels of American government, and from industry, the professions, and the general public. In this respect, the expansion, both in numbers and quality, has clearly served the national interest. It is ironic that this increased service has been accomplished within a system of costs and charges developed for the limited clientele existing prior to 1950.

There is every reason to assume that current demands will at least continue and possibly even accelerate, depending upon the change rate in noneducational activities; but the present dual approach in charges and payments cited by President Benezet is already producing an unhealthy diversity in the capacity of colleges and universities to maintain quality and to make desirable adjustments in their academic and administrative modes of operation.

Maintaining a desirable continuity will require substantial change in the financing of American higher education. The preservation of diversity and pluralism can, and perhaps will, require the introduction of direct Federal support of public and private operating budgets for undergraduate instruction. But such direct support, in the national interest, might too readily reflect the crisis reactions which created the existing unsatisfactory Federal involvement with colleges and universities unless the institutions revise their view of themselves. A hard look at the real current and probable future demand for higher educational service might remove the temptation to reproduce from memory what the future will require. Repeating past performance will help destroy diversity and further widen the gap between what is and what should be.

In at least one important respect, the current dilemma of too much service with too few funds is analogous to the crisis of federalism in the nation. The American Federal system has promoted experiment, diversity, and regionalism. It has contributed to national unity and encouraged pluralism at the same time. Local, state, and national levels of government have all assumed new and often overlapping responsibilities, and each level of government has rapidly increased its service capacity while approaching the limit of its tax sources. The crisis in federalism is similar, then, in broad outline, to the crisis in higher education. Moreover, consideration of policy alternatives for the future of American federalism must also include the requirement of continuity and the necessity for change.

No model of an altered Federal system is available, but agreement exists on a controlling principle which should inform the future of American federalism. There is broad agreement concerning the need to adapt the Federal system in order to promote appropriate decisions at the *appropriate level* of government, and this principle is surely applicable to future fiscal policy for higher education.

Given the dimensions of the fiscal crisis in higher education, it would be helpful, if miraculous, to set aside the tired animosities of public versus private, or research versus teaching, and other such archaic polarities. The national interest will not be served if American colleges and universities are obliged, for financial reasons, to do less than they are doing. If higher education is to avoid provincialism and contribute to new directions in Federal policy, then the central value of educational pluralism as a national asset should be an essential ingredient in the formulation of policy on future financial support.

Diversity among collegiate institutions can be defined by type of sponsorship, clientele served, subjective estimates of excellence, or the number of students served. Considerable lip service is paid to this abstract value, but it has not usually been reflected in Federal actions relating to American higher education.

The systemization of higher education could be a focal point for both continuity and change, with the states acting as conservators and stimulators. Colleges and universities might anticipate new forms in American federalism and develop decision-models involving institutions, states, and Federal agencies that would reward initiative at the level of direct service in the classroom. Many states have established exemplary review procedures which allow for a wide range of variance among different service areas. In addition, the states have developed many methods of direct support for undergraduate instruction, methods which can contribute to the policy considerations affecting future Federal involvement.

It would be a great waste of time to be obliged to invent the wheel over and over again.

Anticipation is often fanciful, but the changes recorded in the recent past in American higher education suggest that institutions which will have to live with the consequences of change should act to influence the pace and direction of events. The central issue of financial support will require a new format and new rules. Disenchantment with large and detailed Federal programs is widespread enough to make innovation possible if not necessary.

Adequate financial support will not provide answers to the problem of student disaffection or of faculty alienation. Nor will it assure a measure of quality across the board. It can provide assurance that collegiate institutions will continue to function and to make efforts toward improvement. Moreover, a more secure financial base will provide time for a reasoned change to occur.

Higher Education as a Right

ALBERT W. DENT

HIGHER EDUCATION in American society—like higher education throughout history—was established primarily for children of the elite or "ruling" families and for the more talented, ambitious, and fortunate children from the upwardly mobile middle-class segment of the population.

Despite the power and prestige of the upper class in this country, it has been the ambitious middle class that has done most in shaping the structure and determining the values and goals of American education. The academic influence of the middle class stems largely from the fact that upper-class children inherit economic security, high social status, and social power. Their social class status with its special privileges is *ascribed*. This is not so for children of middle-class families. They, like their parents before them, must *achieve* adult middle-class status. And even when middle-class status has been achieved, it must be repeatedly validated and nurtured by "good works." That is, middle-classness is more an individual than a family status. In order to maintain high social status, the individual must continue to render socially valuable services. He is expected to strive constantly for success despite the absence of definite, absolute criteria of success. Consequently the middle class, more than any other social segment, has developed its own system of values to support its own standards of excellence.

Middle-class values have proven to be so demanding, sound, and functional that they are generally accepted as norms according to which we have come to judge the desirability and validity of all other norms and the usefulness of other values. And—what is even more relevant to our present interests—middle-class norms and values have become the distinguishing feature of our academic ethos. They determine the "cultural and intellectual climate" of higher education. There is a strong tendency for all colleges, all academic performances, as well as all academic standards, to be judged according to middle-class criteria. Yet the academic community, in the transmission of these values, must continue to re-evaluate and refine them so that they may have wider applicability in our attempts to improve human relations and enhance national strength and respect.

On August 6, 1945, the United States used the first nuclear weapon in the history of warfare. This weapon dramatically signaled the beginning of a new era—the nuclear age. In many ways, this age is vastly different from any preceding. For our special purpose, nuclear power underscored this nation's need for a whole network of new technological skills. Almost instantly, as it were, the United States had to launch a search for a much greater supply of certain kinds of skills already developed and had to develop many entirely new skills. Unfortunately, we cannot afford to wait to recruit these talents from the traditional middle-class families. Our enemies are too close upon us and lower-class people are too restless. In addition to its being morally demanded that all of our citizens enjoy the same rights and privileges, and politically sound to guarantee equality, the masses are insisting upon it. Children of our lower classes are demanding that they be given the privilege to enjoy the good life—American style, now! They should be heeded. This nation must develop all of its human potentials. It must search for and develop needed talents from all segments of society in order to compete successfully with other major nations. The fundamental challenge here is this: Our colleges must find ways of teaching—effectively—students of different cultural and academic backgrounds in the same classrooms.

It is now well-established public policy that equal access to elementary and secondary education is a right for all American citizens regardless of social or economic status. During the last decade, we have been moving rapidly toward public policy establishing higher education as a right to be provided rather than purchased. As we move further in this direction, as I think we surely must, the academic community—trustees, administrators, faculties and students—must broaden their concept of public trust and responsibility even in the face of many circumstances beyond their control.

The academic community must, with broad understanding, adjust itself to necessary continuing change that will serve the needs and demands of succeeding generations, or it will face the alternative of having change forced upon it by less competent sources. That alternative would be too unfortunate to contemplate.

LLOYD H. ELLIOTT

Changing Internal Structures: The Relevance of Democracy

REPRESENTATIVE GOVERNMENT is one means or response which our society has accepted in putting concepts of democracy into practice in Western culture. The functions and workings of government are constantly being remodeled, remolded, and revised in the light of changing social, economic, political, and cultural objectives. So too it has been and must continue to be in the governance of the nation's institutions of higher education.

The purposes of the college and the university have long been well defined, or so we might wish to claim. But to accept that claim is to ignore the many changes that have continuously evolved for carrying forward man's search for a better life—an objective that was never exclusively the province of the university although historians (most of them university scholars) generally ascribed this noble purpose to the institution. Even a cursory view today shows organizations, agencies, individuals, corporations, and new kinds of institutions engaged in the pursuit of knowledge, transmitting knowledge, giving public service, and, in general, expending great effort toward the goal of improving society. This is not to say that the universities and colleges no longer pursue these objectives; simply, they are not, and never were, the exclusive institutions for the pursuit of these goals.

We would all accept, I suspect, John Gardner's statement in 1967 when he said:

> We need in the university community a focussed, systematic, responsible, even aggressive concern for the manner in which the society is evolving.

. . . We need designers of the future. We need to be told how to build a better society, and how to get from here to there.

I would, however, caution against any assumption that the university is the best institution for designing the future, let alone the only one. The campus today reverberates perhaps in part because so many have come to regard the university as the most promising of all institutions for developing cures for society's ills. No longer does the church or the family hold this pre-eminent position, as in earlier periods. The church, to some observers, is alternately too conservative to acknowledge today's problems or too erratic to tackle them in a systematic way. The family in Western culture (and to a degree, in Oriental cultures as well) is no longer the great teaching institution it was for centuries. The state, whether democracy or dictatorship, though seemingly unable to cope with political, economic, social, and cultural crises, is nevertheless today's avenue for action. People turn away quickly from government because of long-standing disenchantment; and, in the default of other institutions, they turn to universities and colleges for commitment and involvement. Government, however, and not the university, is the instrument of public policy; our efforts must be directed toward making government more effective rather than permitting the university to be saddled with a responsibility it cannot meet. To exemplify: the very policy of society toward the university itself is a matter to be determined through the avenues of government. Thus, the extent of scholarly search for new knowledge is now more directly dependent upon government policy than upon any other single factor. And, as noted many times over, the college and the university cannot alone solve social problems.

In a kind of desperation some peoples of the world are turning to the universities to find solutions to major problems, and in doing so are simply making battlefields of the institutions. In this nation our elected representatives are the only ones who have the mandate for such broad responsibility for social policy. The struggle for control of society's policy-making power is, therefore, misdirected when the university is made the object of its contention. And yet, looking about, it would not be difficult to find examples of social programs where institutions of higher learning have exercised judicial responsibilities in assessing their value, have brought about legislation which signaled major changes, and then have become administratively involved in implementing these new programs. Such actions have encouraged the belief that, under the protective umbrella of the educational institution, any cause, no matter how selfish or narrow, could find support.

In another sense the scene of the struggle has simply shifted from the church, from the family, from the local community, from legislative halls, from the economic marketplace, and perhaps even from the Near East or Far East battlefields to the university campus. Whether we look at Latin America, Western Europe, the United States, or the shadows behind the Iron Curtain, there is a growing feeling that they who control the universities will control men's minds and therefore control human actions. We are witnessing, therefore, a fight among individuals, special-interest groups, and coalitions of groups, first, to influence and, then, to control the university. Although this is something of a new phenomenon in the United States, it is not new elsewhere in the world. Simply observing, too, that the object of the struggle is mistaken will not shift the struggle to another arena. It may be more helpful, instead, to examine what relevance democracy has, if any, for changing the internal structure of the college or university so that that institution may better respond to its responsibilities in democracy. Let us examine briefly that structure and the institution's functions.

Governance and the Mission of the University

For several decades the institutions of higher education have been content to follow a routine that permitted professors to teach, in their own ways, each succeeding class of incoming students, to do research in those areas which caught their interest or fancy, and to publicize the results of that research in whatever fashion a constituency might wish. Whether the professors' teaching or research was valid and was well received, critically received, or simply ignored concerned very few besides the professor himself.

As we examine the immense new pressures now put upon the university and the inadequacy of some of the responses to the pressures, it is appropriate to reaffirm that the purpose of a university is above all else "the search for truth." The conditions of that search constitute the defense of academic freedom, and the objective of all governance of the university is to provide the best conditions of learning and teaching that will further the pursuit of truth. As Masefield wrote, "Wherever a university stands . . . full and free inquiry . . . may still bring wisdom into human affairs." Who shall govern the university is therefore not the basic question. It is rather: For what end shall the university be governed? In this context, which might be called the assumptions under which we now proceed, our question becomes one of the relevance of democracy for achieving those conditions of teaching and learning that hold the greatest promise for the pursuit of truth.

But first must come the answer to what constitutes truth. Unfortunately, academic freedom, although a necessary condition for the search for truth, has often been seized upon by some to achieve their selfish ends. Externally the university is subjected to political, economic, social, and cultural pressures; internally it may be subjected to the manipulation of an ambitious administrator, the self-interest of a faculty, and the "causes" of a student group. And yet the very spirit of a university is enemy of all selfish and self-serving interests.

How then can a university be governed so as to maintain the best conditions for the reasoned pursuit of truth? Obviously, procedures must be devised which alert all segments of the university community to obstruction or interference with freedom, right, reason, and truth, and the same procedures must ensure that responsible action accompanies the exercise of the rights of the campus. Otherwise, the conditions of maximum objectivity and reason are jeopardized. And so it seems the university is moving, slowly and painfully, into a complex, delicate system of checks and balances.

By an evolutionary process now reaching over several centuries, the roles of the governing board, professors, students, and other members of the university family are being remolded. Professional organizations, scholarly societies, employers, and many other interests exercise varying degrees of influence on the educational program. So central is the university to the affairs of the world that all societal forces have their effect —sometimes direct, sometimes indirect—on its decisions. The headlines today throw the spotlight on something called "student power." This is not new; the student has long been involved in decision-making in the university. In the Middle Ages, he and his classmates hired and fired professors, begged or stole food, and negotiated with the sheriff.

As cycles come and go, terminology changes. Old epithets give way to new tags, and so "student power" is with us. Similarly, the "power" of trustee, professor, administrator, alumnus, or politician would be equally appropriate. In fact, it is misleading to discuss "power" without including all parts of the university's constituency.

In the forefront in any consideration of "power" is the power of the public, and institutions of higher education have been endeavoring for decades to determine the best means for participation by the public in the governance of the university and in the benefits of its services. Working through a governing board, the public has approved in principle the delegation by the governing board to the faculty of the responsibility for molding academic policy. Standards of admission, courses, programs, and curricula as well as graduation requirements are now quite generally recommended by faculty groups and approved as recommended by administrative officers and trustees. The exercise of this responsibility by the faculty has become widely accepted both within and beyond the university.

A Proposal for Remolding the Structure

How, then, is the university to respond to the newly voiced demand of one constituency or another for more power and influence? And how is the university to be controlled so that it may respond in the most positive, yet institutionally appropriate fashion to needs so expressed? I believe that this new requirement calls for some reorganization of the academic program, and that both the internal and external structure of the university should be remolded.

Within the academic area of the university's work (and this is the fundamental role which the university was established to perform), the objective of reform must be approached by bringing together the various constituencies to gain the contributions of all to the evaluation of the adequacy and relevancy of the academic program. At various times in our history, the public, the church, the state, the scholar, or the student has exercised the primary influence on the subject matter of higher education. In some areas the "employer," public or private, has wielded the greatest authority. In recent years the college and university have been faced with the almost complete surrender of responsibility and authority for subject matter, both its selection and organization, to the individual professor. Under the banner of academic freedom, his authority for his own course has become an almost unchallenged right. He has been not only free to ignore suggestions for change, but also licensed, it is assumed, to prevent any change he himself does not choose. Even in departments where courses are sequential, the individual professor chooses the degree to which he will accommodate his course to others in the sequence. The question then becomes: What restructuring is possible or desirable within the context of the professor's academic freedom?

May I suggest the creation of a departmental advisory body whose membership would be selected from professors, students, alumni, and the public. This body, after a period of orientation, could offer to the department chairman and faculty organized suggestions for change. From representatives of the public, we might expect that the department would receive a direct playback of the expectations of the citizenry, a view of necessities as they arise from the everchanging world, and expression on the relevance of the subject matter to everyday life. Alumni contributions of much the same character could be expected; the alumni, however, would have the benefit of assessing suggestions in light of their college experience and what they encountered after graduation. The input of the professors might be broader than at present if the advisory committee included both professors from the discipline and helpful critics from related disciplines. Finally, student input should be the result of views from majors and from nonmajors, assessing the contributions of courses to specialization as well as to general education. This kind of representative government, by knowledgeable and dedicated persons, could then respond meaningfully to accusations of irrelevance and inadequacy, and the gaps and ignorance that now exist could be replaced by cultivated clarification and understanding.

The organization described above might be appropriate for a single-purpose college specializing in liberal education or for the college of arts and sciences within a university. Professional schools and colleges of a university could be organized on a schoolwide basis. The school of business administration, for example, might be expected to have an advisory council of twelve to twenty-five or more members, depending on the specialized curricula it offers. And so on.

Structure, of course, can be only one element in achieving the objectives sought. Reform of the university will undoubtedly call for some reorganization before it can enjoy any great degree of receptivity. And a most important by-product could well be found in the mechanism that enables laymen, professors, alumni, and students to meet regularly to discuss matters of mutual interest. The university today has found almost impossible the task of bringing students into a closer relationship with alumni and the public. Alumni and representatives from the public can be expected to take a greater interest in students and professors when effective avenues for communication are opened up, and the reverse can also be true. The avenues suggested would help professors and students enter into a new and closer working relationship than the social pressures on the student and the scholarly pressures on the professor now permit.

Students, widely conscious of the generation gap, must be provided better avenues of discussion with alumni and the public, and the agenda of their meeting may appropriately be the college's educational program. Professors, alumni, and laymen must listen regularly and seriously to what students contribute. Mutual concern and mutual respect have little chance to grow unless effective communication prevails.

The objective of university reform and restructuring is clearly the improvement of the educational program. The objective must not be identified with or allowed to become placation of one group over another, a compromise with student power, or a preservation of the *status quo*. The overriding objective must be a more effective educational program for all concerned. No other motive can be allowed to intrude.

If these constituencies can be brought together in a meaningful, constructive manner, solutions to other shortcomings of the university will begin to fall into place. The somewhat mysterious role of the trustee or regent would be clarified; personal needs of students would be examined in relation to the community needs for leadership and direction; and faculty rewards would rest on a broader base. In the final analysis, all parties should be searching for the "knowledge of greatest worth" and for the most favorable conditions of learning and teaching. In today's complex of higher education, advisory committees of the kind herein described could very well become mini-boards of trustees.

The second area of university reform is that of the nonacademic life of the student. The concept of *in loco parentis*, that umbrella under which both parents and personnel deans "sheltered" students for so many generations, must disappear from the campuses. A college is not a parent and can never be one, and present-day transportation and communication make it a farce to believe that such a code can prevail, even if all parties desire it. Parents have held onto the principle through wishful thinking, and all too many institutional officials have been willing to encourage them to believe that the living experiences offered in the college environment would in some mysterious way inculcate in their sons and daughters high ideals and lasting values, of nebulous characterization, however.

Colleges and universities, as managers of housing and dining enterprises, must now work themselves out of the economic bind of mortgage payments that make it mandatory for certain groups of students to use those facilities. I suspect that the best way for institutions to bring the dormitory and dining enterprises into manageable dimensions will be to slow down on new construction and also offer the student a choice in arranging his own living conditions under circumstances acceptable to himself and his family. Such a change of policy suggests also that university-managed housing and dining facilities and their clients (students) must assume the regular relationship of landlord-tenant as found in the rest of society. Any change-over will take time, but it will eliminate nine-tenths of the disagreements originating in the *in loco parentis* concept.

Responsible and Responsive Participation

Reforming of the university today and tomorrow will undoubtedly call up the necessity periodically to reiterate the full length and breadth of academic freedom as it pertains to both students and faculty. In one sense, this principle is being tested to its extreme by those who insist that the university as an institution become involved in programs of social action. Individuals and groups who espouse this stand insist upon a commitment by the university to their cause. Needless to say, if such a course were adopted, those of contrary opinions, who also "search for truth," would be required to surrender to the commitment the university has made, or get out. The search for truth, therefore, must guarantee that even the smallest minority, the single student or the single professor, must still be allowed, in fact, encouraged, to pursue his studies even though the hypothesis he embraces may be shared by no one else.

Advisory councils to departments, schools, or colleges may be used to bridge the gaps which separate the various cultures concerned with the university community itself. I refer to student culture, faculty culture, alumni culture, and the culture of the lay public as it touches the university either politically or economically. In general, a machinery for creative change must be found, whether it be the advisory council or some other, which will provide better for the strength and vitality of the academic community to the end that the shortcomings of educational programs will be remedied. Otherwise the university must either retreat to its monastic background or become a political battleground. Either choice would render the university inadequate in today's world.

The real problem of representative democracy is, of course, the human one: It is difficult for the individual or group to back away from a problem of current importance, study it with detached objectivity, invite other parties to do likewise, explore all possible courses of action, and then join others with appropriate enthusiasm in implementing the solution arrived at—a solution that may be far different from the one first thought to be best. If policies are to be adopted, however, which reflect the very best of which faculty, students, alumni, trustees, and administrators are capable, a thorough, candid, and unselfish effort must be made. It follows that as each voice helps to mold policy, in turn, each must be governed by the same policy.

If broadly representative advisory councils were to be established where serious consideration would be given to the academic programs of departments, schools, and colleges, and if, at the same time, universities were to withdraw from the regulation of the nonacademic life of students, the stage might then be set for some constructive work. Participation of the many often denotes inaction, lack of responsibility, or no courage, and such inertness suggests that some of the myths of decision-making in our society ought to be laid aside. "The buck stops here" indicates a man of conviction and, in the committee-land of Academe, frustration sometimes abounds because of indecision. In the university, however, the tyranny of the individual—student, president, professor, or legislator—is too high a price to pay for "efficiency." We may now be sufficiently mature as a society and as a university to map out meaningful lines of participation by all segments, bring them face to face with the central educational activities of the campus, and benefit from the input of all in the basic refinements of higher education. This would recognize that faculties now hold fundamental power over academic matters, and, furthermore, it would reveal that faculties gained this position by demonstrating, particularly to governing boards and to the public, that they knew more about academic matters than others. The ground rules haven't changed today. If students, alumni, and lay citizens want a voice in the educational program, they must (and I obviously believe they can or I would not suggest an organization that includes them) demonstrate that their points of view and opinions are important to the total job of university education. Student influence on academic matters remains to be weighed on its merits; and, where student opinion withstands the test of cold objectivity, it must be admitted for its true value. At the present time recommendations by faculty bodies on academic matters are, in general, so highly regarded that deans, presidents, and governing boards, while often still required to give formal approval, generally give such approval without question. Advisory groups of the type here suggested—which would weigh student, as well as other, opinions—could, through serious efforts, achieve similar respect.

If creative change, as John Gardner uses the term, is to find a haven in the university, the institution must be governed in such a way as to guarantee that questions will be raised at all levels and from all constituencies and that, once raised, such questions will have full consideration. Representative democracy calls for procedures both within and without the university that will offer a careful sifting of requests and suggestions, followed by systematic consideration by the entire community, after which recommendations for action can be made. In reality, the divisions among interest groups within the university and even beyond its boundaries are both exaggerated and artificial. Aside from the small group of anarchists who wish to destroy the colleges and universities, it must be assumed that all individuals and groups—professors, students, administrators, alumni, trustees, and the general public—are first of all citizens of, and friends to, the university. A university's survival or even its adequate nourishment for continued good health, would, therefore, be greatly endangered today without the ongoing participation and support of each group. How ridiculous it would be to cut off the university from intimate liaison with the public; and equally ridiculous would be the requirement that the professor submit his course outline for approval to the students who have just registered for his seminar or to the alumni who have returned for a reunion.

Most of the difficulty that has arisen in recent years on campuses can be laid to the efforts of special groups to use the university in ways in which this institution cannot be used; to manage the campaign for civil rights; to conclude the war in Vietnam; to protect the oil depletion allowance; or to defy society's generally accepted ethical or legal standards. Infringements on freedom and breaches of order occur when individuals ask the university to encourage, to legalize, or to allow activities or behavior which the rest of society rejects. In this respect representative government on the campus is no different from the representative government of our political life.

Internally, the university in American society must have a structure organized along democratic principles and provided with safeguards against authoritarian take-over. Harold Dodds, writing in 1962 in *The Academic President*, noted that "academic leadership has shifted from the Napoleonic approach of earlier years to a more democratic, representative form of governance by conference." Sound organizational structure can encourage participation and, in practice, can actually teach responsibility. The university professor has been characterized as "one who thinks otherwise." And Walter Lippmann has written, "Where all men think alike, no one thinks at all." The governmental structure of a university must be such as to admit either the professor or any other member of the community who chooses to think otherwise, and that same structure must encourage all to think seriously about the matters at hand.

Objective Participation in Governance

In the final analysis the university must be run by the power of truth and logic, and the best governance will be that which provides a fair hearing for all voices. The common objective of all voices is the creation of the best possible educational environment in order that study and search may be carried out with the least interference. Teaching and learning require both freedom and order. Without freedom, there is intellectual bondage; without order, there is academic chaos. Infringements on freedom and breaches of order occur most frequently when groups, whether within or beyond the university, pursue their own objectives at the expense of the basic purposes of the institution.

Patrick Henry said, "Don't tread on me," and the student today is pleading, "Don't fold, spindle, or mutilate me." Yet the importance of the individual is often considered today unrealistic, romantic, youthful, impractical. On the other hand it is precisely the relationship between the individual and the organization which has the most profound effect on the student's membership in the community that is the university.

And I would suggest that the ultimate test of the structure of an institution is the effectiveness by which the structure aligns the individual to the organization and its goals. In the university, each person has his own mosaic of individual pursuits, and his accommodation with the purpose of the institution is, therefore, a most delicate and critical task. However, such pursuits are never completely separated from the larger society of which the individual and the institution are members. Advisory councils which provide bridges of communication among students, public, faculty, and alumni may help to restore these groups to the greater unified society instead of contributing to greater divisiveness. The generation gap is but one of higher education's problems of communication.

The framework of checks and balances in colleges and universities has given rise to the now old-fashioned committee system, but until something better comes along, the committee remains the best means for rational and exhaustive consideration of academic affairs. The suggestion of one more committee—this time an advisory group—will be looked upon as the last straw on the academic camel's back. However, without the committee, action is too often taken in response to pressures and is, therefore, lacking in objectivity. Appropriate committees provide the mechanism for meticulous and exhaustive study. There is, as yet, no worthy substitute. Let us now simply expand the bases of both committee representation and scope of deliberation and enjoy the greater dividends accruing from the wealth of their contributions.

The committee system, after all, has proved itself to be flexible enough to promote academic freedom, strong enough to protect individual rights, and manageable enough to enlist understanding and support far beyond the immediate university family. As we bemoan the academic backache brought about by the weight of the multitude of committees, we must ask whether the burden is too great a price to pay for the kind of governance under which the university may best reach its objectives. That which is good for alumni—or administrators, or the general public, or students, or professors, or trustees—may also be good for the institution as a whole, but each proposal remains to be examined with as much objectivity as can be mustered.

Any power except the power of truth is self-serving power and has no place in the university; the power of ideas and the conditions that best serve their pursuit remain the only proper weapons for use in the intellectual arena that is the university. Power without truth is a falsehood and incompatible with the campus; and, since the power of a university is truth, it follows that the work of the university is the continuing struggle for truth.

Said another way the university is to be governed by all hands who have an interest. Since the New England town meeting is impractical, all who have an interest must be appropriately represented in such a way as to enlist their wisest participation, and to the end that scholars of all ages may seek the truth.

Today for thee and tomorrow for me.
Cervantes, *Don Quixote*

EDWARD SCHWARTZ

Student Power—
In Response to the Questions

DURING 1967–68, I wrote a variety of tracts and articles outlining my sense of what student power in universities should mean, and what it should not mean. One of the latest of these appeared in the September 1968 issue of *Mademoiselle*. As in earlier statements, I tried to spell out the general propositions of the program—student control over student institutions and rules; student-faculty cooperation on matters relating to the curriculum; student involvement in matters basic to university life, such as admissions and investments—and then proceed to place the program in a context of educational theory. The effort has been to formulate a coherent rationale for our arguments and to communicate this rationale in terms which could be understood readily.

I admit, however, that this approach has raised as many questions as it has answered. Why do students want power (as distinguished from *why* should students *have* power)? What is the competence of students to exercise power? Over which areas of university life? In our view, what changes in the university will be necessary if students are to be accorded power? Each of these questions has been asked, explicitly or implicitly, at meetings of the educational establishment where the issue of student power has been raised.

Consequently, my intent here is to deal with several of these questions in a fairly precise manner. I have always contended that the discussion of student power is more a battle about educational theory than it is a debate between corporate and democratic theorists, as much a discussion of the kinds of decisions that are made in universities as it is an argument

56

over who should make them, and as involved with trust between people as it is with the structures through which people move. Yet to understand the relationship between these general themes and the specific points of contention between the establishment and the students, one must deal with specifics.

Some Whys of Student Power

Why do students want power in universities? Some argue that they really do not. J. W. Anderson, writing in the June 30, 1968, issue of the *Washington Post*, observed that, "The slogan 'Student Power' is misleading. The students do not want power, in any conventional sense of the word. They are not demanding seats on boards of trustees, and they do not see themselves as future administrators. They wish the university to be run with more regard for them, but they do not wish to run it themselves."

College presidents who recently have read student manifestoes demanding seats on the board of trustees doubtless would dispute this claim, and Anderson partially contradicts himself elsewhere in his piece by describing a protest at Roosevelt University in which the administration capitulated on precisely this demand. Yet Anderson is correct in one important respect—the demand for student power begins only after students become dissatisfied with the university policy. If students are satisfied with their institutions, they are more than willing to let the establishment govern them.

The experience of the author's alma mater, Oberlin College, is indicative. For years, students petitioned the Oberlin administration and faculty for change in campus social rules, with little success. Ultimately, they lost confidence that either group would agree to student wishes. At that point, they demanded power to make those rules for themselves, on grounds that only they had to obey the rules and that the Oberlin rulers did not understand or share student sentiment. The desire for power sprang out of disenchantment with policy.

On the other hand, Oberlin students rarely suggested that undergraduates should be involved with curriculum planning. The reason was simple. When asked, "Do you feel that you are getting a good education at Oberlin?" most students replied, "Yes." It is only in the past two years, when student leaders began to question aspects of teaching and the curriculum, that the demand for joint participation in decision-making about curriculum has arisen. In 1967–68, two students sat on the faculty educational policy committee and many important changes were adopted.

Hence, just as the American colonists endorsed a Declaration of Independence only after they had thrown tea in the Boston harbor, the student community demands student power only after requests that involve policy matters are rejected, or ignored. Often, administrators counter undergraduate pleas for power with a counter-plea for "trust in the university community." What these presidents fail to recognize is that student power movements develop because trust has broken down —for whatever reason, the students no longer trust the establishment to make decisions on their behalf. Not surprisingly, administrators who use this argument meet with little success.

Further, the degree to which a movement for student power is militant depends largely upon the process by which administrators reject a specific set of student demands. If the president, or dean, or professor fails to give the student a hearing; or if he seems less than receptive to extensive discussion with students; if, in short, he rejects a proposal because students initiated it, then he will be subjected to a revolution in short order. He may be subjected to a similar response if, despite his best intentions, he is inaccessible to students—the problem in most multiversities. In both cases, students feel that, not simply their proposal, but also their identity has been insulted.

Even the president who tries to "understand" and "reason" with his students may face a student power movement. Tolerance does not mean agreement, and if the areas of disagreement between students and administrators are sufficiently broad, then the demands that the students will make on their institution will broaden as well. A dean at Oberlin tried to be understanding. His approach to social rules, however, dated to the Oberlin of 1930. No amount of "rational discussion" could bridge the chasm between institutional and undergraduate values. Demands for student control over the rules were the result.

If student disagreement with university policy leads to demands for student power, administrative opposition to a particular *set* of demands, more often than not, explains their resistance to student power in general. Of course, both sides can argue their case in the most elevated and theoretical terms. Yet specific points of conflict often lie in the background. The dynamics of university battles are suggestive—the dean and president ally with the students when they seek power over the curriculum, since neither one exercises much power over this area; and the faculty is more than willing to cede student power over social rules, finances, and even issues involving recruitment and investments. Everyone in the university argues for student power at some point, provided such power is granted over somebody else's turf. Students become "rash, immature, transient, inexperienced, and incompetent" to a university official only when they challenge an area of governance over which that official exercises special control.

Consequently, one cannot consider demands for student power over given areas of university life without also considering the context of the policy questions that the students have raised. I doubt that any administrator would resist the accordance of institutional authority to undergraduate students if the students proposed, "We agree with what you're trying to do, and we want to help." Administrators often urge students to say just that. Yet student power is not sought in so submissive a spirit. That is the crux of the matter, and institutions will have to deal with it as an active force. I must outline each area of the student power program and unravel the debate surrounding it.

"Control over Their Own Affairs"

Should students maintain control over their own affairs—organizations, student governments, speaker programs, finances, dormitory rules, social life? Those of us who argue this case point both to the proposition of democratic theory which states that he who must obey a rule should make it, and to notions of personality development which encourage the accordance of responsibility to those who must learn to accept it. Administrators retort that students aren't "ready" to assume this kind of responsibility, that they need guidance and control in doing so, and that they fail to consider the "long-range interests of the institution."

Yet what lies at the heart of these administrative objections? When a college president or dean speaks of the "long-range interests of the institution," he inevitably has in mind some short-range student misdemeanor that will jeopardize them. It is essential, then, to consider forms of student activity that threaten administration policy. In earlier periods, I might have listed the invitation of controversial speakers to the campus, or the creation of radical political organizations, or the publication of illicit doctrine in the campus newspaper as being among central administration headaches. The growing acceptance of student rights among administrators has reduced friction surrounding these issues, however, and concomitantly reduced certain barriers to student power. Yet despite substantial reforms on a few campuses, battles over parietal hours and intervisitation remain fierce. Here, appeals to the "long-range interests of the institution" reflect essentially political considerations. Proposals to grant students control over their own rules—in the knowledge that those rules will be liberalized—conjures up visions in administrative minds of angry alumni, aroused parents, and incensed legislators railing against promiscuity and decadence in a presumed citadel of reason. Professors worry about the relationship between their school's "image" and its status. Frequently, both administrators and faculty ask, "How can you say that only students are affected by social rules when other segments of the campus may also suffer consequences of student behavior?"

At base, such arguments are symptoms to students of the *inability* of the professor or the administrator to govern rather than evidence of his strength. Men who decide on questions of "image" in our society are not among the specimens most admired by the younger generation, particularly in institutions designed to retain a critical independence from the surrounding society. Fear of controversy has silenced too many people from fighting injustice—permitted too many social crimes to remain untended—for the young to embrace this fear in higher education. In this sense, "student power" as a slogan may be an indirect plea for university power—a demand, an expectation, that universities should make decisions about their internal affairs based on the preferences of the people who live in them, not on the whims of people who surround them. If the administrator admits that he agrees with public sentiment, after using it to justify his stand, then he worsens his position. He emerges as a man who would hide behind a pile of alumni letters rather than defend his own beliefs—again, a coward, who merits little respect from students.

Of course, none of this is meant to imply that administrators who bluntly announce their desire to regulate campus sexual behavior will meet widespread undergraduate approval. That presidents and deans cloud such announcements behind rhetoric or politics is, in part, a tribute to student intensity of preference in matters of their nonacademic life. Young people, simply, are fed up with our society's obsession with personal and private morals, particularly when the obsession obscures the nation's disregard for a number of social morals. Intimacy between male and female should be a matter between the two, not between them and the world. Those who delight in determining rules for human interaction of this sort fall into a general category of people in our country who construct barriers to honest relationships of all kinds. Here again, young people are trying to break down those barriers. The cultural premise from which they spring has wrought so much social havoc as to render insignificant by comparison the cases of premarital pregnancy which arise from misuse or nonuse of birth control devices. Indeed, many students suggest that the helpful approach to the "relationship" question is the provision of birth control devices to prevent pregnancy, not the enactment of rules to prevent intercourse. The one facilitates a relationship; the other inhibits it. Students believe in facilitation.

The issue of student power over social rules, then, is enmeshed in the over-all generational battle over personal morality. Most universities would reject the approach deemed most helpful by students—the distribution of contraceptive devices in the dormitories. Yet institutions create real trouble when they exercise their value preferences in the other direction. Why should administrators *care* about student sex life? They seem to care about so few other areas of student personal growth and development—too few, in fact—that their choice of this particular behavioral pattern seems ludicrous. Indeed, that prestigious universities are abandoning these rules leads many of us to believe that the schools which retain them merely expose deficiencies in other areas of their programs. If institutions spent as much time generating an exciting educational climate as they do imposing rules, they might find that public reaction to their rules would diminish. This is the kind of question which students are raising—the question of priorities—and universities have been slow to answer it intelligently. Hence, the demand for student power.

On Teaching and the Curriculum

The quest for student power over curricular areas stems from a similar concern. A desire to sit around tables with professors discussing departmental matters is only a partial motivation for the demand. Indeed, in the past, many students were afraid to participate in faculty meetings— they respect their professors in a way that they do not respect their deans. Yet the challenges to university teaching and curriculum content have become sufficiently widespread as to delegitimize professorial stature and to loosen student self-restraint. Now that students are "flexing their muscle" in this area, there is little question that their demands will grow in intensity.

Here, too, much of the debate is theoretical. Students insist that, as learners, they should have a say in what they learn, and in how they learn it. After all, the students argue, they pay to receive an education. To these charges, professors respond that students lack the academic training to make appropriate judgments on curricular matters, that they are moved more by questions of popular taste than they are by standards of intellectual excellence, and that their participation in curricular decisions would erode a basic tenet of professional academic freedom.

Yet, as with demands for control over rules, specific grievances concerning teaching and the curriculum lie at the heart of student demands for shared power over the classroom. Each of these must be delineated.

To start, it is important to recognize that much of the student criticism about the classroom reflects discontent with the style of teaching rather than the content of particular courses. Dull lectures, perfunctory examinations, papers graded without substantive comment, lack of classroom discussion, inaccessibility of the professor, all these rank much higher on a list of student gripes than complaints that an English professor chose to teach *Hamlet* rather than *King Lear* in a Shakespeare course, or that a political scientist was a behavioralist rather than a traditionalist. Student Course and Teacher Evaluations are more critiques for teaching than they are proposals for curricular revision. The medium outweighs the message.

In raising these kinds of criticisms, moreover, students are challenging the areas in which professors have the least claim to professional competence. College teachers are not trained to be teachers; they are trained to be political scientists, economists, biologists, and philosophers. If they were trained to teach, and encouraged to teach well, perhaps there would be fewer student complaints about the quality of teaching. That they were not, however, renders foolish their argument that "professional competence" should be the standard against which student participation should be weighed. Conversely, students are not competent political scientists, economists, biologists, and philosophers, but they are competent judges of good and bad lectures, adequate and inadequate discussions, helpful and deficient comments on papers. Hence the area in which student critics can be most acute is the area in which the professor's skill is least developed—a condition which leads to enormous friction.

Indeed, faculty resistance to student power in the area of curriculum may reflect less concern about student "incompetence" than resistance to the kinds of questions which students are asking—uncomfortable questions about teaching which many professors do not want to consider. The academic faces extreme pressures to establish himself as a scholar, and he will argue that this task is far more related to his advancement than is any special attention paid to his students. Some claim to be bitter about this state of affairs. Bitter or not, they see little they can do to change the situation and they resent those who would demand teaching of them, when teaching doesn't pay off.

Yet, if faculty response to criticism of teaching is negative, then student power over the curriculum should become not simply a desirable goal, but an essential goal, to those who wish to create higher standards of teaching in universities. To whom else is the question of teaching more important? Departmental chairmen are interested in attracting distinguished scholars. University presidents may be interested in hiring national celebrities. Publication is the route to achievement of both goals. Only the students are solely concerned about good teachers and good teaching and will judge professors almost exclusively on that standard. If interest in a subject is a prerequisite to developing competence, then students may well have the greatest competence on the campus to evaluate teaching.

The real source of tension between students and faculty becomes even clearer, moreover, when one realizes that other kinds of student curricular proposals have met with some success. Undergraduate complaints about emphasis on grades and pressures to compete led to quick and widespread acceptance of pass-fail. Student pleas for "relevance" are yielding quiet revolutions in the designing of courses in the social sciences and humanities. Requests for "learning by doing" are being met slowly through the development of community action curriculum projects, which should become commonplace within the next five years. Greater flexibility in requirements, new opportunities for independent study, interdivisional majors, even student-taught courses all have become "respectable" innovations for a university to consider. It is only when the nature of the *relationship* between student and professor is challenged— through questions about teaching, about the teacher's availability outside the class—that the student faces all the familiar arguments about his "incompetence." Yet such arguments merely verify what students suspect —that professors are reluctant to develop relationships with students, that they may have to be pressured to do so.

On the Quality of Institutional Life

Students should participate in decisions basic to university life—the third general principle of student power. College presidents cringe in horror at this notion. "Which areas?" they ask. "What are students competent to decide?" "Do students want a say in *everything?*"

This sort of gut reaction reflects as much general presidential insecurity as it does hostility to students as a pressure group. I doubt if there are many professional groups more self-pitying than college presidents, who spend their lives bemoaning the number and variety of constituencies to which they must respond. Frankly, having spent two years in the office of the National Student Association, during which time I had to react to such diverse groups as the Central Intelligence Agency and the Students for a Democratic Society, the Ford Foundation and the "Dump Johnson Movement," the Columbia student strike and the American Council on Education, I am somewhat less sympathetic to all this pouting. Yet I can see that a college president who fancies himself the harassed intersection of a myriad of opposing vectors might become reluctant to add yet another interest group to his list.

Nonetheless, the "Oh, how pressured we are!" argument becomes downright obnoxious when attached to a notion of bureaucratic efficiency. As one prominent educator recently put it, "Why, we've got a job to do—turning out doctors, and lawyers, and engineers. If we spent all our time in this dialogue business, we'd never get anything done." In that one brief comment was embodied every notion about higher education which students are determined to change: that young people are "objects" who have to be churned off an assembly line for society; that the success of the educational process should be measured in terms of the number of students who can be processed; that interaction, discussion, mutual decision-making are hindrances, rather than assets, to education. The future "doctors, lawyers, and engineers" are tired of being viewed only as such. The future poets and social activists are quite prepared to destroy a system that treats them in this manner. Yet the educator's sentiments, I am sure, are widely shared.

The matter is complicated further inasmuch as, here again, the student demand for a say in basic university decision-making reflects a concern that new factors be considered among the criteria in making decisions. The introduction of a new variable does not make an equation easier to solve. Students feel, however, that certain variables must be weighed if

just decisions are to be made by university administrations. Justice is not
a function of efficiency. Indeed, justice may depend upon *inefficiency*.
Yet students demand that considerations of justice outweigh those of
efficiency.

They demand the consideration of justice, particularly in areas of university policy that relate to political and social questions of the nation.
Among the areas involved are research grants, investments, recruitments,
relationships with government agencies, extramural housing projects in
ghettos, admissions—in short, all the areas about which the Students for
a Democratic Society has expressed the greatest concern. When some of
us argue that students should be accorded an institutional voice in certain
of these areas, we meet the familiar arguments about competence. As
with professors and deans, however, the presidential reference to competence often clouds a more central objection to considering concerns
which students might raise about certain decisions.

Take the area of university investments as an example. Whenever I
suggest to a university president or educator that students should have a
say in where the institution invests its money, I am met with the reply,
"Oh nonsense, students don't understand how to invest money, and we
don't have time to train them. Even I don't fully understand these
things."

The argument is well-taken, but misses the point of the students' demand. Even if most undergraduates could not evaluate whether an investment were an appropriate financial risk, they most certainly could and
would point out that Mississippi Power and Light Company (in which
Harvard invests substantially) may not hire Negroes, that the Chase
Manhattan Bank helps support the economy of South Africa, and that
the Dow Chemical Company manufactures Napalm for the war in Vietnam. They might make similar points about acceptance of grants from
the Defense Department, the Central Intelligence Agency, or the Institute for Defense Analysis. About the market, students know little;
about social issues many students are extremely perceptive and sensitive.

The real issue surrounding the accordance of student power over many
of these areas, then, is the policy question—whether administrators will
agree that the political stance of universities should be an important consideration in institutional decision-making. Such concerns are, indeed,
inefficient. Occasionally, they even involve economic costs. Yet students
would contend—often through vigorous means—that failure to confront
these issues yields even greater moral and social costs. They find it strange

that a college president who lauds student efforts to combat racism in the South becomes furious when the same student points out that a university project or investment contributes to racism. They feel that if the president is a morally sensitive man, he will want his students to raise these kinds of considerations, since so few people in the university, and even fewer outside it, are raising them. When the president rejects responsible contentions of students, they can reach only one conclusion— and they act on it.

What Kind of Rule?

What I have tried to suggest throughout this piece is that the debate over student power involves more than just the question, "Who rules?" It also involves "What kind of rule?" and "What are the qualities of humane rule?" The impact of social movements for civil rights at home, for peace in Vietnam, has led to a demand that all institutions, and particularly those whose presence is felt immediately by the young, act humanely. University intrusion in private love affairs is deemed inhumane; professional disdain for teaching is deemed inhumane; administrative obliviousness to the social concerns of students is deemed inhumane. In every case, students are trying to inject a new sense of political and social responsibility in a society that appears to have ceased to honor either.

When leaders of the society, and of the university, resist the kinds of changes which students propose, the students then demand institutional power so that they may enact the changes themselves. Bob Dylan's exhortation that fathers and mothers should "Get out of the way if you can't lend a hand" is as clear and vibrant an expression of this feeling as any which has been offered. The student demand for power further tests the university's humaneness. A university which is decent to its students will grant student power as an expression of trust and as an indication that it sympathizes with the student concerns. When the university administration or faculty rejects the student cries for power—often by using arguments which skirt the real issues and insult the students' integrity— the young's image of the corruption of the old order is reinforced.

Yet the young will no longer accept corruption without a fight. Those who miss this sense of urgency do so at their own risk. What young people lack in argumentative skill and political experience they make up for in growing tactical sophistication and a willingness to apply it. They are determined to win points, and, judging from the pace of events, they probably will. The question is no longer whether, but how; no longer how far, but how fast; and these depend, essentially, upon the ability of an old order to move, to change, and to grow.

Changing Internal Structures

LINCOLN GORDON, ROBERT JOHNSTON,
M. K. CURRY, JR., BERTRAM H. DAVIS,
DOUGLASS CATER

Oases of Freedom
LINCOLN GORDON

THE PAPERS of Lloyd Elliott and Edward Schwartz both provide substantial materials for a discussion of university structure and governance. Elliott's is the more analytical, while Schwartz mixes analysis with a kind of advocacy in which overly colorful pejoratives detract considerably from the force of his arguments.

Elliott properly begins at the beginning by explicitly restating the purpose of the university as the advancement of learning and the objective of university governance as the best conditions of learning and teaching for furthering the pursuit of truth. In Schwartz's paper, some passages imply a similar concept of the university as an institution devoted to the advancement and transmission of knowledge and understanding, but other passages suggest sympathy with the notion that the university should be a springboard for the revolutionary restructuring of society as a whole.

From these divergences follow important differences in the premises for reforming university governance. Elliott explicitly posits a basic consensus—except for a few anarchists whom he apparently feels can be safely disregarded—among all the interest groups, inside and outside, full time and part time, involved with a university community. These groups obviously differ in special interests and backgrounds, but not in their broad objectives. From this premise follows the conclusion that reform in governance requires, not a radical restructuring, but rather

68

new or better devices to improve communications among the various groups and to reweight the inputs of their respective influences. Elliott's main recommendation to this end is his proposal for departmental advisory groups. In this broad area, Schwartz again is ambiguous, sometimes implying basic consensus on objectives but at other times conjuring up a sort of Hobbesian state of nature—the warring of every man and group against every other—a state in which the life of the university would soon become, as Hobbes put it, "poor, nasty, brutish, and short."

On one critical issue, the two authors disagree clearly and explicitly. Elliott believes that the essential character of the university as a free marketplace of competing ideas requires that the university as such *not* be institutionally committed to specific public causes or programs of social action. Schwartz, on the other hand, wants universities to take a "political stance" on issues of concern to students and seeks student power to ensure that that stance is congenial to student opinion.

On this fundamental issue, I believe that Elliott is right and Schwartz wrong. Universities occupy a highly privileged position as oases of untrammelled intellectual freedom, bolstered by the practice of professorial tenure and by the custom of free debate. They enjoy a unique status as institutions supported by government, directly or indirectly, but whose members are uninhibited in their criticism of government and other social organizations. In Europe and Latin America, they normally enjoy the additional protection of autonomy from interference by the ordinary civil police. These privileges have been won through centuries of hard-fought battles, and they are among the first to go whenever liberal democracy is replaced by one or another form of totalitarian government. (I am aware that a certain vogue has been achieved by a current pseudo-philosophy which claims that our freedoms are really shams disguising the thought control exerted subliminally by a "military-industrial power complex," but I always wish that its adherents could spend some time in universities in Russia, China, Cuba, Argentina, or in the Germany of the 1930s, in the hope that even their reluctant minds could scarcely remain oblivious to the difference. Perhaps the current experience in Prague will have been at least a temporary lesson for them.)

Obviously, an institutional stance must be taken by any university on issues involving its own institutional life, even though some of these may be fraught with controversy. Its admissions and hiring policy cannot trim between being segregationist or integrationist; it must choose. It must decide whether or not to include in its programs offerings which are strongly desired by some sectors of the community but may be hotly opposed by others. If it is located in a city, its actions are bound to be intertwined with the complex of urban problems which are at the forefront of public attention nowadays. (On this point, I was astonished to notice Schwartz's statement that "universities should make decisions about their internal affairs based on the preferences of the people who live in them, not on the whims of people who surround them." Laying aside the coloration of the word "whim," I had supposed that it was precisely this attitude which has been the target of so much student criticism at Columbia University.) Universities must evidently also take an institutional stance on matters of public policy directly affecting higher education.

Beyond these important, but limited, areas of direct institutional concern, however, I believe it fundamentally wrong for universities to take *institutional* stands on matters of public policy, no matter how clear-cut the moral issues may appear to student or faculty minorities or majorities at any given moment. Elliott rightly points to the constraints that such a stand would impose on majorities or other minorities who hold different points of view. It is of the essence of academic freedom that all these individuals and groups be able to hold and express and defend differing points of view without constraint. Where this self-limitation has been abandoned under pressure from powerful student or faculty groups—as happened not many years ago at the venerable University of San Marcos in Lima—the effect has been to destroy the university as a center of free inquiry and free teaching and learning.

This is why I would take issue with Schwartz's position on university investments. His line of argument would cast as campus political issues certain decisions whose actual political effects are trivial (such as university holdings of Chase-Manhattan securities in relation to *apartheid* in South Africa). It would be an absurd distraction from the central purposes of a university to promote embattled student politicking on a few shares of Chase-Manhattan or Dow Chemical or IBM or Polaroid or U.S. Treasury bonds. If students are sufficiently concerned with United States policy toward South Africa to want to make it a cause, there are far better ways to organize their pressures than politicizing what is now an essentially nonpolitical mechanism for deciding on university investments.

Similar considerations, both of pragmatic nature and of principle, lead me to oppose student or faculty membership on boards of trustees. This idea is mentioned only briefly, but evidently with favor, by Schwartz, and is referred to by Elliott only in his odd phrase on "the somewhat mysterious role of the trustee or regent." In my mind, the key point here is that proposals for student or faculty membership on boards of governance imply a role for trustees which it has taken a century of patient evolution to eliminate and which should not be revived. As Elliott rightly states, trustees today *de facto* do *not* concern themselves with academic appointments and promotions, the curriculum, or the details of student affairs. Their trust is essentially one of looking to the maintenance and growth of the financial and physical corpus of the institution and overseeing its broad developmental policies. The willingness of public-spirited laymen to fulfill this role without interfering in professional concerns is a feature of American university organization greatly envied in other countries. It should not lightly be discarded.

As to the substance of structural reform, I agree with both authors on the need for greater student participation in curricular design and in control of student affairs. Both papers, however, seem to me to beg one critical question which has been woefully underdiscussed in the outpouring of argument concerning student power. This question has to do with the nature of student representation and the relations between student representatives and their own constituents.

On many campuses, it is a standard complaint of the activists that elected student councils are "passive," mere "sellers-out to the establishment." The activists seem to feel that the intensity of their own moral convictions—or perhaps the superiority of their tactical skills in what they call "winning concessions"—makes them legitimate spokesmen for entire student bodies. But this is an arrogant claim and not really defensible. If in fact the great majority of students feel that they are at the university in order to study—to grow in intellectual and humane stature while acquiring professional insights and skills—the mechanisms for student participation should ensure that this majority is appropriately represented. And whoever the representatives are, there should be arrangements to ensure that the views they advance are favored by their constituents and are not merely their own personal predilections. Especially in large institutions, this is no easy task, and it warrants much more discussion than it has yet received.

More Than Lip Service

ROBERT JOHNSTON

Dr. Elliott's and Mr. Schwartz's principal conclusions seem to me to be as follows: Large numbers of college and university students (here and abroad) are administratively and psychologically alienated from the form and content of their education and from the processes of achieving change in their educational institutions. That is, there are few if any mechanisms on more than a handful of campuses by which students can exert a reasoned, significant influence on either the substance of the education they are offered (what they are asked to learn) or the way in which it is presented to them (regardless of their approval or disapproval), their positive or negative evaluations of what is being done, and the depth of their feelings on this question.

Mr. Schwartz addresses himself mainly to enumerating and explaining the students' concerns which, through long neglect on the part of those in charge of educational institutions, have given rise to cries for "student power." Among the concerns are teaching and curriculum which ignore the diversity and depth of students' interests; universities that have allowed themselves to become deeply enmeshed in national and international affairs that the students find repugnant; universities that support, if not implant, a life style heedless of values that many students think should be taken much more seriously; systems of institutional repression which inhibit innovation, protest, and change in even the most basic areas of student concern, such as dormitory rules and the enforcement of standards of conduct irrelevant to the processes of learning.

Mr. Elliott discusses the complementary question, alternative methods of governance, and proposes a more open decision-making process. His plan involves a larger circle of discussion of all university questions, principally through freer standards of information sharing developed with numbers of strategically placed advisory committees.

As a journalist who has had a long-time interest in educational problems, it seems to me these two interests of the authors—involving students in the processes of education and at the same time seeking to invest far more resources than we now do in improving these processes—merit first priority in assessing directions for institutional change. We know very little about what "education" means, how it takes place, and what its specific short- and long-term benefits are. But we certainly do know that unless large amounts of institutional resources—time, money, and talent—are committed to improving the educational process, we are going to see very few important changes from the highly unsatisfactory present situation.

And we know, further, that although these resources are a prerequisite, they will hardly be sufficient unless they are used in direct cooperation with the students whom they are designed to benefit. We see everywhere too much education and not enough learning. Only students can learn; they cannot and must not be taught *to* or *at*; they must be active, in fact the most active, participants in the educational process. It is absurd to assume, as the present educational system seems to, that the high degree of student participation which must precede efficient learning will be automatically forthcoming in a classroom and university setting which in fact allows for no participation at all, only acquiescence.

The two papers thus seem to me to offer adequate discussions of some of the students' problems and some new directions to pursue in solving them. One should, however, be clear about the limitations of the advisory committee approach, as proposed by Dr. Elliott. First, if advisory committees are to be effective, those who are to be advised must be willing to share information concerning the problems under consideration. For all their rhetoric about free discussion, universities now are run in an extremely secretive manner. Unless the concerned parties will agree beforehand to discuss issues freely, then advisory bodies are doomed to misuse and disuse. A second prerequisite for an effective advisory group is its strategic location close to the people and issues with which it will be concerned. In curricular matters, for example, departmental student advisory groups have in many institutions worked out well, whereas college-wide curricular advisory groups have been totally ineffectual.

Moreover, at the same time that institutional renovators are fiddling with new committee systems, they would do well to streamline the present system. Everywhere major logjams hamper change and innovation. Efficient centers of decision making are needed—small committees or officials empowered to give authoritative go-aheads to experiments and new developments—so that a new idea does not have to make its way through a dozen hostile committees and be subject to a blackball by any one of them. (Berkeley's Board of Educational Development, created two years ago, has been given a small but effective role of this kind.)

Dr. Elliott's and Mr. Schwartz's papers, beyond their concern for the longstanding neglect of the students' position in the processes of teaching and learning, raise additional serious questions which are best seen in the following contradiction between them. Mr. Schwartz points to the students' concern with developing a very different life style from what their families have known and into which their colleges have sought to socialize them. It would be a life style incorporating, as he says, an increased "moral sensitivity."

Dr. Elliott, on the other hand, thinks universities should opt out of the struggle over social problems and social decisions in which they have become enmeshed. He opposes the "assumption that the university is the best institution for designing the future" as inimical to the university's basic goals. But alas, to define these basic goals he falls back on a cliché, "the reasoned pursuit of truth." Such a phrase must be put in the same category as Mr. Schwartz's concern for "moral sensitivity": so general and vague as to serve only as a cover for a multitude of sins and vested interests.

Lurking behind Dr. Elliott's pursuit of truth are all the same problems as attend Mr. Schwartz's "moral sensitivity": entanglement in the role of arbiter or—worse—battlefield, with a range of extra-university interests which are at best tangential and at worst disastrous to the university's classic and I think most appropriate role as principal custodian in the preservation, creation, and transmission of knowledge.

If student activists on the one hand and university administrators on the other were to pay more than lip service to this classic concept of a free university, a number of important implications would become clear; and most of them, I think, say more for the acuity of the students' perceptions of their universities' proper roles than for the perceptions of their more traditional guardians.

First, student activists have courageously and appropriately developed civil rights and political and other New Left movements into strong forces for change outside the umbrella of university protection, usually without even invoking university prestige. Marxists would say that students were developing a class consciousness.

Second, as students, they are, in the classic conception of the university, free agents in their societies. The university, acting *in loco parentis*, is inimical to this concept and puts the university in a position of monolithic authority vis-à-vis its students. This extraneous authority and responsibility can only serve to confuse the true issue of the best relation between teacher and student for learning.

Thus, university communities, as opposed to the university itself, are entirely appropriate (even desperately necessary) places for the development of alternative life styles for the future. On might even say that students as a class (or community, depending on your preferred terminology) have already played a very significant and productive role in this respect, but they have been most successful when they have gone outside the university's institutional structure to do so.

Third, the student activists have, with great care and considerable tactical ingenuity, stripped away the pious phrases that the traditional guardians of education have used to defend or to hide their own excursions into nonacademic affairs. The interpenetration of national vested interests and university skills and needs has been thoroughly exposed by careful reporting and analysis by the New Left. Clearly, there will be no relenting on this issue until universities are restructured, in fact as well as in theory, as the *independent* guardians of knowledge, bound to no government, no elite, and no one point of view.

Fourth, and pragmatically, it seems clear that those who control and are responsible for universities have conceived much too large a role for themselves. Universities must be able to fulfill their classic essential functions. Students, beyond their immediate concerns with the acquisition of new knowledge, are outside this sphere of proper interest. Student government, student rules, student publications, ought to be left *entirely* in the hands of students and be placed completely outside the university's institutional structure. The students can thus organize their lives, and their present and future life styles, as they see fit.

Fifth, it is clear that a proper balance between the university's role in the transmission of knowledge and its role in the creation of new knowledge has not yet been worked out. The former has been receiving almost no attention, compared to the latter, so that in this area students have every right to make demands on the university for a redress of the balance. And it must follow, as night follows day, that an effective redress of the balance will involve a great deal more participation and give-and-take in the processes of teaching and learning than now exists.

If, therefore, one limits one's conception of the university to the classic role of preserving, transmitting, and creating knowledge, the ambiguity of "moral commitment" *vs.* "pursuit of truth" disappears, and the responsibility for and control of social change and innovation is placed back where it belongs—with the society as a whole and with its members. Likewise the dilemma of institutional change (what changes are needed, and how best to achieve them) is very much clarified. With goals and purposes well defined, criteria of achievement and compatibility are much more easily arrived at. With these institutional responsibilities clarified, the kinds and degrees of participation required of everyone involved will become clear. Institutional change at that point is no longer a problem of power, vested interests, democracy, or whatever, but simply of commitment to the basic ideals of one of the world's oldest social institutions—ideals that have been severely jeopardized by the last twenty-five years of American academic administration.

The Nemesis of Creativity

M. K. CURRY, JR.

LLOYD ELLIOTT raises the critical question: Is our form of government relevant to the current demand to change the internal structures of higher education so as to provide viable skins for the new wine of a revolutionary age? To put it another way, he asks whether democracy, as we know it, provides an adequate frame of reference for the radical changes which the students, quasi-students, and faculty members of this generation are fighting to make the new norms of governance and operation and acceptable goals and objectives in higher education? Or, to phrase it still another way: Is there any traceable, significant, logical connection between the implications of democracy and the drive to change the internal structures of higher education in America today?

The answer to the question in any of its forms may rest on: (1) our definition of democracy; (2) the nature of the purpose of higher education; (3) the definition of the structures within which higher education takes place today; and (4) the meaning of the tumult: What are the changes being sought really intended to achieve?

President Elliott's reference to "representative government" as "one means or response which our society has accepted in putting concepts of democracy into practice in Western culture" calls to mind John Stuart Mill's great treatise on political philosophy, *Considerations on Representative Government*, the first book to expound the modern theory of democracy and to defend this kind of democracy as the best form of government. Perhaps a review of Mill's theory will shed some light on our definition of democracy and on the role of higher education in implementing its purpose.

Mill, On Representative Government

To Mill, democracy meant nothing less than universal suffrage which at least occasionally permitted all citizens to take an active part in the government, by the personal discharge of some public function, local or general.

Mill did not think, however, that every form of government was possible for every people. He believed that there are "conditions of society in which a vigorous despotism is in itself the best mode of government for training the people in what is specifically wanting to render them capable of a higher education." He thought that three conditions must be considered in determining whether a form of government is suitable to a given country: (1) The people for whom the form of government is intended must be willing to accept it, or at least not so unwilling as to pose an insurmountable obstacle to its establishment. (2) They must be willing and able to do what is necessary to keep it in existence. (3) They must be willing and able to do what is required to enable it to fulfill its purposes.

Clearly these three conditions must be taken into account when we judge the form of government within any community of a given country which is committed to representative government. By this token, it should apply with equal relevance to institutions of higher learning in that country.

Mill also considered the criteria by which we are to judge the goodness of a particular form of government. According to him, the best government is "one which fulfills the purposes for which governments are established." Mill then defines the purposes of government and concludes:

> The merit which any set of political institutions can possess consists partly of the degree in which they promote the general mental advancement of the community, including under the phrase advancement in intellect, in virtue, and in practical activity and efficiency; and partly of the degree of perfection with which they organize the moral, intellectual and active worth already existing, so as to operate with the greatest effect on public affairs.

According to Mill, representative government is the best form of government for large populations because it promotes, to a greater degree than any other form, "the general mental advancement of the community," and because it utilizes, in better fashion than any other government, "the moral, intellectual, and active worth already existing" in the community. In support of the first point, Mill contends that self-government will benefit men because of the influence it has in improving their character. Here he makes use of one of his favorite themes: the superiority of an active character over a passive one.

The best kind of person, and the happiest, according to Mill, is one who is not content merely to remain what he is, but who constantly tries to improve himself. He will not be satisfied with simply conforming to the customs and prejudices of his community but will blaze a new trail in a new direction. He will also be continually learning; he will be willing to embark on unusual paths of thought and action for the sake of discovery. Such a person will be an individualist in the best sense of the word, and he will be truly free.

Mill affirms that "this active type of character is greatly encouraged by self-government, whereas other forms of government suppress it in varying degrees. Indeed, for many men, participation in government may be the first step toward liberation from the chains of custom and conformity."

Mill contends also that not only is the mind of the citizen improved by participation in government, but also his moral education is furthered. The citizen must put aside selfish considerations and consider the common good. "He is made to feel himself one of the public, and whatever is for their benefit to be for his benefit." He argues that self-government promotes the common good by enlisting the energies of all the people, thus putting to the best use possible their existing good qualities. It most efficiently protects the rights and interests of the people, because each person is the best defender of his own rights. Since direct self-government is practicable only in a small town, representative self-government must be the truly ideal form for large and populous states. To protect the minority against the tyranny of the majority, Mill proposes *proportional representation*.

Proportional representation results in a legislative assembly that is more truly an exact image of the divisions of populate opinion that can otherwise be obtained. And it seems *just* that the assembly should mirror the country as a whole. But it must be remembered that *justice*, however important it may be, is not the only consideration to be taken into account when setting up governmental machinery. A government must also be able to govern efficiently, and to do so requires a considerable measure of *stability*. "A good government must strike a balance between the demands of justice and those of stability. It must not let the search for justice paralyze it into inaction; nor must it, for the sake of efficiency and stability, fall into the injustice of dictatorship or tyranny."

Now, many have pointed out that proportional representation seems to encourage instability in government, though of course it is not the only cause of such instability.

Obviously, the great problem facing the university today, in the midst of a technological revolution which makes possible more and more efficiency and which permits a larger and more diverse enrollment, is that of meshing properly and effectively the yearning for *justice* with the requirements of *efficiency* and those of *stability*. The students equate *justice* with *freedom*, and absolute justice with absolute freedom. The administrators and board members, and sometimes the faculties, who are also concerned with *efficiency* and *stability* think it necessary to limit freedom and to defer justice. Their efforts to do so leave them open to attack from the students who cry now for more and more proportional representation in the decision-making process. The resolution of this problem will probably come from a clearer definition of the roles in representative government.

Perhaps the real question is: Who governs in a representative government? Mill was more concerned with the problem of who should *not* govern than of who should. According to him, one thing is certain, "the representative body ought not to govern." He insisted that "there is a radical distinction between controlling the business of government and actually doing it," and therefore he opposed administration by representative bodies. He thought one man might decide and act more ably than a body of men. He saw the function of a representative body in matters of administration as "not to decide them by its vote, but to take care that the persons who have to decide them shall be the proper persons." Thus, according to Mill, "Deliberation, and *only deliberation*, is the proper function of the representative assembly."

More recently, Walter Lippmann, writing in *The Public Philosophy*, echoes the same idea when he argues that the proper separation of these two functions is necessary to the health of the government. We may extend these remarks to include the governance of the university.

Finally, Mill made the point with regard to universal suffrage that "it is the greatest educational means for raising mankind to a higher level." Said he, "Whoever, in an otherwise popular government, has no vote, and no prospect of obtaining it, will either be a permanent malcontent, or will feel as one whom the general affairs of society do not concern. . . . It is a personal injustice to withhold from anyone, unless for the prevention of greater evils, the ordinary privilege of having his voice reckoned in the disposal of affairs in which he has the same interest as other people."

Representation in University Governance

Now, as President Elliott points out, the mission of the university is above all else "the search for truth." The conditions under which that search is carried on, including academic freedom, is "the objective of all governance of the university." All are intended to ensure the best conditions of learning and teaching that will most effectively and efficiently further the pursuit of truth. Thus, as Masefield indicates, the real issue is not "Who shall govern the university, but rather: For what ends shall the university be governed?"

Within the framework of John Stuart Mill's delineation of the function of representative democracy, it would appear, there is room for change in the internal structures of modern institutions of higher learning so that the more effective and efficient pursuit of truth will be promoted. President Elliott proposes a remolding of the structure to include all segments of the academic community in the process of evaluating the adequacy and relevancy of the academic program. Recognizing that the public has already approved the principle that the governing board will delegate to the faculty the responsibility for molding academic policy, Elliott proposes that participation in the evaluation process be extended to the students, the alumni, and the supporting constituencies. The participation would be achieved through the creation of a departmental advisory body composed of professors, teachers, alumni, and the public. This body, after due study, could recommend to the department chairman and faculty suggestions for change. President Elliott recognizes the nonacademic life of students as a second area in need of reform. He suggests that the concept of *in loco parentis* is obsolescent and offers instead the idea of participation by the students themselves in the rules governing their nonacademic activities. I should think most colleges and universities would be willing to implement this proposal if they received from the students responses that are responsible and will guarantee the necessary measure of order in the midst of the new freedom.

If, as Mill suggested, the capacity to act responsibly grows with the opportunity for meaningful participation in the decision-making process, the caretakers of higher education must recognize the necessity of involving the students in more and more phases and at deeper and deeper levels of evaluation. This is not to suggest that the administration or the faculty should turn over the governance of the institution to the students and pre-empt for them the time and energy which they should devote to the development of skills to perfect the search for truth. Rather it suggests that the viability and flexibility of the democratic process should be proved to work satisfactorily in a program geared to producing the leaders for our form of government and our society.

The main problem is that administrations, faculties, and governing boards all too often succumb to the *nemesis of creativity*, in Arnold Toynbee's phrase; they lose the bent for creativity developed in one crisis situation (perhaps when they were students) and become the reactionaries and opponents of any and all change when succeeding generations of students come along, dreaming and yearning to build a new world order. If the capacity for renewal can be recovered in all segments of the university community and the responsible commitment to the search for truth can be raised above petty, selfish desires, there is a possibility that the university can survive this era of radical change and emerge as one of the creative forces that will fashion and mold the new society.

I have said nothing directly about Edward Schwartz's stimulating paper on student power. Mill's discussion of representative government is germane to his topic. Suffice it to say now that in an age of rising expectations, the insistence on student participation in the decision-making process in the university will increase, particularly when the governing boards, the administrations, and the faculties allow such a great gap to develop between the theory of democratic government and our actual practices. These groups must close the gap or students will move to try to control or destroy the system. Whether students would do better is debatable, but at least they may come to know from experience what the alternatives are like. The students, once in power, would also know the "nemesis of creativity." But society moves forward on the eternal eagerness of youth to succeed where their elders have failed. In the interests of progress, loose them and let them try!

The Constant Observers

BERTRAM H. DAVIS

AT A TIME when group power more and more becomes an end in itself, President Elliott usefully reminds us that the ultimate power of a college or university is truth and that a structure of institutional government can be justified only to the extent that it assists in fulfilling an institution's purpose. If we place too much emphasis upon group power, we are likely to create the expectation—if we are not already acting upon it—that power should pass into the hands of those who can muster the greatest numerical support or raise the loudest voices in their own behalf. But in a college or university, which is both an intellectual and a social community, the power of decision should reside with those who are best equipped to exercise it, whatever their numbers, and ideally each group should acknowledge the appropriate authority of the others and the extent to which its own authority may be shared.

President Elliott has also wisely recognized that, in attempting to advance its purpose, an institution should not deny itself the counsels of any group that has a proper interest in the institution. His proposal that advisory bodies be established for departments and separate colleges is a comprehensive one, intended to provide the faculty with the leavening experience of students, alumni, and representatives of the public. No doubt, as he suggests, the thought of another committee will provoke the inevitable groans, and it may be that an institution can devise somewhat simpler arrangements for enlisting such comprehensive assistance. The important point, nonetheless, is that such matters as curriculum, faculty evaluation, and the institution's relationships to the community run the risk of being unsatisfactorily resolved unless those who hold the power of decision seek out a variety of informed opinion.

President Elliott has, in fact, thrown down a challenge to all of us. Faculties, he says, achieved fundamental power over academic matters by demonstrating that they knew more about them than did other groups; but they are challenged to recognize that other groups may have something vital to contribute to their deliberations. The alumni, the public, and the students are challenged to "demonstrate that their points of view and opinion are important to the total job of university education." Of these groups, the students of necessity will play the most significant role, not merely because they have had the best organized support, but also because they are constant observers of the effects of institutional policy and by and large have reacted intelligently to it.

Like all slogans, "student power" may be self-serving. Yet even under a self-serving slogan, Mr. Schwartz provides a rationale for student participation in institutional affairs which should serve our colleges and universities well. One may be totally unconvinced by his discussion of institutional investments. One may argue that at one point he has failed to distinguish between curriculum and teaching. One may note an inconsistency in his first questioning whether an administration should care about the student's sex life and then his suggesting that it should *facilitate* intercourse between the sexes. (Some persons, of course, will be appalled at the suggestion.) But it is difficult not to be persuaded by his more significant arguments that students do have valid insights into the quality of teaching and that they ought to have an influence upon the curriculum designed to prepare them for living in a society of which they are often astute observers. His organization's attack upon the *in loco parentis* concept has steadily won supporters, although not all of them would happily relinquish to students the total control over student affairs that Mr. Schwartz desires.

The battles in these areas are old ones, and it is a mistake that over the years the students have steadily been repulsed: their role in institutional affairs has in fact been more influential than the record would lead one to believe. The student's evaluation of faculty members, if not openly solicited, has somehow been conveyed, and perhaps rare is the department meeting in which the reaction of students has not influenced decisions affecting the status of departmental members. Anyone having taught any length of time can recall incidents a good many years ago when students took matters into their own hands and through the threat of disruption, or some other unpleasantness, compelled a modification of institutional practice. What is needed now is the formalizing and clarifying of a role that has been essentially haphazard and ill-defined, as though we were afraid to confess that it existed. What is essential is a procedure that would dislodge student-based rumor, hearsay, and prejudice from our faculty and administrative discussions and replace them with responsible student opinion.

Of such a procedure the colleges and universities will surely be the beneficiaries. They will be the beneficiaries also if simultaneously they conduct re-examinations of the roles of their faculties and the procedures established for the exercise of those roles. It is gratifying to have President Elliott recognize the pre-eminent role of the faculty in academic matters, including the status of its own members. Perhaps the mere fact that a leading educator takes this role so much for granted will have a beneficent effect, for we ought not to conclude that it is quite so universally recognized as one might infer from his comments. It might be argued, in fact, that the differences in faculty role from institution to institution are far more striking than the differences in student role, for students have ways of exerting their influence which faculties for good reasons have eschewed; merely as subscribers to an institution's services they have had an authority beyond the faculty's reach.

Ultimately, we will do well to remind ourselves constantly of the foundation stone on which our institutions rest. If an institution's purpose is the pursuit of truth, we must adapt its structure and its procedures to that purpose, and we must seek the counsels of all those who can assist us in the quest. We must also vest primary authority for institutional matters in those who have shown themselves best qualified to exercise it. Any other arrangement invites the chaos which is threatening to engulf us.

Are We at Runnymede?

DOUGLASS CATER

MY PERSPECTIVE is that of a political analyst, one who is used to watching government and who would like to turn and watch universities for a time.

In reading the papers and in reviewing various discussions, I have asked myself at what point in the history of government can the university really be said to be. Are we at Runnymede, where the barons of the NSA and SDS and the rest are negotiating a Magna Carta? Or are we approaching that miracle at Philadelphia, and can we expect a full-blown constitution to emerge for the government of the university? Essentially, it seems to me, what we are discussing is the constitution of higher education.

It is curious that the time lag that has occurred in the development of a constitutional form of government, with its recognized apportioning of powers, should be paralleled in a university. The house of intellect, one might have thought, would be ahead of government. In the evolution of the United States Government we recognize, as one of its peculiar geniuses for the preservation of freedom, that our Founding Fathers called for a separation of powers.

Richard Neustadt refined that very perceptively when he said that "we don't have a separation of powers at all. We have separated institutions sharing powers, and this sharing process has become, in the American form of government, a very complex and still evolving process."

Our Constitution was devised by a group of men who fervently believed that that government is best that governs least. In recent years we have had to evolve constitutional arrangements to meet conditions under which governing least is by no means governing best.

Hence we have a living Constitution, which we do not read as a hard-shell fundamentalist reads his Bible. I think by comparison the university is still in a prehistoric age; except in rare circumstances, I see no evidence of a living constitution, written or unwritten, for the disposition of power. Mostly, the system seems to evolve from ad hoc arrangements made to deal with emergencies. We have no clear and accepted doctrine of the separation of powers by which, as new circumstances develop, a more modern constitution can evolve to meet the modern reality of the university. It seems self-evident that the modern university, like modern government, cannot retreat into the old philosophy that governing best is governing least. The university cannot today, either by choice or by circumstances, be an insular body.

If, as Dr. Elliott says, the pursuit of truth is the university's governing purpose, we must recognize that much of truth is no longer to be found solely in the cloister, that truth has become an organized search. It involves many alliances and entanglements outside the university, and they are not all amenable to clear black and white definitions. There is going to be increasing need for those outside the university, for those in the entangling alliances, to understand what the constitutional power structure of a modern university is. Where does the buck stop, and which particular buck stops where?

In perspective, in a university governed by separated institutions sharing powers, I must admit to a certain amount of bafflement over devising a clear-cut role for the student. Though I sympathize with a great many of the frustrations that have been expressed by them and their elders, they are not new. When I was a graduate student at Harvard, being sustained by a handsome fellowship, I left the university before getting my sought-after Ph.D. because I no longer felt a sense of relevance. As a first point, I think much of the complaint about being "talked at" rather than "talked with" points to a pernicious problem in the communication system in the university.

Second, I believe that activism on the part of students is educational. In my day I was one of the founding fathers of the National Student Association (well before, I might add, we ever dreamed of approaching CIA), and, when I look back on what taught me most during university days, I think these periods of activism were certainly as educational as anything in the classroom.

Third, I believe that protests by students do yield benefits and that the sheer history of student protests makes it evident that this is a role for students to pursue.

Yet some paradoxes trouble me in a time of mounting student unrest, mounting student claims for student power. The first paradox is that although there is a mounting assertion of student power, there seems to be declining interest in representative student government. In fact, student government, as I understand it, on most campuses has become passé. There seems to be no real interest in majority rule. I would suppose that the relative secrecy of an SDS convention could be compared to the secrecy of the trustees in making some of their decisions.

On the cutting edge of student power, there seems to be an effort by a posse of students to assert and claim power, yet without clearly defining the meaning of *power*. I think participation, within various limitations, is obviously vital for students: it is the right to be heard in orderly processes, obviously a well-meant, well-sought objective.

If power means the right to decide, then students are verging on territory that needs very clear definition, for here we reach another paradox. Mr. Schwartz mentions a special quality of humaneness among students: I wonder whether some chemical change takes place in us when we (most of us were students) cease to be students. Where did we lose that humanity? In a recent letter, a magazine asked me to write an essay for them entitled "Why I Sold Out." (I plan to do it after I know a little more in time.)

The exercise of power requires making what are called "51–49" decisions, where the difference between the superior good and the least bad is marginal. It requires that, having once made a decision, we must not, as Dean Acheson once put it, pull up the roots every morning to see whether the flower is growing. It requires a certain obduracy in sticking to a policy or program so that its worth can be either proved or disproved—this is what the exercise of power in governments and universities regularly involves.

How does the student, who is in the learning stage in life and who should be free of this kind of commitment, become involved as an active power factor in a university environment? Power is not an unfettered privilege to be sought after. In defining student power, there needs to be a great deal of precision, hard-headed analysis, and recognition of what is a right role for a student to play while he is still in the learning process and before he joins the more involved participating process.

In the evolution of constitutions, whether for governments or for universities, the arrangements of power are not always spelled out to the last crossed "t" and the last dotted "i." Justice Holmes once said that some things have to be stated obscurely before they can be stated clearly. There are many interstices in living constitutions. It requires a great deal of civility among those who share in the power process of constitutions not to test the last ounce of endurance in challenging others who share in that process. John Gardner has noted that the miracle of any social organization is when it works, not when it fails—a thought that should linger in our minds.

Democratic constitutions for governments and for universities remind me of the bumblebee: scientists tell us that, aerodynamically, the bumblebee can't fly. Somehow it does, and there will always be a great deal of miracle and mystery in the whole process.

[In] America . . . . no natural boundary seems to be set to the efforts of man; and in his eyes what is not yet done is only what he has not yet attempted to do.

Tocqueville, *Democracy in America*, Part I

FRANKLIN D. MURPHY

Some Reflections on Structure

CONSTANTINOS DOXIADIS, with his usual lucidity and perspicacity, refers elsewhere in this volume to the fact that any system, be it a human structure or a human institution, has an anatomical or structural component and a physiological or functional component. He stresses that we should be seriously concerned with the physiology—the function—and not be hypnotized by the structure. Yet at the end he does point out that we really must not forget the structure if we want an organism that can function viably. Just as the nineteenth-century biologists were preoccupied with description and structure, so in our time there is a preoccupation with function, biochemistry, physiology, and so on, which sometimes seems to me to understress the necessity for precise, thoughtful, and intuitive thinking about structure.

Much has been said by thoughtful people about the function of the American college and university—and its occasional dysfunction. I present here some reflections on the structure—without which there can be no function—that is, on governance and administration.

Structural Antecedents

The European university, as it evolved from the thirteenth century on, was essentially an unstructured enterprise. It was an almost spontaneous drawing-together of a community of scholars. There was much intellectual activity, functioning within a very rudimentary, almost unicellular structure; this structure grew not by a plan but by evolution, for even a community of free-wheeling scholars needed some kind of mechanism

88

to permit their dialogues to proceed in some constructive, reasonable way. What executives these institutions had were professors elected by professors.

Thus the European university has grown much like Topsy, in evolutionary fashion, to its 1968 moment of crisis. Make no mistake about it: just as we are preoccupied with the American university and its deep and serious problems, so our antecedent institutions in Western Europe have deep and serious problems, no less dangerous than those we confront.

We now see many thoughtful studies being made of ancient institutions in Britain, with what must seem to the British very radical recommendations for streamlining structures, for giving twentieth or twenty-first century recognition to how the new community of scholars can function. In Germany, students and politicians raise serious questions about the authoritarian tradition, which is presumed to support the right of the scholar to structure his life as he wishes—and the public and the student be damned. There has been in France a very different situation since Napoleon's reforms. A highly centralized structure is being torn apart, not deliberately or because of committed anarchy, but because the structure has simply never matched and kept pace with the evolution of the function. The dinosaur didn't die because anyone was out to get him; he died because the evolutionary process was simply not capable of changing his organism to deal with a new, suddenly altering environment.

In the United States we have had a somewhat opposite historical tradition. Our universities were established, not by a spontaneous gathering-together of a community of scholars, but by a deliberate intention on the part of thoughtful and interested men to build something called a university for very pragmatic purposes—not merely to explore man and his environment and the history of thought, but to serve the society.

Even Harvard College was established in the first instance with a highly vocational commitment to the production of well-trained clerical technicians, if you will. But no matter what its obligation or the objective, the American university was established by an appointed, self-perpetuating governing board, under circumstances of certain religious or public requirements, which by whatever mechanism it saw fit would then appoint faculty. It was the board who went out to draw together the community of scholars, under some plan of action, and that board also appointed a chief executive officer to keep the shop and to assist them in assembling that community of scholars.

Later, the American people, with their Yankee sense of pragmatism, decided that a laissez faire system could not serve all the needs of the growing young American Republic and created the land-grant, public institutions. But here again the principle was the same—not a spontaneous drawing-together of scholars but the deliberate creation of a system with a governing board, usually appointed by the government in some fashion, who in turn appointed a chief executive officer. Then together they assembled the body of scholars.

In both cases, in the United States, the university governing board represented less the scholarly interest than the public interest. In the European case, a board or university council represented the scholarly or internal interest. One reason the European university in our time has perhaps not so well served the technological requirements of a changing society is that its governing board has been preoccupied more with the interests of the scholars than with those of the society.

In Europe, we now see, by one means or another, radical recommendations for change, which I think arise out of sheer necessity and because the public recognizes that higher education is not a mere desirability; it is not merely a cultural badge. It has become a necessity for any society that wishes to advance effectively in a complex industrial and social world. It is the public interest, then, which forces reorganization. The public interest will, in my view, increasingly be expressed in the European revolutions today.

In the United States, the problem is to achieve a balance, in a somewhat different way, in terms of government, so as to serve the scholarly or internal interests more appropriately in decision making and administration.

The Governing Board

My first proposal: In the United States we must develop a new pattern, with at least one or more members of every governing board being persons who have had professional experience in higher education. In some ways, all complex institutions, regardless of their ultimate objective, have elements in common. Can we imagine any major industrial corporate board which had as a kind of unwritten mandate or common law tradition that no one with industrial experience would serve on the board? It would be inexcusable, and it would be stupid.

I am convinced that, in these latter days of specialists, universities have—not deliberately but almost by inadvertence—fallen into unnecessary traps of one kind or another. They have not admitted to the fundamental dialogue that must be carried on in a governing board those with intuitive insights who should be there. Some may say, "But the president is on the governing board. Does he not represent this kind of experience and insight?" Not entirely. The president is quite properly an institutional leader, and to some extent his objectivity can be questioned.

There are in this country today men and women of great skill, experience, and judgment who have left the higher educational community for a variety of reasons and whom institutions could call upon to provide this kind of service. It seems to me that the public interest can be well protected by using this kind of educational experience at a time when the university is often in deep confusion.

The Office of Chief Executive

My second major point: The office of the president or chancellor has become impossible—not merely in its demands on the mental and physical health of the incumbent but in what the office itself requires. Within my lifetime, the American university was comfortably isolated, up some tributary of the mainstream of society, where scholarly life went on in isolation, in a kind of Mr. Chips environment. Now we have *really* said goodbye to Mr. Chips.

The American college and university now has come into the mainstream, whirled about by currents of pressures almost unpredictable even fifteen or twenty years ago, and subject to the rising expectations of all segments of society—students, government, industry, adults (because of the increasing complexity of knowledge needing continuing education at an even greater rate). All of these pressures have put upon the university a load of obligations and a mass of expectations that are literally enormous in sum total. Yet the university's structural response has been practically invisible. It has been a Parkinsonian kind of response. New problems? Add a few more vice-chancellors. New areas of interest and knowledge? Add a few more schools and departments. It has been an additive and therefore totally unconstructive approach to the exponential growth of expectations and requirements.

My proposal in this case, then, is that large and complex institutions (smaller institutions are getting larger and more complex than they like to admit) should create *two* principal offices in the administration of the institution. Here again I turn to the corporate model. The office of chairman of the board should become a full-time, paid officer of the institution. He should be the chief *executive* officer. He should carry the title because in our society titles are important. Our institutions must deal with all segments of society, and presidents and chancellors know that when they say, "I will send our vice-chancellor or vice-president," they are asked, "Aren't we more important than that?" A full-time chairman of the board would have primary responsibility in the areas of finance, legislative and public relations, budget, and, in general, contacts with the exterior world. The president would become the chief *education officer* of the institution, with primary responsibilities for relationships with the faculty and the student body and for all the important internal plans and operations of the institution.

Unless the present office is separated into two parts, almost co-equally important, the role will become intolerable. The president's role will decrease in efficiency to a point where no one is really running the shop very well at all.

My third point: No matter whether this role is single or double, it will still be an enormously time-consuming job or pair of jobs. As it is structured today, no other institution in American society is called upon by more people to do more things under more intense pressure than the university. I feel that every governing board should *require* its chief executive officer or officers to take a sabbatical leave as often as do its faculty members.

A great deal of talk goes on, sometimes evolving into nonsense, about the importance of creativity within a university faculty. But nobody ever talks about the need for creativity within a university administration. We suffer from those fourteenth-century conditioned reflexes (or Oxonian and Cantabrigian reflexes) in saying that after being a dean or vice-chancellor for two years, a man can go back to the "really creative" business of counting angels on the head of a pin. Today creativity in administration is just as important and necessary, if the university is to survive, as creativity in discovering knowledge.

My next point is that no matter how the office of a chief executive is eased, divided, or streamlined, institutions ought to think seriously about —and perhaps put into the contract—a maximum term of ten or some other number of years for a university president or chancellor. In my experience, with certain notable exceptions, the chief executive of an institution makes his greatest creative impacts in the first five to eight years. He may need a few more years to follow through on the implementation of these creative impacts. Beyond that, however, the housekeeping function inevitably becomes larger, and much of the vitality, drive, and creativity declines.

How is it possible to ask a man to take such a job, to give up other kinds of opportunities for continuing development, for ten or more years, and then ask him to return to limbo? I have no doubt that boards of trustees can write such contracts and include in them guarantees against an uncertain economic future. The guarantees, involving very few dollars, would ensure the opportunity for a leader to act objectively and without fear of ultimate retribution.

Faculty and Student Participation

The role of administration in the educational process varies around the country. Much is said today, mainly by university presidents and administrators, about the increasing erosion of the quality of the undergraduate curriculum—one of the main reasons, in my view, of much unrest within student bodies. Everybody bemoans the exponential growth of research, the increasing loyalty of the university professor, not to the institution or the student, but to his discipline or even to his particular panel on the National Institutes of Health. The university president talks about this, but nothing happens, because, as universities are structured, he really cannot do much about it except exhort in speeches and papers or say, "The regents gave the curriculum to the faculty long ago, and there isn't anything I can do about it."

I question whether we can continue down to the twenty-first century the relatively minor role of the chief education or executive officer in shaping the direction and quality of the curriculum. If the executive is not given some increasing authority—not necessarily final decision-making authority—it is hot air to talk about the important role the American university will play in dealing with such problems as the urban crisis, because most of the faculty will be coping with the enrollment problem.

Mainly, because of faculty inaction, not administrative inaction, the student plays much too minor a role in the affairs of the university. I do not think there are many important decisions in the university that can be made by students in the context of the over-all university pattern. However, enormously important roles can be played by students in definitive, substantive policy making, in participation not only with the administration but with the faculty. In my experience, student participation is greater, by a magnitude of a hundred, in those areas in which the administration has authority than it has ever been in those areas in which the faculty is presumed to have some authority. If participation is the name of the game, and I believe it is, students are talking to the wrong people when they talk to the university president. They should talk to the faculty, who defend them in public (sometimes irresponsibly) but steadfastly deny them a right to participate in faculty councils.

Let us be very clear about the vast difference between the logical right of a student to participate in dialogue, on the one hand, and stretching of the principle of academic freedom to permit anarchists to tear up an institution. University life depends on reasoned dialogue, and as long as there is reasoned dialogue, there will be something called a university. But these absurd baroque, rococo bits of philosophy that float around these days within the university community, attempting to justify the negativist or the anarchist in his preoccupation—like the arsonists— with the beauty of the act, with the beauty of destruction, these simply have no place in our society.

Such actions will tear down the university community. Somehow, administrations and our faculties must be able to make sophisticated distinctions between the properly upset and concerned student, on the one hand, and, on the other, the anarchistic, negativistic nihilist.

For the concerned students, let us bring them in much more fully than ever before. For the others, let us deny them any right to be members of the academic community.

PART 2

POSSIBILITIES . . .

The optimist proclaims that we live in the best
of all possible worlds; and the pessimist fears this is true.
James Branch Cabell, *The Silver Stallion*

gambit *is a type of chess opening in which a player sacrifices a piece or pawn in the hope of greater gain later, and, by reasonable extension, the first move, especially with an implication of cunning, in any contest or negotiation.*

H. W. Fowler, A Dictionary of Modern English Usage

C. PETER MAGRATH

Student Participation: What Happens When We Try It?*

AFTER MORNINGSIDE HEIGHTS, Berkeley and Mario Savio may seem ancient history to weary and battle-scarred university deans, presidents, and trustees. Yet the discontents that these events symbolize are of very recent vintage. Viewed in perspective, the student activism that began in the mid-1960s has stimulated, with remarkable speed, student participation in the government of American colleges and universities.

The following are random illustrations of what has been happening; with a change of datelines, they could fit any number of places. A large number of students decide, with well-publicized threats, to defy dormitory regulations concerning rights of visitation with members of the opposite sex; the university authorities then modify the challenged regulations. Massed numbers of students disrupt traditional on-campus recruitment visits by representatives of a chemical company or by members of the United States Armed Forces; faculty members also become engaged, and the college or university suspends on-campus recruitment or modifies the ground rules for such visits. Controversial speakers and commencement day guests, including such "incendiary" figures as the Vice-President or the Secretary of State, become involved in incidents that disrupt their speech-making or the ceremonial proceedings; the university authorities and the faculty-student groups that sponsor

---

*The following description of student participation is based on my experience as chairman of the Advisory Committee on Student Conduct at Brown University during November 1966 through May 1967. At that time I was a member of the Department of Political Science at that university.

97

speakers respond in diverse ways, sometimes seeking to reaffirm in classic libertarian terms the rights of guests and speakers, but more commonly deciding *sub silentio* to bypass the problem by not inviting to the academic groves those whose presence might precipitate demonstrations.[1]

A number of things have happened in these various incidents, but their common denominator is that students participated in the making of rules—in the governance of the university. Such participation is, of course, informal and, because it has its genesis in an issue of the day, usually spasmodic. But the fact of participation nonetheless remains.

My thesis, in short, is that student participation in university government has already proved itself a reality at many colleges and universities and that, with dramatic suddenness, virtually any school may be similarly affected, no matter how bucolic its setting, no matter how remote its traditions and students seem from the more obviously "radical" environments of Berkeley, Harvard, City University of New York, or Wisconsin. Clearly, "participation" of this kind is figuratively, and sometimes literally, participation in the streets and before barricades. It has an anarchic tinge to it that—perhaps pleasing to those few with nihilistic mentalities—will produce chaos and eventually destroy any institution in which it becomes the students' *modus operandi* of participation. It is my further thesis, therefore, that the problem for America's colleges and universities is to move toward more formal, more institutionalized modes of student participation. A number of schools have already done so, but, as we all know, the development of a structure for participation is a complicated matter. "Participation" is hardly a self-defining word. To speak of student participation in the government of the university tells little about either its content (whether students are to be encouraged merely to advise or are to be given significant quanta of structural power) or its scope (whether it includes only rules for social conduct or extends to academic-curricular or other matters). This essay will describe the move of Brown University from essentially informal to formal student participation in the making and en-

---

[1] While I agree that the terrible divisions induced by the Vietnam war stimulate many of the on-campus protests and add a profound emotional dimension to them, I believe that student activism is a consequence both of the changing nature of the university (primarily a function of size) and of the discontents and doubts stirred by the nation's severe social problems. These antedated the Vietnam war, and will postdate it too. The destructive student activism at Columbia University seems to me an example.

forcing of rules for student conduct, and will evaluate the preliminary results. It will conclude with some speculations on the issue of student participation.

The Background

During 1965–66 Brown University with its coordinate women's college, Pembroke—about 5,000 undergraduate and graduate students—became increasingly tense over student conduct rules and disciplinary proceedings. The main components of the "social system," as the students called it, were as follows. The dean of the College of Brown and the dean of Pembroke, in consultation with the president (who clears major policy decisions with a committee of the University Corporation), had primary responsibility for making and enforcing student conduct rules. These rules, in part written and in part based on informal traditions and understandings, could be, and often were, modified in response to purely *advisory* proposals made by the Brown and Pembroke student government organizations. Their content was the subject of growing discontent and pressure from the student governments and the campus press. The main issues were parietal visiting hours in the men's dormitories (about nineteen hours per week), the requirement that essentially all out-of-state women live on campus, the curfew regulations which applied to all resident women (markedly more permissive for juniors and seniors), and a rule that made the women liable to disciplinary sanctions if they stayed overnight in "unapproved" places—hotels, motels, or men's apartments. The enforcement of these rules in 1965–66 was exclusively the prerogative of the deans' offices at Brown and Pembroke with informal right of appeal to the president.

Early in the 1966–67 academic year, however, an attempted modification in the rules-enforcing procedures weakened the old procedures without substituting new ones, and contributed to a growing restiveness. At the end of the preceding semester, the University, at the request of the faculty, created two all-faculty boards—the Board of Review for Disciplinary Cases and the Board of Review for Academic Freedom —each with six elected members. Unfortunately, their responsibilities were ill-defined, although the assumption was that the Disciplinary Cases Board would be concerned primarily with student misbehavior and the Academic Freedom Board would serve as an appellate forum for students and faculty alike with complaints about possible constraints on their right to express themselves freely or to hear controversial speakers.

Unluckily, before the new boards could be organized and staffed, a disciplinary case developed at Pembroke that drew wide attention. A young woman who frequently broke the explicit "unapproved" places regulation was suspended by the Pembroke dean's office for a few weeks within the semester. At this point things began to heat up. She appealed her suspension to the Disciplinary Cases Board (finally organized), but her case went undecided. The board split on whether it had appellate authority over deans' decisions, or whether it was to serve merely as a nonappellate mechanism for resolving disciplinary prosecutions initiated by deans if a student opted to have his case decided by the faculty board.[2] Student and faculty supporters of the suspended student rallied around the slogan "no academic punishment for a social offense." The matter then went before the Board of Review for Academic Freedom, which responded with an advisory opinion that certain University disciplinary procedures and regulations interfered with "the full freedom of students in the learning process," and that this appeared to be such a case. The Pembroke student, it suggested, had been temporarily exiled from the benefits of the academic community.[3] All these points, as well as the propriety of the Academic Freedom Board's intervention, were then raised at faculty meetings without being resolved. Amid much emotion and eloquence, the faculty became hopelessly divided over how the two boards were to operate and on the more general question of the proper faculty role in disciplinary cases and their relationship to academic freedom.

Meanwhile student protests increased, with rallies and marches and with articles in the *Brown Daily Herald*. Soon after, the Brown and Pembroke student governments unanimously passed resolutions asking President Ray L. Heffner to create a rules-making body with final authority for all student conduct matters, to be composed equally of administration and student representatives. Similarly, the Boards of Review for Academic Freedom and for Disciplinary Cases requested

[2] Subsidiary disputes further complicated the issue: whether an assistant dean had erred in failing to apprise the student of her right to have her case decided by the faculty board (which technically existed but was still unorganized at the time of the incident), and whether it was appropriate to suspend students for a brief period *within* a semester.

[3] Letter of Board of Review for Academic Freedom to President Heffner, Nov. 1, 1966; published in the *Pembroke Record*, Nov. 8, 1966.

President Heffner to appoint a committee that would explore student conduct issues. Although not directly related, a November 1966 incident heightened campus tensions. A speech by General Earle Wheeler, USA, chairman of the Joint Chiefs of Staff, culminated with a small group of students jumping on the stage and trying to encircle him. Some ineffectual punches were thrown, and one student was arrested by local police.

The Advisory Committee on Student Conduct

On November 15, in response to these problems and diverse pressures, President Heffner appointed an Advisory Committee on Student Conduct. Its members consisted of two undergraduate students (the student government presidents of Brown and Pembroke) and one graduate student, three administrators (the senior deans at Brown, Pembroke, and the Graduate School), and three faculty members. Each person had one vote, and I was named chairman. Our mandate was a sweeping one:

> To examine the relationship between student conduct and the proper atmosphere of a university; to consider the present state of student conduct at Brown University; to examine present rules and codes of behavior in The College, Pembroke College, and The Graduate School; to consider the procedures by which such rules and codes are amended and enforced; to consult with appropriate individuals and groups; to make recommendations to the appropriate authorities.[4]

The president's action had the effect of easing campus tensions. Not only did the committee's establishment imply that change was on the way, but the committee itself gave early evidence that it took its mission seriously. The committee's report was promised for well before the end of the spring 1967 semester, and President Heffner directed the three deans to give priority to the committee's work. He agreed to my request for funds to obtain secretarial aid and, more important, funds to conduct a survey into the attitudes of the undergraduates, their parents, the faculty, and alumni toward student conduct issues.

The survey's primary value was the cathartic opportunity it gave faculty and students to express their views on the disputed issues. More than 4,000 questionnaires were sent out to nine university-related groups, and the total return rate was nearly 70 percent. In addition to the survey, the committee canvassed student-conduct procedures at a sample of other schools, took testimony from faculty and student or-

[4] Letter of President Heffner to the author, Nov. 15, 1966.

ganizations and from individual faculty members, students, and university officials. In all, it held thirteen hearings involving fifty witnesses and received numerous written communications. These hearings were, at the witnesses' discretion, either open or closed. The open sessions generated wide coverage in the campus press and, in conjunction with the survey, communicated the message that the committee was hard at work.

The committee met usually three times weekly. Much could be said about its work and internal problems, but my most lasting impression is how, over a five-month period, we moved out of our institutional roles and perceptions. The two undergraduates especially were initially suspicious and thought of themselves as mandated delegates; they unquestionably perceived the administrators and faculty similarly. As we worked on administrative chores, heard testimony, discussed issues, and finally voted on recommendations, we developed a sense of unity in which the vital considerations became, not administrative convenience or what students would prefer, but what was good and viable for the *entire* University. In the end, the Advisory Committee's twenty-eight recommendations were unanimous.

In a way, this is overly rosy, for the "esprit de committee" developed only slowly and as a result of very frequent meetings under the pressure of a campus crisis. Then too, the consensus was a result of the wide knowledge about student conduct matters gained through the expenditure of much time and thought. These matters are a normal preoccupation of administrators, but the task of becoming better informed and making serious recommendations placed severe demands on the faculty and, especially, on the student committee members. At one point, my Brown student colleague, an intelligent person and a moderate activist who knew how to apply pressure on administrators, complained to me that the work was interfering with his studies and leaving him no time for anything else. "If you students want to govern the university and really play the administrator role, not just pass resolutions and make demands," I told him, with a grin, "then you've got to give it the time; this is the price you have to pay for true student power."

The problem of constructive student participation—participation that gets down to the "nitty-gritty"—is of course difficult. Students are birds of passage who usually lack the expertise and sophistication to function effectively on complex university affairs until their junior and senior years. Within a year or two they graduate, but the administration and faculty are left with the policies they helped devise. A student generation lasts for four years; colleges and universities are more permanent.

Committee Recommendations

The Advisory Committee on Student Conduct divided its recommendations (which subsequently were endorsed with virtual unanimity by the administration, faculty, students, and trustees) into two general categories: those proposing new substantive rules, and those proposing structural arrangements for making and enforcing future student conduct rules. The philosophic underpinning behind the first category of recommendations is best described by two passages from the report:

> The phrase "in loco parentis" presumably means that a university stands, for purposes of control and discipline, in the same relative position to the students as the parents do. But we know of no legal code that imposes such an obligation on the University, and the "in loco parentis" phrase is commonly cited in a disparaging fashion by those who criticize existing student conduct rules and who fear an excessive paternalism on the University's part. In our view, the concept of "in loco parentis"—if indeed it can be dignified by calling it a concept—is essentially irrelevant to the problems confronting Brown University. . . . [A] university community such as Brown, which includes young people in various stages of developing maturity, must have a certain number of basic student conduct regulations. It must also express its legitimate concern through counselling and education. But the University, while undoubtedly an "alma mater" to many of its sons and daughters in a certain nostalgic sense, is not equipped to serve as a surrogate parent for its students. Most Brown and Pembroke students are fortunate in having parents, and parental control is properly their—not Brown University's—responsibility.

> *   *   *   *   *   *   *   *

> Assuming for the moment that moral standards with regard to alcohol, drugs, and sex are changing what should a university's response be? If radically permissive standards of behavior are indeed emerging, there is no need for a university to endorse them. A university, after all, is composed of members of our contemporary society, and such a university community cannot be expected to establish codes of behavior that differ radically from contemporary moral standards. A university can be expected to serve as a continuous forum where the consequences of certain kinds of behavior are evaluated in the light of student interests and problems.[5]

[5] *Community and Partnership: Student Conduct at Brown*, Report of the Advisory Committee on Student Conduct, Brown University (1967), pp. 11, 13–14.

The major recommendations of the rules included the following: that curfews be eliminated for junior and senior women; that seniors, with parental permission, be allowed to live off campus; that the overnight destinations of women students no longer be subject to university regulation; that student government units in both men's and women's dormitories be allowed to set the hours of visiting with members of the opposite sex and the rules governing the visitations, subject only to the restriction that visitation would be unacceptable during "those nighttime hours when people are normally sleeping and those morning hours when people are dressing and preparing for the day ahead"; and that the university not forbid the possession of alcoholic beverages in student rooms, yet noting the state law prohibiting the sale to and possession of alcohol by persons under age twenty-one.[6] More negatively, we recommended that the university take a position prohibiting sexual intercourse in its residential units; that students possessing, using, or distributing marijuana, LSD, and other hallucinogens and narcotic drugs be made liable to disciplinary sanctions; and that on-campus student protests whose distinctive character is physical force or physical obstruction be made subject to University discipline.

Two points are relevant in evaluating the Advisory Committee's recommendations. First, each member of the committee significantly modified his initial view on most issues as we gained understanding of them. Second, the student members were invaluable contributors to the understanding reached. They instructed the deans and faculty members not only on student attitudes and behavioral patterns, but also on how certain possible rules would appear to the student body and the kinds of impact they might produce. Questions put to students on an examination may wrongly, though understandably, be misinterpreted by the respondents; the same phenomenon can exist with student conduct rules and guides. The students also learned, and when the recommendations were released, the undergraduate student government leaders were able to explain effectively—if not always with enthusiasm—the committee's concern with drugs, uninhibited sexual behavior, and general considerations of the University's reputation and its relationship to the community. A cynic might say the students were neatly co-opted into supporting establishmentarian values. But students can also play the co-optation game, and many would regard the committee's recommendations as extremely permissive.

[6] The committee also recommended that temporary suspension within a semester was an inappropriate sanction.

The second category of recommendations, dealing with machinery for making and enforcing student conduct rules, were an outgrowth of our own successful experience. In essence, we recommended a perpetuation of the Advisory Committee in the form of a twelve-member University Council on Student Affairs (UCSA), which is now in operation. It consists of three deans or their representatives, three professors elected by the faculty, and six students—five undergraduate and one graduate selected by the student government organizations. The UCSA elects its own chairman from among the three faculty representatives, and each member has one vote, with the majority ruling, and ties regarded as a negative vote.

The Council's jurisdictional responsibilities extend to all noncurricular student conduct questions and to all serious disciplinary cases in which the student affairs deans believe that suspension or expulsion from the university may be justified. Its rule-making function is to serve as the campus agency for proposing to the university president new or modified regulations, and the president must respond to its proposals. He is free to modify or reject them, but the explicit assumption is that he will customarily accept them, especially when they are unanimous.

The Council's role in disciplinary cases works as follows: A student charged with a serious rule infraction has the option of having his case decided *either* by the appropriate dean's office or, alternatively, by the UCSA. The disciplinary sanctions need not be the most severe possible —suspension or expulsion. In either case, students have the right to appeal verdicts and punishments to the president, and they are protected by a number of explicit procedural safeguards such as written notification of charges, the right to present testimony, and the right to have assistance during the hearing. These arrangements institutionalize significant student participation in all social and disciplinary affairs. The Advisory Committee expressed the rationale this way:

> On the matter of making and enforcing social policies and student conduct rules, we believe that the University's common interests can best be identified and pursued through a partnership process. More specifically, it is our conviction that the students' role should be very substantial. First, social and student conduct policies and procedures impinge directly and almost exclusively upon the students; their impact, moreover, is doubly significant at a primarily residential university such as Brown. Second, we believe that students are more likely to act maturely and responsibly within a social system which they help to create and to enforce.

It is equally desirable that the University establish a formal mechanism which can provide a continuous forum for the discussion of the University's social system and which can authoritatively recommend adjustments and changes as experience and needs indicate. The proposed University Council on Student Affairs is designed with this end in view. It will blend the perspective of deans, faculty, and students, and its recommendations for future policy changes will be informed by their experience in administering and enforcing the existing student conduct rules. . . .[7]

Results of the Survey

Although the recommendation for the administration-faculty-student Council was voted before our survey results were available, the poll on preferences for student conduct structural arrangements confirmed its acceptability (see Tables 1 and 2). More important, it disclosed a strong consensus among the University's diverse constituencies favoring student involvement in the making and enforcing of social conduct rules. The categories of persons polled were: Brown and Pembroke students, parents of Brown and Pembroke students, older Brown and Pembroke graduates (Classes of 1930 and 1940), new Brown and Pembroke graduates (Classes of 1959, 1963, and 1965), and the faculty. One question asked, "Who should *make the rules* about student conduct in 'nonacademic' matters?" A second inquired, "Who should *enforce the rules* by hearing cases and deciding punishment in matters of 'nonacademic' student conduct?" In both cases the respondent could indicate a preference for student representatives, for deans, or for designated faculty. He was also informed that he could circle more than one if he favored "sharing" the rule-making and rule-enforcing functions.[8]

The percentages reported in Tables 1 and 2 undoubtedly contain some distortions. For example, the personal popularity of the then dean of the College probably accounts for the relatively high number of Brown students (14.9 percent) and recent Brown alumni (24.4 percent) indicating a preference for "deans alone" in rules enforcement. Similarly, faculty responses may have been affected by the imbroglio that developed in the first experiment involving deans and faculty in rules enforcement. The message of the survey is, however, clear: an overwhelming majority of respondents in every category—alumni, faculty,

---

[7] *Ibid.*, p. 8.
[8] Respondents were also permitted to specify another solution; the less than 9 percent who made such a selection are excluded from Tables 1 and 2.

TABLE 1: *Responses to: "Who Should Make the Rules about Student Conduct?"*

(1967 Brown University Survey)

Respondents	N	Percentage of Responses Favoring Responsibility By:						
		Students Alone	Students and Deans	Students and Faculty	Students, Deans, and Faculty	Deans Alone	Deans and Faculty	Faculty Alone
Brown students........	444	9.9	21.4	13.7	35.4	3.8	3.6	1.6
Pembroke students.....	365	12.9	16.2	15.1	45.2	1.1	0.3	1.1
Brown parents.........	473	1.1	26.4	32.1	16.5	7.4	7.2	4.7
Pembroke parents......	351	3.4	21.9	24.8	25.9	7.1	8.8	2.8
Brown old alumni......	169	3.6	26.0	25.4	17.2	9.5	6.5	5.3
Brown new alumni.....	316	7.6	24.4	16.5	29.7	8.5	2.5	2.2
Pembroke old alumnae..	131	3.1	33.6	19.8	27.5	4.6	4.6	0.8
Pembroke new alumnae..	208	9.6	20.7	17.8	33.7	1.4	2.9	1.4
Faculty...............	314	10.5	15.3	8.9	34.7	9.9	7.0	3.2
Total.............	2,771	7.0	22.1	19.5	29.9	5.9	4.9	2.6

Note: Responses do not add to 100% because of the elimination of miscellaneous and inapplicable answers.

107

TABLE 2: *Responses to: "Who Should Enforce the Rules about Student Conduct?"*

(1967 Brown University Survey)

Respondents	N		Percentage of Responses Favoring Responsibility By:					
		Students Alone	Students and Deans	Students and Faculty	Students, Deans, and Faculty	Deans Alone	Deans and Faculty	Faculty Alone
Brown students........	444	8.3	19.6	11.5	27.9	14.9	8.1	3.4
Pembroke students.....	365	12.1	17.3	15.6	39.7	3.6	3.6	1.9
Brown parents.........	473	1.9	25.6	29.0	16.7	12.1	7.4	4.0
Pembroke parents......	351	5.1	24.2	20.5	23.6	10.5	9.1	3.7
Brown old alumni......	169	3.0	25.4	22.5	14.8	18.9	4.7	4.7
Brown new alumni.....	316	8.2	23.1	12.7	18.7	24.4	5.4	1.3
Pembroke old alumnae..	131	4.6	31.3	17.6	23.7	9.2	6.1	1.5
Pembroke new alumnae..	208	18.8	21.6	15.9	25.0	5.8	3.4	2.4
Faculty...............	314	10.5	19.1	4.8	23.6	19.1	14.0	2.2
Total.............	2,771	7.8	22.3	16.8	24.3	13.2	7.2	2.9

Note: Responses do not add to 100% because of the elimination of miscellaneous and inapplicable answers.

parents, and students—favored a student role in both the making and enforcing of social conduct rules. Of the 2,771 respondents, 78.5 percent favored involving students in some rules-making capacity, most preferring a sharing of powers, while only 15.5 percent of the respondents chose one of the "alone" combination. Among preferences for systems for rules enforcement, 71.2 percent of the respondents favored a system that would involve the students, and only 23.9 percent favored one of the "alone" combinations (a figure made high by the popularity of the Brown dean).[9]

These statistics—incompletely analyzed here—reveal a widespread acceptance among presumably concerned adults of the idea that students should in some formal way be worked into policy-making and enforcement in social matters. Admittedly, our survey respondents may be thought to be disproportionately representative of upper middle class and upper middle "Eastern sophisticates." In my observation, however, they are not notably radical in matters of political attitudes, social conventions, and tastes, and the responses shown in the tables may well be representative of emerging national attitudes among college- and university-related adults. The American society, it is well to remember, encourages independence and the early assumption of responsibilities by young persons. "Participatory democracy," the slogan of New Left militants (rhetorically catchy if operationally meaningless), is one thing; carefully defined student participation in rules-making and rules enforcement is quite another. College students, an Advisory Committee colleague wrote perceptively, are "developing into citizens rather than subjects." [10] Participation through such arrangements as the Brown University Council on Student Affairs is part of that process.

A View of UCSA's First Year

How, in practice, have Brown's new social system and its University Council worked? Based on the first year of existence, it must be pronounced, I think, a qualified success. The report of the predecessor Advisory Committee resolved a number of outstanding issues and re-

[9] The faculty proved to be the most conservative of the respondents in favoring a role for students in both rules-making and rules enforcement. Whatever the significance, the faculty responses throughout tended to be the most extreme, both in permissiveness and restrictiveness.

[10] Erwin C. Hargrove, "Rather Citizens Than Subjects," *Pembroke Alumna,* October 1966, pp. 6–9.

moved the tensions that had troubled the campus. It was received with a great deal of enthusiasm and created a brief period of administration-faculty-student good feeling that, given the restlessness of today's students and the complexity of certain social conduct issues, could not last.[11]

Two examples drawn from the UCSA's first year (1967–68) illustrate the point. The Advisory Committee's report recommended that the hours for visitation by members of the opposite sex in dormitories be essentially set by student government units at the residential level. The only forbidden time for visitation would be late nighttime and early morning hours, such as between midnight and 11:00 A.M. on weekdays. There was no student government dissent from this recommendation in the spring of 1967; quite the contrary, it was regarded as a great victory that settled a five-year debate over "parietal" visiting hours. But when the new academic year began in September a number of residential units at Brown (not at Pembroke) ignored these guidelines and voted twenty-four hours of visitation. The Brown student government endorsed the right of the dormitories to do this, and it demanded that the UCSA recommend to the president a no-restriction policy on visitation hours. The Council, after some long and acrimonious sessions, declined to do so. It finally broke an internal stalemate by proposing to President Heffner, who accepted the recommendation, that dormitory visiting hours might begin at 10.00 A.M. and extend to 1:00 A.M. Sunday through Thursday and to 3:00 A.M. on Fridays and Saturdays.

Many observers would regard this as a rather un-Victorian approach

[11] An early partial dissent was expressed by Edward Schwartz, president of the National Student Association, during a 1967 interview:

"I'm told, for example, that the McGrath [sic] Report has created this student-faculty committee to deal with social rules. Now I was arguing today that students alone should deal with social rules. It seems that the McGrath [sic] Report will be very difficult to revoke.

"What I've suggested to some people is that the students examine faculty social life, not as a gossip column, but what is the character of faculty social life here? Do you have a sort of 'Who's Afraid of Virginia Woolf' situation? Is there wife-swapping and things like that? Then the students should write a report on faculty social life and insist that if this ever becomes public it would be very bad for the image of Brown. The faculty is clearly incapable of handling its own social affairs and this student-faculty committee should undertake some investigations of rules which the faculty would have to allow since, afer all, Brown is a community and we all have an interest in what each other is doing. That might poke some holes into the seriousness of faculty members determining the way students run their social lives."

Interview in a Brown undergraduate journal, *Res Publica*, January 1968, p. 25. It is not clear whether Mr. Schwartz, a leading representative of the NSA Establishment, had actually read the Advisory Committee's report.

to relationships between the sexes. But the point of view of dissatisfied students was well summarized by the *Brown Daily Herald*, which editorialized that "the superficial issue of '24-hour parietals' is an insignificant one," since the new liberalization was a vast improvement over the past:

> What is at issue, however, is a divergence of philosophy, present even in the Magrath Report, regarding the maturity of the student and his ability to make his moral decisions himself. On the one hand, a dormitory's residents are mature enough "to determine their own parietal visiting hours . . ."; on the other hand, they are not mature enough to know which hours should be "unacceptable or restricted."
>
> Students maintain they are capable to judge—and in fact, as residents of the housing units who will have to live by these rules, the *best* to judge—which hours are "unacceptable or restricted." The criteria here are convenience, effect on the housing units' members, and moral considerations. By removing this decision from those it affects, the Council is in no way contributing to the spirit of personal responsibility for personal conduct that can nurture more self-reliant undergraduates at Brown.
>
> Fundamentally, the self-determination of parietals was rejected because the UCSA's administrative and faculty members do not believe students are fully responsible members of the University community.
>
> For students to tolerate this view, for students to obey rules formulated from this philosophy, would be for students to act not like independent adults but like obedient children . . . students are no longer willing to be treated like children.[12]

The Council, despite a renewed request from its Brown undergraduate members, has so far refused to change its recommendation, and the visiting hours issue has provoked no further public controversy on the campus.

Far more serious was the Council's first disciplinary case involving a CIA recruiter's visit to the campus and all the bitterness and frustration engendered by the Vietnam war. In a fairly typical case, fourteen Brown and Pembroke students, including a popular student government leader, were charged with obstructing the entry of the CIA recruiter to a room where he was to interview students who had asked for appointments. The protestors of the recruiter chose to have their fate decided by the Council. Following a lengthy session devoted to taking testimony from all involved, hearing students who appeared as counsel for the defendants, and deliberating, the UCSA adjudged the protestors guilty of

12 *Brown Daily Herald*, Oct. 31, 1967.

forcible obstruction on the University's premises. Recognizing "the sincerity of the convictions of the students that informed their actions and their anguish over the implication of the issues for the fate of the nation," the Council nevertheless unanimously concluded that there is "no place in the University . . . for dissent by physical confrontation." It ordered them placed on disciplinary probation, a sanction making the offenders liable to suspension or expulsion were they to be found guilty of a similar offense during the remainder of the academic year. The Council further recommended that University policies "in the matter of recruiting be thoughtfully reexamined in the context of the University's functions and aims." [13]

President Heffner and the faculty subsequently undertook this reexamination and the guidelines that emerged seem to have won over-all campus approval.[14] Some of the anti-CIA students denounced the UCSA proceedings as a "sham," and the *Brown Daily Herald* criticized the Council for allegedly being unjudicious in its procedures. But the verdict and the sanction—which had the support of all the student members—was generally regarded as correct and fair.

Internally, however, the Council did not always work smoothly. Some university officials believe that the student representation (half of the UCSA membership) is excessive, while the Council's student members expressed disappointment at what they described as a "we-they" attitude on the part of most administration-faculty representatives. In turn, some of the administration-faculty members on the UCSA perceived the students as similarly frozen in generational attitudes and biases. This situation, probably inevitable, was intensified by the fact that the students on the UCSA regarded one of the faculty members as having a dim view of the Advisory Committee's recommendations and the Council it created. In a conversation with me, this faculty representative, whose attitudes toward students tend to be conservative, described the student government representatives on the UCSA as "functionaries" who—perhaps because of the pressure of time—rarely did their homework prior to Council meetings. "They're just officeholders," he commented, also adding that it was a "misuse of faculty time" to involve it, as the Coun-

---

[13] *Ibid.*, Nov. 10, 1967.
[14] The student government was chagrined that the faculty committee which explored the recruitment issue did not include student representation. Another 1967–68 advisory committee that made recommendations to the president on the confidentiality of student records did consist of administration, faculty, and student representatives, each with voting power.

cil did, in disciplinary cases. The problem, in his view, is a "corruption of function" that places teachers in the difficult position of having to discipline their students for social misbehavior when the proper faculty function is to teach academic subjects in the classroom. In fairness to this faculty representative, it should also be reported that he described the UCSA as "a good thing" that served as an "avenue of communication" between administration, faculty, and students. He claimed that, despite his reservations, he had given the Council "a fair shake" and that many of its first-year problems were a consequence of its newness.

Although the major concern here is with student participation in social conduct matters, such participation is usually combined with *faculty* participation, and the suitability of faculty representatives is at least as delicate as the caliber and attitudes of student representatives. No one wishes to censor faculty selection procedures according to any ideological constraints; yet faculty committees on committees often act casually in making their nominations, which are tantamount to election. Many faculty members, exceedingly gifted in research and teaching are, for reasons of temperament or indifference, ill-suited to fulfill delicate roles on student affairs and disciplinary committees. At the very minimum there should be an understanding that only those who accept the principle of student participation and the further principle of faculty involvement in the concerns of committees such as the Brown UCSA should accept election to them.

Despite its inevitable problems, the new Council deserves a C+ or perhaps a B− for its first year's labors. This, in effect, is the evaluation of Pembroke's Dean Pierrel who has commented, "Right now our path is a very rocky one and the meetings of the Council are too often reminiscent of the Ford-UAW negotiations. However, I am persuaded that we *must* do everything possible to make this work, at least for the present, for the likely alternative is serious disorder and disorganization in which students and the university alike will suffer." [15] There is no way of empirically measuring these things, but my own strong belief is that the availability of the Council made possible a speedy and equitable resolution of the explosive CIA recruiter case in a manner superior to such alternatives as a disciplinary decision by the university administration alone, or by a hastily formed *ad hoc* committee of some kind. There were about five other disciplinary cases in 1967–68 serious enough

[15] Rosemary Pierrel, "Student Power," 1968 speech (Mimeographed).

to warrant use of the UCSA; in only one of them did the students elect to have their case (involving a violation of dormitory visiting hours) decided by the Council.

One final function performed by the UCSA should be noted. In response to a faculty vote, which itself came in response to various student proposals, the UCSA was asked to appoint two temporary faculty-student subcommittees that sponsored a number of open forums on outstanding campus issues and the general question of the University's responsibilities in its city and state relations. This suggests that a structure of the UCSA type, if available, can be adapted to deal with both sudden emergencies and with less crisis-laden problems that may concern a university.

A Consideration of Academic and Curricular Affairs

If students are becoming citizens instead of subjects on social conduct matters and are properly given formal and heavy voting representation within university structures, must—or should—the same development occur in academic and curricular affairs? This difficult question can be treated only briefly here, but it is relevant; formal student participation in the social area will bring with it demands for similar participation in other areas of university decision-making. Much of the rationale justifying it in the social conduct area can, at least superficially, be transferred to the academic-curricular area. Certainly, to paraphrase a statement in the report of the Brown Advisory Committee on Student Conduct, quoted above, the quality of a faculty and the content of a curriculum "impinge directly" upon students. But, unlike conduct rules, they do not impinge "almost exclusively" upon the student; many other considerations are related to the question of student involvement in curricular and faculty affairs. Colleges and universities are for students, but they are not for students alone. Quite aside from the major issue of student competence to participate directly in the hiring, firing, and rewarding of staff, the allocation of budgetary resources, and the making of curriculum decisions, universities especially serve a diversity of research and public service functions that, at most, concern students only indirectly.

It is nonetheless self-evident that quality of faculty and curriculum vitally affects students. My present view is that student evaluations of the effectiveness of faculty in the classroom should be taken account of, but as an informal process. Student evaluations of faculty competence are too often based on superficial criteria; charm, humor, and rhetorical polish, without regard to content, play a disproportionate part in the evaluations. Here the wisest policy is one that allows for student influence on its merits; carefully prepared student proposals, based on a broad understanding of curricular affairs, deserve to be considered by administration and faculty alike.

During the 1967–68 academic year at Brown, for example, the student government on its own initiative sponsored an evaluation of the university's curriculum, whose philosophic premises have been unchanged since 1945. The outcome, a report of 400 pages, is an impressive document that searchingly examines the existing curricular assumptions and methods of teaching and, with great specificity, proposes major revisions. Known as the Magaziner-Maxwell Report, after its two very talented undergraduate authors, it has stimulated considerable interest. A special subcommittee of administration, faculty, and student representatives, appointed by the University's Curriculum Committee, has spent many hours discussing the report's proposals, and they will undoubtedly receive consideration by the full Curriculum Committee and the faculty in 1968–69. Whether or not the Magaziner-Maxwell Report directly leads to a major restructuring of the Brown curriculum and teaching techniques, it will probably stimulate some desirable reforms and a healthy re-examination of the established system.[16]

In my view, student participation on such curricular affairs should be an explicitly advisory one, but there should be formal channels for transmitting this advice and a clear expectation that administrators and faculty will respond, if only to say, "No, thank you," to the suggestions. For its pertinence, however, I wish to quote the comment of Professor Newell M. Stultz, a Brown political scientist, who chaired the Curriculum Committee's subcommittee that conducted a preliminary evaluation of the Magaziner-Maxwell Report:

> It seems to me that curriculum committees do two sorts of things: they initiate policies, and they monitor the implementation of policies. . . . I rather believe that students should have a formal and continuing role in the policy-making function. I cannot see that it would be particularly useful to have students as monitors. I believe students can usefully serve in a policy-making capacity simply because my experience

---

[16] Not surprisingly, the Brown student government is demanding voting representation on the Curriculum Committee.

is that they do have ideas, often good ideas, that should have a means of being articulated when policies are being considered.

Some might think the student role should be advisory. If the proportion of student members to all members is fairly small, say no more than 15 to 20 percent, then in fact they would have an advisory role. They might vote, but only when the other members of the committee (or structure) were importantly divided might the student vote become significant. What this means, then, is that students would have an established channel for communicating their ideas at the policy-making level, and they would have the chance to express their opinions on all issues of policy that were decided. They would not themselves likely be able to determine the result. Power would be largely symbolic.[17]

On Balance

There will be increasing student participation in the government of American higher education, both formal and informal. Its mode and manner of expression will vary according to the diverse circumstances and traditions of our colleges and universities, though, as the present trends already suggest, I strongly suspect that most of this participation will manifest itself in the social conduct aspect, as distinguished from the academic-curricular side, of higher education. University administrators and trustees and regents, not to mention many professors, are uneasy about this trend, and understandably so. It is new to the vast majority of colleges and universities, and it will bring with it problems, though these will be, I believe, less disturbing than ones caused by the exclusion of students. Whether we like it or not, this development primarily reflects a distrust of the large and complex universities that have developed so rapidly and so spectacularly in recent years. Their bigness and the inescapable impersonality of their bureaucracies, along with a heightened concern in our society for *formal*, institutionalized guarantees on behalf of individual rights and procedural due process, fuel the demand that students be given a substantial role in the government of the university. On balance, this can be a healthy and vitalizing thing if—and this is one of the biggest words in the English language—it is carefully defined and ultimately limited, and if students are made to accept responsibility for the choices and policies that are influenced by their newly acquired power. I feel that such an arrangement as the Brown University Council on Student Affairs does precisely this. It is also absolutely essential to insist, as the report of the Brown Advisory

[17] Memorandum to the author, March 29, 1968.

Committee on Student Conduct did, that the university not be analo-
gized into a miniature civil state overlaid with all the minutiae and
procedures of the public legal code. It is not, moreover, a sort of experimental populistic democracy where everyone has equal political influence regardless of the issues and interests at stake.[18]

The events of the spring of 1968 in which student activists, some
misguided and some nihilistic, seized buildings and made hostages of
deans, trustees, and presidents—events dramatized by the paralysis of
Columbia University—may make this essay's discussion of reasonably
polite and rationally conceived student participation seem remote. Certainly if, to use the apt phrase of the *New York Times*, a "fascism of
the left," comes to dominate the actions of substantial minorities of
students, no report and no council on student affairs can prevent turmoil. But I doubt that this will happen if the nation's leading universities provide opportunities for formal student participation in the
making of social policies and in the processing of disciplinary cases,
while, at the same time, unequivocally drawing the line against informal
student participation that parades, literally, as physical and violent protest. It is perhaps significant that one of the causes of discontent behind the turmoil at Columbia University was the absence of a student
role in disciplinary cases.[19]

Legitimate demands for peaceful and rational student participation
in university affairs should not be linked and confused with the violent
and destructive actions of that small but dangerous minority of students
whose actions indicate a total lack of comprehension of what a university is, what it does, and what it can be. In my judgment, institutionalized student participation in the social conduct area, as in the
case of Brown's tripartite administration-faculty-student council, can
perform a vital function in negotiating disputed issues. And, if it unfortunately becomes necessary, when students overstep the boundaries
of civilized conduct, such a council can serve as a disciplinary agency
that is perceived as representing legitimate authority by the major
groups who participate in the life of the university. Most students, I
believe, are reasonable when treated reasonably, and I am confident that
they can be made to see that their own best interests do not lie with
those who see the college or university as a political battleground and

[18] Logan Wilson, "The Abuses of the University," address delivered at Michigan State University, March 10, 1968, argues this point cogently.
[19] *New York Times*, April 27, 29–30, 1968.

whose tactics can make the educational process its first casualty. "I take the side," declared one frustrated Columbia student barred from an academic building, "that I have the right to go to class." [20] The overwhelming majority of American students, I think, would agree.

[20] *Ibid.*, April 26, 1968.

[But] here's yet in the word 'hereafter' the kneading, the making of
the cake, the heating of the oven, and the baking; nay, you must
stay the cooling too, or you may chance to burn your lips.

Shakespeare, Troilus and Cressida

ALLAN P. SINDLER

A Case Study in
Student-University Relations*

TODAY'S STUDENTS AT CORNELL and elsewhere in the nation are pressing
for greater freedom to direct their own lives both on and off the campus,
to shape university policy, and to engage themselves in the controversial
and critical public issues of the day. These goals are pursued with vigor
and a variety of tactics that promise colleges and universities much spir-
ited disagreement and conflict for the future. Whatever one's view of
these student goals, it seems evident that the sensible resolution of disagreement will depend on ground rules governing university and student
interaction, formulated to be as full, clear, persuasive, and equitable as
possible. An educational community, by its very nature, has a special obligation to accommodate change through legitimate procedures and the
exercise of rationality, avoiding both the inertia and conservatism said to
be inherent in large institutions and also avoiding any uncritical acquiescence to student demands because of coercive pressure. If students' view-
points are pressed in orderly ways, are received without prejudice, and are
subjected to the considered judgment of the educational community, the
present period of student challenge may have invigorating and constructive effects for university life. Much of the outcome will depend on the
sensitivity and farsightedness of faculties and administrations across the
land.

* The reader should know something of my background as author of this case
study. My discipline is political science, and until recently my interest in student-
university relations was that of the typical academician. My qualifications here rest
essentially on my chairmanship of Cornell's Commission on the Interdependence of
University Regulations and Local, State and Federal Law, which played the central
role in the changes adopted at Cornell.

119

This paper concentrates on but one of the problems of student-university relations—that of university principles and practices in the regulation of student misconduct. It is a question that increasingly agitates students and provokes their demands for change. My case study reports how one university, Cornell, responded to student challenge in this area. The account focuses mostly on the substance of Cornell's new policies and procedures, but it also concerns the more general question of effective student participation in university affairs.

The Formation and Work of the Commission

As of 1966–67, Cornell was believed by many to be among the most liberal of universities in its practices encouraging student extracurricular and academic freedoms. Like most universities, however, Cornell had not operated by a deliberate, explicit, and internally consistent set of principles and policies on the topic. The last large-scale internal reform of student conduct matters had taken place in 1958, and had not been broadly explored since. A succession of three controversies between students and the University in the academic year 1966–67 uncovered a need which led to the formation of a commission.

One controversy concerned an allegedly obscene story in a student literary journal. Its unfolding included an initial action on campus by Cornell's own safety force, the subsequent involvement of public authorities in prosecution, a near-riot by students stimulated by an attempted arrest on campus, and an ultimate judicial decision that the story was not obscene. Another dispute erupted over the issue of whether a recognized student organization could make use of the University facilities ordinarily available to it in order to solicit pledges from students to burn their draft cards. The final disagreement concerned the manner in which University officials were cooperating with public authorities in curbing student use of marijuana; especially it concerned the University's disposition of information gained through its questioning of students.

In the course of these disputes, student spokesmen raised searching questions concerning the University's role in law enforcement relative to student conduct. Although unable to present a full and consistent position of their own, they succeeded in demonstrating that the University's stands also lacked those characteristics. Persuaded that the students had raised important matters requiring speedy resolution, the administration and the faculty responded by establishing a University Commission to do the job of review and recommendation. The University Commission on the Interdependence of University Regulations and Local, State and Federal Law, which was appointed on May 10, 1967 and requested to work through the summer and report by September, was charged with a broad mandate:

> Its report should include findings and policy recommendations in the broad area of student affairs and conduct, law enforcement on campus, the interdependence of university regulations and local, state and federal law, and university procedures in all these areas. The reports of the committees which are considering judicial procedures and freedom of expression and artistic standards should be integrated into the Commission's recommendations.

The thirteen-member Commission comprised roughly equal proportions of faculty, students, and administration. The student members were a principal officer of the student government, a leader of Students for a Democratic Society, and two others prominent in student organizational life. The administration complement included the vice-president for planning, the vice-president for student affairs, the University counsel, the director of resident instruction of the College of Agriculture, the dean of the College of Arts and Sciences, and the associate dean of students. "Pure" faculty included professors of music, electrical engineering, and (as chairman) government. (Within the administration group, all but the vice-president for student affairs and the University counsel were also faculty.) The representative composition of the Commission undoubtedly contributed to its importance and legitimacy, although the members did not operate primarily in their respective roles. Rather, they behaved for the most part as concerned individuals seeking guiding principles on which they and the Cornell community might agree. Judging by the strength of the *Report* and its favorable reception, this sharp modification of constituency role-playing may suggest one effective way of coping with the inevitable facts of conflict and change on college campuses.

The Commission issued its *Report*, endorsed by all members, on September 27, 1967.[1] Its length and complexity—over forty single-spaced

[1] The Commission met twenty-five times from May 29 to August 23, 1967, in sessions lasting two to four hours or longer. During the first month it took testimony from faculty, administrative officers, and students and from community law enforcement officials and local attorneys interested in the Commission's activities. It also received written communications from students and faculty. The remaining time was devoted to the issues and to writing the *Report*. Notes of meetings were taken and testimony was recorded as means of assisting the deliberations.

pages—reflected the breadth of its mandate and the variety of subjects to be considered. The *Report* attempted to present principles for a student conduct code setting out University jurisdiction and action, to distinguish code enforcement from law enforcement, and to delineate the appropriate role of the University in each sector. In addition, a revised adjudicative system for University handling of student violations of the conduct code was proposed. Finally, the *Report* reviewed and proposed a position on each of the following "policy problem areas": freedom of artistic expression (including the obscenity controversy), political advocacy, dissent, and civil disobedience within and outside the campus (including the controversy over solicitation of pledges to burn draft cards), and student involvement in marijuana (including the controversy over University cooperation with public law enforcement authorities in investigating drug use).

In light of the subject's importance and the *Report*'s complex substance, the administration distributed widely both the document and a summary of it—to faculty, administration, trustees, campus and local newspapers, and attorneys and public officials of the city and county. During October and November, Commission members spoke on campus before various groups, explaining the *Report* and soliciting reaction to it. The November faculty meeting was devoted to the same purpose.

The Commission was dissolved in mid-November except that the Faculty Council (the executive committee of the faculty) asked the chairman and the other faculty members to prepare legislation drawn from the *Report* for Council and faculty action.[2] The proposed legislation was handled as two packages. The first proposed a *University Statement of Principles and Policies Governing Student Conduct* which, after administration acceptance and Council endorsement, was adopted by the faculty in February 1968 as legislation. During the process some useful alterations were made, but essentially the *Report*'s position remained intact. The second package proposed legislation altering the University's adjudicative structure for handling student misconduct, and in May 1968 the faculty adopted legislation that combined parts of that package and another set of recommendations from other Cornell bodies.

The *Report*'s discussion of "policy problem areas" was excluded from the legislation and, instead, was referred to the student drafters of a new conduct code and to the Faculty Committee on Student Affairs (the

---

[2] At the present time, authority in the broad area of student conduct and activities has been delegated by the president to the faculty.

standing committee empowered to ratify and interpret that code). The draft of a new code (which must be consistent with the already-adopted *University Statement of Principles and Policies*) was submitted in May and, as of this writing, is being reviewed closely by the Faculty Committee on Student Affairs. After review, revision, and approval by other faculty and student elements, its adoption in fall 1968 by the Faculty Committee on Student Affairs will put the last of the pieces in place. For better or worse, Cornell will then operate in the area of student misconduct by a new set of principles, policies, regulations, and adjudicative procedures.

Student Misconduct, Cornell's Jurisdiction, and the Law

As indicated above the major substantive elements of the *Report* were embodied in the now-official *University Statement of Principles and Policies Governing Student Conduct*. Since the *Statement* is reprinted at the end of this paper, my commentary can be selective.

Two polar positions on regulation of student conduct may be identified, neither of which, in my judgment, is considered by the large majority of the Cornell community, including students, to be appropriate to its needs. At one extreme is the "service facility" view: the institution focuses on providing, through its formal learning resources, the opportunity for students to acquire a higher education. Being concerned essentially with academic training, not with student conduct in nonacademic or extracurricular matters, such an institution can rest content with a handful of rules designed to protect the formal academic environment. The other extreme is the full-blown *in loco parentis* view: the institution asserts or accepts the role of surrogate parent with respect to the total development and welfare of each student. Such an institution presumably would have an ever-constant concern for all student conduct, expressed through many and varied regulations. The Commission *Report* urged:

> . . . the "service facility" position truncates the meaning of education and impoverishes the concept of an educational community. . . . [The *in loco parentis* position] involves a university in almost limitless obligations of dubious connection with its central purposes, and it demeans students as members of the educational community.

The *Report* sought to express Cornell's commitment to an in-between position that emphasizes and encourages the affirmative aspects of community but shears off the arrogance and interference associated with the extreme *in loco parentis* view. It also contains explicit statements to guard against any misinterpretation by students or others that Cornell's position in any way rejects genuine concern for its students.

Such a perspective makes nonacademic student conduct an appropriate area of regulation by the University. The touchstone of such regulation, however, should be the strengthening of responsible student freedom and maturity. Hence the inclusion in the *Statement,* as one of the two principles termed fundamental, of the following University commitment (Principle II):

> The University's approach to student conduct emphasizes the University's obligation to promote the personal freedom, maturity and responsibility of students.

The other fundamental principle (Principle I) undergirds and directs the entire *Statement* and will be restated in the new student code as establishing the jurisdictional parameters of University regulation. It commits the University to confine its regulation of student conduct to protect its special interests as an educational community, and defines those interests independently of law, law violation, or punishment for law violation. Law enforcement as such is deemed mostly the province of public authorities. Although the definition of the University's special interests is necessarily general, the new student code is expected to elaborate specific offenses derived from it, and it is intended that a student can be subjected to University discipline only when charged with violation of a specific code offense. No catch-all phrases will be included among such offenses, thus eliminating any attempt to protect the "image" or "reputation" of Cornell, to punish actions which "discredit" the University, or to impose discipline for "conduct unbecoming a Cornell lady or gentleman." The "exceptional" extension of University jurisdiction permitted in Section 2 will be subject to safeguards designed to prevent its abuse.[3] Through such means the concept of "University interests" will be given its proper narrow interpretation and not be so broadly construed as in effect to embrace all student misconduct in all places—as to become but a thinly disguised *in loco parentis* role or law-enforcement role.

[3] Use of this provision is anticipated to be of the order of one or two cases every few years. A decision to charge a student under this section of the code would involve the judgment of the dean of the University faculty and the vice-president for student affairs, and the case would be adjudicated through the usual procedures and machinery, which involve students no less than faculty. Further, University discipline would be confined to a choice between no penalty and suspension/expulsion, because the opportunity to impose a wider range of penalties invites excessive use—and therefore, abuse—of this provision.

The remaining six "supporting principles and policies" comprising the *Statement* complement and implement the two fundamental principles just discussed:

III. This provides explicit confirmation of the clear implication of Principle I, namely that the boundaries of Cornell's jurisdiction turn on criteria divorced from the question of law and the public jurisdiction.

IV. Extensive public investigation or policing of student law violations on campus doubtless would have an adverse effect on the interests of the University community. Yet this factor cannot be permitted to convert student misconduct not otherwise a code offense into a code offense, since this would overturn the basic distinction drawn between Cornell and public jurisdiction. By this backdoor route, law violations per se could come to be considered as code offenses, a position contradictory to both fundamental principles of the *Statement.*

A literal reading of the clear distinction drawn thus far between University and public jurisdiction might wrongly suggest that Cornell has boxed itself into choosing among unpalatable alternatives. Since the University, like any good citizen, is a friend of the law, do these principles mean that Cornell has to turn over to the police every student it suspects of any law violation, no matter how technical or petty the offense? While this would result in the clear assignment by the University of law enforcement to law officials, it would also doubtless embitter student-University relations and destroy the mutuality of trust required for a viable educational community. Do these principles mean, on the other hand, that Cornell is subscribing to a "lawless" campus in a literal sense? Hardly, since the University has no authority to declare or make its community a sanctuary exempt from the reach of the law. Do these principles mean, then, that Cornell is issuing a standing invitation to public authorities to come up and police the campus? Such a situation, on balance, would scarcely promote the University's pursuit of its educational interests. Yet is not public policing of the campus necessary if, on the one hand, Cornell is reluctant to turn students automatically over to public jurisdiction for every breach of the law and, on the other, it is insistent on confining its own jurisdiction to misconduct violating the code, not the law?

The effective answer to these questions lies in the content of the code, that is, in the categories of misconduct deemed to harm the University's interests and hence held to be punishable by the University. Most student misconduct on campus which breaks the law will also likely, for other reasons, transgress the code, for example, physical abuse, theft, unauthorized entry into facilities, property damage.

Does the *Statement's* distinction between the student code and the law then become mostly terminological, having been drained of substance? Emphatically not. The present code, soon to be replaced, states that a student "may also be subject to disciplinary action for conviction of a violation of civil or criminal law. . . ." The implications of that position are markedly different from the rationale and consequences of the formulation under discussion here. The effect of dissociating code offenses from law violations per se is greatest for student misconduct which might violate the law, but not the code, for example, some categories of draft resistance activity conducted on campus in an orderly way. More generally, the University's adherence to these new principles permits it to define the severity of offense and penalty by its own relevant criteria, and not simply by automatic emulation of how the law defines and handles the misconduct.

V. The University ordinarily will handle student misconduct violating both code and law in such a way that dual punishment is avoided. This means, barring exceptional circumstances, a voluntary waiver of the exercise of Cornell jurisdiction if the student was apprehended by the police and his case is being processed as a law violation. However, when University officials apprehend a student for campus misconduct which breaks the law as well as the code, the University will attempt to keep at least the minor law violations entirely within its own jurisdiction as a code offense. The latter policy derives not from any *in loco parentis* viewpoint, but from the point earlier discussed that student trust is impaired when a university routinely assigns all minor infractions of the law by students to the public jurisdiction. The feasibility of the policy obviously hinges on the development of appropriate understanding and working relationships between University and public officials, and on the willingness of the complainant or victim to let the matter be handled by the University.

VI. In many "university towns" the practice has developed for public officials to return students apprehended for less serious law violations to the university's jurisdiction, on the expectation that the university will impose through its disciplinary procedures a substitute punishment for court-imposed penalties. Although often well-intentioned and humane in purpose and in accord with the wishes of all parties, this practice represents an undesirable application of the *in loco parentis* tradition and contradicts both fundamental principles of the *Statement*. It retards the development of responsible student freedom and it clouds the otherwise clear distinction between public and institutional jurisdiction by committing the institution to act as a *de facto* community law enforcement agency. The provisions of VI thus explicitly prohibit Cornell from initiating or participating in such arrangements.

The prohibition extends, however, only to the use of Cornell's disciplinary authority in place of the ordinary disposition of the case by public officials. Cornell is prepared to cooperate with law enforcement officials and with student defendants in many other important ways, because it recognizes the need to offset the student's disadvantage associated with his absence of roots and his transiency in the local community and because of its humane obligation to extend assistance to a student in trouble. Cornell's cooperation is meant to assure that a student's position before locally administered law is not worse than that of his counterpart non-Cornell local resident. Public officials often have been able to work out arrangements other than prosecution or imprisonment for young Ithacans who are first-time offenders or minor law violators. Equivalent procedures not involving the use of the University's disciplinary power doubtless can be developed for Cornell students who run afoul of the law.

VII. It is explicitly recognized that Cornell's needs as an educational community should at all times condition the scope and methods of its cooperation with public officials in law enforcement, and may at times confine or preclude its accommodation of requests for its cooperation. The University should take particular care not to confuse its law enforcement and code enforcement roles when investigating student misconduct, in part because a student's rights as a citizen may be denied and because evidence not admissible in the courts may result. Even more important, University insensitivity to the confusion of its roles may have larger consequences detrimental to the health of the educational community.[4] The Commission *Report* put this legitimate anxiety well:

> Mutual good will and trust should undergird University-student relations, perhaps most especially in the sensitive areas of regulation of student conduct. It seems imperative, therefore, that students be able to assume that when they cooperate with University officials for purposes of investigations of Code violations, they will not later be dis-

---

[4] The concern which produced VII derived from the 1966–67 campus controversy on the manner of Cornell's cooperation with law enforcement officials in investigating student involvement with marijuana. The policy here developed is, of course, of more general import.

mayed to learn they were cooperating unwittingly in the quite different matter of law enforcement. If University actions make such an assumption chancy—meaning that a student cannot be sure with which jurisdiction and for what purposes he is being asked to cooperate—then students may choose not to cooperate at all and to demand, instead, a formal judicialization of every stage of Code enforcement. Such a change, together with the underlying shift in student perception of the University from trusted ally to mistrusted adversary, would inaugurate a new and bleak period of student-University relations.

VIII. In the likely eventuality that the University will be subjected to criticism for its failure to act in a particular and perhaps controversial instance of student misconduct, VIII provides a summary explanation and justification. Some student misconduct will fall outside the University's jurisdiction and thus preclude University action. And for some student misconduct falling within the University's jurisdiction, if public authorities seem disposed to handle the matter, the University may elect not to act in order to avoid imposing dual punishment on the student. University inaction, as doubtless Cornell's constituencies will have to be told again and again, implies no condonation of the misbehavior. As the *Report* wryly noted, "Society is not defenseless, after all, when faced with law violators, even when they are Cornell students."

The Revised Adjudicatory System

The revised adjudicatory system adopted by the faculty in May 1968 was, as noted above, a version that drew from several sets of recommendations, all of which shared the direction of change. Over-all the legislative outcome was consistent with the main themes of the *Report* with one exception to be discussed below.

The structure of the ongoing adjudicative system, introduced in 1958 and more recently subjected to growing dissatisfaction, comprised an all-student lower board and an all-faculty review board. Although the faculty board has mostly upheld lower board verdicts, the exceptions often related to controversial areas such as allegedly private behavior (especially parietal rules and sexual behavior) and political advocacy and dissent (office sit-ins, interference at a University event, and the like). Students were virtually unanimous in condemning the review authority of the faculty board, and early in 1968 several members of the student board resigned in protest of the overruling of a decision. Students not only saw their role as limited to advisory, but also regarded faculty board decisions as being taken with insufficient knowledge of or sensitivity to student attitudes and their rationale. In addition, the system had shown no great capacity to anticipate or defuse incipient campus controversies over one or another area of student activism. The Commission's *Report* labeled this inertia as "damaging strategy, . . . since it accentuates the willingness of students to escalate conflicts and confrontations to crisis proportions in the sure knowledge that crisis, at least, demands and gets fast attention." This setting clearly signaled both the necessity and the direction for revision.

The *Report* proposed, as a remedy for these deficiencies, a redistribution of authority between the adjudicative boards. The faculty board would retain mandatory review authority only in cases where the student board imposed suspension/expulsion penalties or where the student defendant appealed to it. In either situation, it could only approve, reduce, or vacate the penalty set by the student board. This system, it was hoped, would invest the student role in adjudication with integrity and responsibility as well as with authority, while protecting the defendant's rights by an appellate procedure free from the risk of an increased penalty. Given the Commission's preference for retaining an all-student initial board, this proposal reflected the judgment that no nonstudent mechanism could be devised to provide review of allegedly "wrong" student board decisions without it also taking on the fuller, resented role of the current faculty board.

Under this proposed system, it would not be possible to rectify those instances of defective justice in which the student board held for an unwarranted exoneration or for overly light penalties. The Commission believed, I think, that this was a tolerable price to be paid for assuring effective student participation in the adjudication of student misconduct. Cornell, as an institution and as an educational community, could likely survive an occasional miscarriage of justice in favor of the student defendant. What was felt to be more important was the retention by the faculty of its capacity to protect the proper policy content and interpretation of the code. The Commission's *Report* thus sharply distinguished between the student board's verdict in a given case and its rationale and policy interpretation. If the latter were felt to be in error, the Faculty Committee on Student Affairs [5] could affirm the proper meaning or appli-

---

[5] The FCSA is now inaptly titled. Its voting membership since early 1968 includes two students, and that number will likely be increased in the near future.

cation of the code provision in question. This would then serve as binding instructions to the student board in its handling of subsequent cases.[6]

The University faculty meeting of May 1, 1968, accepted the redistribution of power between the two boards, but altered their composition to establish both as joint student-faculty boards. Each was to be a nine-member board, with five students and four faculty on the initial board and the reverse ratio on the appeals board. The former was to have a student chairman, the latter a faculty chairman; neither could vote except to break a tie. The commentary at the meeting suggested that the concept of a genuine educational community and of student-faculty interchange of views was believed to be better served by jointly composed boards than by retention of the boards as presently constituted. Some who supported this change did so, I suspect, less from a commitment to the concept of community than because of anxieties that Cornell might be moving too rapidly in the direction of "student power." [7]

The faculty also endorsed the creation of a new mechanism, proposed by the Commission's *Report*, which in my judgment has the greatest potential for developing a truly community-wide perspective on, and responsibility for, the regulation and adjudication of student misconduct. Called the "University Student Conduct Conference," this new body will be chaired by a faculty person appointed by the Faculty Council and will be composed of all members of the two adjudicative boards, the vice-president for student affairs, a representative from the dean of students office, and a representative from the Faculty Committee on Student Affairs. The Conference's scope of concern is no less broad than the far-ranging area of student conduct itself, and although its authority is limited to the making of recommendations, it surely can develop into a highly influential and respected voice on such matters. For example, the Conference could be expected to provide a forum for a focused exchange of views

---

[6] If, for example, a student board held that a prolonged office sit-in by students constituted an exercise of the right of petition, and not a violation of some specific code provision, its verdict of innocence would be final. The FCSA, however, could review the policy and code implications of that decision, and then could instruct the student board for its handling of future cases that such circumstances violated a designated code provision. If a student board ignored such instructions or persistently refused to impose any penalties for certain categories of code violations, then presumably the time would have come once again for revision of the adjudicatory system.

[7] In addition to the impact of events on the Cornell campus, many faculty could not help being affected by the tragic situation at Columbia University, involving student occupation of buildings and subsequent massive police action on campus, which had begun a scant week before the Cornell faculty meeting.

among members of both adjudicative boards, for proposing interpretations of or changes in the code, for standardizing penalties for categories of offenses, for reacting to rationales underlying decisions of the adjudicative boards, and for identifying and discussing problems in advance of their eruption as campus disputes. The Conference, in short, constitutes a remarkably flexible mechanism which provides all elements of the Cornell community with effective access and which promises considered and timely discussion of important matters relevant to student conduct.

Some Observations on Student Participation and Influence

This case study has treated the development of new University policies on a subject which, by objective standards, should have the most direct concern to students. What role did students play in the reformulation of the regulation and adjudication of student misconduct? No single or simple answer can be given.

The student contribution was most direct and dramatic at the very outset, in precipitating and defining the controversies which persuaded the University to undertake reconsideration of its policies. The Commission was the child of student protests against the application of University rules and practices to such varied student activities as publishing a literary journal, soliciting pledges to burn draft cards, and smoking marijuana. Not unexpectedly, the crisis eased and student concern softened once the Commission was established, since that development recognized that student claims merited and would receive serious review and implicitly suggested that revision of current policies was likely.

At no time after the formation of the Commission was student input ever again so tangible, direct, or intense. Student interest revived slightly during the fall after publication of the *Report* and when Commission members, including the student members, were on campus circuit on behalf of its recommendations. Yet student reaction can best be characterized as affirmative by default: there was a quiet acquiescence and an absence of adverse commentary rather than explicit commendation or enthusiasm.[8] Few organized student groups chose to present their views

---

[8] Student criticism of the *Report* was almost entirely confined to the marijuana issue, and some faculty expressed uneasiness on the same matter. The *Report* urged that use and possession of marijuana, as well as trafficking in marijuana, be made a code offense, but that the University might sensibly elect to concentrate on the elimination of trafficking and to rely on means other than disciplinary authority to reduce use. The student drafters of the new code inherited the problem, and thence

to the Commission, student attendance at the post-*Report* campus meetings was slim, and only a thin trickle of student suggestions or reactions, verbal or written, came to the Commission's attention.

Some explanations for this relative quiescence can be offered. The short time between the Commission's initial meeting in May and the end of the term permitted few students to appear, and by the opening of the fall term the Commission had ceased official meetings and was working on its *Report*. Still, any group that wanted to register its views with the Commission had adequate opportunity to do so, and student passivity in the fall remains untouched by this explanation. Since only an activist student minority had ever been exercised about University regulation of student conduct, the somewhat mysterious cycles of student activism provide another explanation. In the 1967 fall term, the attention of Cornell activists was directed to off-campus locales and issues, and there were no major campus incidents or confrontations. When normalcy returned in the spring term, in the form of campus protest activity against recruiting by the military services and by Dow Chemical Company, student spokesmen began urging the faculty to make its decision soon on the various proposals for a new adjudicative system. That student attention should be episodic, and linked to the events of the day, is neither unexpected nor a characteristic peculiar to students. Still, making due allowance for the dulling effects of the placidity of the fall term, the impression remains that student involvement was unusually low for an issue that had agitated the campus a scant few months earlier.

The apparent satisfaction of students with the *Report*'s proposals undoubtedly provides a good part of the explanation. The interest of students (as most of us) is more sustained on matters that offend than on those that please. Student (and faculty) reaction to the *Report* should be measured affirmatively by the absence of brickbats hurled, rather negatively by the absence of bouquets proffered. Yet student satisfaction is itself partly a function of student expectations and attitudes toward the University, which pushes the question back a stage.

In my judgment, the root explanation lies in the complementary, indeed, symbiotic relationship between student activists' perceptions of the University and the receptivity to self-defined student interests of the ad-

---

it has come to the Faculty Committee on Student Affairs. The most probable outcome is that trafficking in marijuana will be a code offense, use and possession will ordinarily be a matter to be referred to clinical or counseling services, and no action violating the code will be excused because the student had acted under the influence of drugs.

ministration and much of the faculty. Cornell's activists doubtless share the general mood and ideology of their counterparts on other campuses, but not to the degree of committing themselves to viewing the University as an establishment agent that must either be radicalized or undermined. Luck undoubtedly plays a part here, but characteristics of the students' immediate environment which are not simply fortuitous contribute importantly. There is student awareness, for example, of the willingness of the administration and faculty leaders to meet with student spokesmen, to exchange views seriously and with reasonable candor, and to set in motion fuller and more representative inquiries (such as the Commission whose work is recounted in this paper) when the scope and intensity of student interest and pressure warrant. Student activists groups, knowing that they can gain access to officials who will hear them out seriously, may well choose to remain wary and skeptical of the University, rather than bitter and hostile.

Students' perceptions of their place at the University make unfeasible any adherence to procedures by which students merely propose, but administrators and faculty fully dispose. Cornell has learned that lesson. It was neither an accident nor unusual that one-third of the members of the Commission here reported were students, and that the Commission took pains to provide many opportunities for students to react to the *Report*. Students are voting members of some University committees, including the Committee on Academic Integrity, which handles cases of academic cheating, and the Faculty Committee on Student Affairs. Evidence from many campuses makes it apparent that more systematic incorporation of student representatives in the structure of university government is a high-priority item on student agenda. In a sensible effort to shape that development in order to avoid disruption and discontinuity, Cornell has appointed a University commission, composed of faculty, administrators, and students, to recommend guiding principles for the greater inclusion of students in Cornell's policy-making and administrative processes and machinery.

The new commission also will consider the important and tangled problem of how to secure representative students for such University service. To date Cornell students have been less concerned with this problem than with the antecedent one of enlarging student membership on various University committees and formal student input in various University functions. The question, however, is just around the corner; students, like today's Negroes, will not long be content to have their representatives chosen for them or through mechanisms they consider unresponsive or irrelevant to their interests. Cornell's selection of student participants has thus far made connection mostly with Student Government, but the reader may have noticed that this case study has made virtually no reference to that organization. The important student-initiated movements at Cornell for the past few years have all originated outside Student Government. Knowing that it could not survive by continuance of "Mickey Mouse activities," but unable to mobilize student backing of its attempts to take on new and relevant functions, Cornell's current form of student government was formally abolished by student vote in the spring 1968 term. An alternative structure remains to be devised in the coming academic year. Given this virtual *tabula rasa*, the new commission can be highly influential in suggesting new modes of student representation and government suitable to the serious desires of students to participate effectively in University affairs.

My final observation returns to the theme advanced in the first paragraph of this paper. I believe strongly in the observation of the Commission's *Report*, made with reference to its proposals to revise the adjudicatory system, that they were "premised on the belief that students are likely to behave more maturely and responsibly, and with genuine affection for the total community, in a system of justice they themselves shape, interpret and enforce." I see no reason why the soundness of this belief is exhausted on student conduct matters. Faculty and administrators are being challenged by today's students to rethink matters thought closed, to be receptive to change, to experiment, and to innovate. To accept that challenge doubtless will be painful for many of us, but not to do so may well be crippling to the universities we serve and thus far control.

Cornell University Statement of Principles and Policies Governing Student Conduct

Derived from the Report of the University Commission on the Interdependence of University Regulations and Local, State and Federal Law, September 27, 1967, and including amendments by the Faculty 2/14/68.

Non-academic student conduct is an appropriate area of concern and regulation by the University. This Statement sets forth basic principles and policies shaping the scope, manner and standards of that regulation. Particular attention is given to the determination of the parameters of University jurisdiction, the protection of the special interests of the Universiy community, and the relationship of University to civil jurisdiction and of the

Student Code to law. Other aspects of University policy governing student conduct, such as standards of fairness in the adjudication of Student Code offenses, are treated in other University legislation and are not included in this Statement.

Fundamental Principles

I. The University, as an educational institution, has a special set of interests and purposes, the protection and promotion of which are essential to its effective functioning. These are, with respect to the governing of student conduct:

a) The opportunity of all members of the University community to attain their educational objectives

b) The generation and maintenance of an intellectual and educational atmosphere throughout the University community

c) The protection of the health, safety, welfare, property and human rights of all members of the University community, and the safety and property of the University itself.

While these interests and purposes necessarily lie within those of the larger civil community, it is appropriate that the University's governing of student conduct be focused upon and limited to their support.

1. The University's responsibility for student conduct is distinguishable from society's.

The University's governing of student conduct through its enforcement of the Student Code shall be carefully distinguished from the enforcement of general community law, which is the responsibility of public officials. The University shall make its sanctioning powers over students serve its educational goals, rather than duplicate general police functions already well represented in law and public law enforcement.

2. The essential purpose of the University's governing of student conduct is to protect and promote the University community's pursuit of its educational goals.

Ordinarily, University jurisdiction shall be confined to student conduct which has an adverse effect on distinct interests of the University community, as set forth in (a), (b), and (c) of I above.

Exceptionally, University jurisdiction may be extended to include grave misconduct demonstrating flagrant disrespect for the basic integrity and rights of others, whether or not the student's offense involved the University community or constituted a law violation. Such misconduct calls into question continuance of the student's membership in the educational community, either because

(a) his presence would adversely affect the ability of others to pursue their educational goals, or

(b) his misconduct grossly violated standards of behavior requisite to the maintenance of an educational community.

II. The University's approach to student conduct emphasizes the University's obligation to promote the personal freedom, maturity and responsibility of students.

Supporting Principles and Policies

The following principles and policies set forth the basis for University regulations consistent with the Fundamental Principles and provide appropriate correlation between the governing of student conduct by the University and law enforcement by the civil community of which the University is a part.

III. The presumed or proven violation of law by a student neither compels nor precludes University jurisdiction, and is deemed irrelevant to determining whether the conduct falls within the University's jurisdiction.

IV. The presumed or proven disruptive effect on the University community of extensive investigation by public officials of student conduct is deemed irrelevant to determining whether the conduct falls within the University's jurisdiction.

V. In situations of overlapping jurisdiction where student misconduct violates both the law and the Student Code, the University ordinarily seeks to exercise its jurisdiction so as to avoid dual punishment of a given instance of student misconduct.

Therefore, the University shall adhere to the following policies in determining whether to exercise its jurisdiction with respect to student conduct violating both the law and the Student Code:

1. When the student is apprehended by University officials, the University shall seek to handle all but very serious breaches of the law as a Student Code violation within its own jurisdiction. The University shall seek to cooperate with public officials so that its exercise of jurisdiction ordinarily will not be followed by community prosecution of the student's misconduct as a law violation.

2. When prompt public prosecution of the student is anticipated or is under way, the University shall not exercise its jurisdiction until public officials have disposed of the case, unless exceptional circumstances compel otherwise.

3. These policies must be based on jurisdictional understandings and procedures jointly developed and periodically reviewed by University and community officials. To the maximum extent feasible their content shall be made known to the Cornell community.

VI. When public authorities apprehend a student for law violation, whether or not the misconduct is a Student Code violation also, the University neither makes nor permits use of its disciplinary power as a substitute mechanism for the law. Therefore, the University shall neither request nor agree to special advantageous disposition of a student's case by police, prosecutors, or judges solely because of his status as a University student. The University shall refuse to accept remand of students charged with or convicted of law violations for the purpose of imposing disciplinary punishment.

Nonetheless, the University, recognizing that the absence of roots and family in the local community may place students at some disadvantage when involved in law violation, stands ready to assist student defendants and to cooperate with public officials to promote equitable application of the law. Should a student charged with law violation request assistance from the University, a University representative shall advise him and, if requested, shall facilitate the student's employment of suitable legal counsel. If the student defendant consents, the University ordinarily shall cooperate with the requests of appropriate law enforcement officials for programs of probation or rehabilitation.

VII. The University's cooperation in law enforcement, at the request of public officials, shall be exercised in each particular case with a view to safeguarding the interests of the educational community, especially student confidence in the University.

When the University acts in a law enforcement rather than a Student Code enforcement role with respect to students, the Cornell community or the students questioned shall be informed fully and promptly of that changed context of inquiry and investigation.

VIII. The University's inaction with respect to known instances of student law violation implies no University support, approval or indifference, but simply reflects

    a) When no Student Code violation is involved, its respect for the bounds of its responsibility for student conduct

    b) when a Student Code violation is involved, its concern to avoid imposing a dual punishment for the same instance of misconduct.

Student Participation

JOSEPH WHALEY, JOSEPH M. HENDRICKS,
ROBERT D. CLARK, MARTHA PETERSON

The Freedom to Control
JOSEPH WHALEY

DEAN MAGRATH and Professor Sindler have presented perceptive reports of two cases in which orderly change in university governance, at least in the realm of student nonacademic behavior, was made possible. In each case, the key was the explicit recognition by university authorities that the situation was too serious and complex to be handled by established procedures. At Brown, the president apparently realized that campus tension was mounting to possibly explosive levels, and he acted at once to move the university toward identification and solution of the underlying problems. According to Dean Magrath, the result was an easing of campus tensions. At Cornell, the administration and the faculty together seem to have responded rationally, despite the very tense atmosphere on campus, by recognizing that there existed nonroutine problems which might require very real changes in university policy. They then acted, in good faith and without much delay, and Professor Sindler reports that Cornell students were by and large satisfied.

Had the true nature of these crises not been recognized, and had the authorities—those individuals, whoever they may be, who actually control the formulation or implementation of policy—decided instead that some "get-tough" policy was indicated, Cornell and Brown might well have been the scene of a confrontation which would have embittered student-university relations for years. I would like to suggest why this is so. It involves the relation between the power of the students and the limited means available to them to exercise that power.

138

In this context, power may be characterized as the freedom to control the lives or actions of others continually despite any objections they may have and with or without their explicit consent. In this sense, heads of educational institutions have traditionally been very powerful in relation to many of the people associated with them. Faculty members evolved the shield of the tenure system to protect themselves from capricious use of the university's power over them. Students, by and large, have had no such shield.

Until recently, students in this country tended to accept this vulnerability, if they thought about it at all. This widespread acceptance derived in part from the premium that American society places on the possession of academic degrees. Most students, realistically recognizing the odds against persons without degrees, cheerfully or cynically performed the tasks required by the university, regardless of the intrinsic value of those tasks. Draft deferments have compounded the incentive to stay in school, since even those male students who support U.S. foreign policy do not all feel an obligation to put their own lives on the line.

Thus, although some university practices may appear senseless to intelligent and reasonable students, the many persuasive reasons for not rocking the boat have been a built-in discouragement of criticism, based on an implied threat that the university's power may be used punitively.

University power over students is applied both subtly and openly, through displays of force. For example, a dean often has at his disposal a gradation of means which range from refusing to admit a student, notifying parents, entering a black mark on a student's record, referring to a disciplinary committee, altering grades as a punishment, suspending or expelling the student, and even calling in the police. Faculty members, for their part, exercise control by their assigning of grades, by their deciding whether a student will continue in their department and whether he will be granted a degree, and ultimately by their possibly writing references to an employer or graduate school. This spectrum of possible hidden or direct retribution faces any student who questions an act or practice of the university. Many students have seemed to reason that it is better to keep silent, since graduation is only a few years away.

Fortunately, not all students keep silent. Some voice their criticisms, sometimes responsibly and sometimes not. One common criticism, which apparently underlay the unrest at Brown and at Cornell, is that the university enforced a system of social regulation for students without bothering to discuss it with them or justify it to them.

At this point, I suggest that civilized society requires that disputes be settled, if at all possible, through the use of reason and with patience. Only if these fail to lead to agreement is force an acceptable means to resolve the dispute. Sadly, the standard student experience has been that the university wants not discussion but obedience. Traditionally, the university first applies psychological force (such as the hidden pressures just alluded to) and ultimately physical force if the student still does not conform. It does not necessarily matter whether the student is ever persuaded of the validity of the university's requirement. (Note well that this principle seems to apply to curricular matters as well as to social regulation.)

Unfortunately for some boards of trustees, administrators, and faculties, students have also used force in several recent and successful experiments. If they failed to try reason and patience first, possibly it is because reason and patience had never really been attempted with them.

At Cornell and Brown, the legitimate grievances raised by the students led to changes through processes orderly and conducive to rationality. The application of reason and patience paid off, both for the students and for the universities. Elsewhere, students have occasionally resorted directly to force without first attempting in good faith to persuade, using reason and patience. The consequences have not always been constructive.

Students who feel that persuasion has not worked or will not be taken seriously do not have a wide range of means available for applying force. They cannot easily adjust the severity of their actions to the gravity and complexity of their dissatisfaction, unlike deans or faculty members, who can choose from among an assortment of potential pressures. Student economic leverage is negligible (see M. de Jouvenel's essay), and in many institutions students are allowed no effective and timely participation in the formulation of the decisions which affect them. The only weapon they can use is their ability to embarrass, and even ultimately to immobilize, the institution itself. It's all or nothing, when the university is seen as being unwilling to listen or to respond.

This student weapon has a major drawback that intensifies the seriousness of any crisis in which it is used. It does not lead naturally to the development of positive, reasonable proposals which will constitute a basis for university action leading to needed reforms. Rather, it encourages authoritarian personalities in the administration and in the general public to show their worst qualities and thus aggravate the students even more by demonstrating that authoritarianism.

Perhaps at Cornell and Brown, the student body might never have reached the "critical mass" of tension and frustration which, in the presence of determined leadership, could have been turned by any spark into a confrontation. In any case, however, the intensive efforts described by Professor Sindler and Dean Magrath seem to have led to an institutional insurance policy of sorts—better university-student understanding.[1] The process may be worth trying elsewhere, if time permits.

From Behind the Ivy Walls

JOSEPH M. HENDRICKS

PROFESSORS MAGRATH AND SINDLER describe genuine responses by the administrations and faculties of their respective universities to student demands for participation in formulating and implementing policy on student conduct. These responses resulted in a portion of authority for student disciplines being distributed to students. In both instances, however, the faculty and administration retained considerable, perhaps dominant, authority in this area. Student participation in this process was not *pro forma*, but at the same time the protests were primarily limited to specific areas which directly affected students only, and even in these areas, the universities were not called upon to undergo radical change.

Professor Magrath deals briefly with student interest in curriculum, and Professor Sindler comments favorably upon the prospect that students will not limit their demands for change to the area of student conduct. Both writers note the acceleration in student protests and would probably agree that their papers are "interim reports" which will require updating as the students' quest for power continues.

The protests at Brown and Cornell were of such a nature and intensity that the universities could absorb them by bending traditional structures. However, students are now demanding power in determining policy which faculty, administration, and trustees have never happily shared with each other. Although one of these centers of control may on occasion side with students against another on specific issues, they will individually and collectively be less responsive to student pressure as it becomes increasingly evident that the vested interest of all may be

[1] Editor's note: The above was written a year before the 1969 disturbances on the Cornell campus.

challenged and all may be called upon to relinquish power in controlling the university.

The typical response of faculty and administration has been to interpret student protests as "communication problems," and they have seldom taken seriously the claims that unrest is rooted in the belief that the entire program of higher education is largely meaningless and irrelevant. The strategy employed in dealing with these communication problems, therefore, is to involve students in token roles, assuming that they will be satisfied with merely being consulted and advised in decision making but not involved in the actual determination of policy, which abides in the hands of faculty and administration. The memorandum from a member of the Brown Curriculum Committee to Professor Magrath concerning participation of students on the committee is characteristic of this posture:

> . . . students would have an established channel for communicating their ideas at the policy-making level, and they would have the chance to express their opinions on all issues of policy that were decided. They would not themselves likely be able to determine the result. Power would be largely symbolic. (p. 47)

Students surely know the difference between "symbolic" and "determining" power, and it is the latter that they now demand.

Insistence that students accept symbolic power is increasingly viewed on campuses as the same kind of response that the civil rights movement received from the nation. The earlier stages of the movement were guided by the assumption that the demands of black people could be met by merely altering "the system." As long as this assumption prevailed, the movement received general national support: but, when black protests began to probe beneath the surface of white vested interests, the system could not, or would not, relinquish power in response to persuasion. The language of black protest then changed from persuasion to force, and there developed among black leaders distrust of any accommodation with established interests. Finally the message of black militants was that "the system" could not be altered to include black people. Rather, it must be destroyed and remade with black people participating both in architecture and construction.

If such a critical juncture has not already been reached on some of our campuses, it is being approached with alarming speed. If relations between students and the university continue to deteriorate to such a deplorable state, all will be losers, and the principal loser will be the university. As another response to the crisis, the university could reaffirm its faith in students, admit that it is already being remade, and welcome students into the continuing reform process.

Despite the turmoil and tragic violence, student protests not only have forced higher education to define problems which have long needed attention, but also have been the principal force in setting the direction of institutional change. Students have confronted higher education with the reality that teaching has become a lost art, and their complaints have accelerated debate over the failure of graduate schools to prepare teachers. They have exposed higher education as a system that encourages faculty to give first allegiance to their guilds and to fulfill the demands of industry and government before attending to student needs, thus subverting the university's stated aim and purpose. Student involvement in the community has led to demands that curriculum be relevant to the great problems of our time and that the academic program include learning through service. Gradually universities have followed student leadership from behind the ivy walls into the community to address themselves to the ghettos, mental health, air and water pollution, penal systems, and many other problems which no responsible institution of our society can longer ignore. Students also are appropriately protesting investments by governing boards that tend to maintain and perpetuate immoral social structures.

Student unrest will continue to intensify tensions between university administrations and their several constituencies; but traditional relations with these constituencies have blocked the path to change, and there is little reason to believe that substantial reorientation with these constituencies would have occurred without student pressure. It is to be hoped that the claims of these constituencies will come to be measured by educational merit rather than by their economic and political power.

It now appears that students will have a dominant role in matters directly affecting them, such as student services and conduct. They will press their demands for partnership with faculty, administration, and governing boards in determining university policy on a broad scale. Their demands, like those of their partners, should be measured only by educational merit.

The Immemorial Path

ROBERT D. CLARK

THIS COMMENTARY on two excellent papers is given against a background of some student unrest and disturbance at San Jose State College during the year 1967–68. The major events were as follows. Black students made dramatic charges of racial discrimination. The charges were followed by a week of open hearings and, in consequence of threats from a much aroused external community, a football game was canceled. Then, four students, in the presence of several hundred more or less militant sympathizers, interrupted an ROTC drill. Next, a demonstration against Dow interviewers on campus escalated from some fifty or sixty militants to more than a thousand angry protestors when the police, trying to make their way through two to three thousand curious but resistant onlookers, resorted to the use of tear gas. Mexican-American students threatened to disrupt commencement exercises; as a result faculty members, fourteen graduating students, and two or three hundred people from the stands staged a walk-out.

The gains from the disturbances were considerable. (1) Steps were taken to reduce discrimination against blacks; in particular, an ombudsman was appointed to deal with injustices and frustrations arising out of the racial problem. (2) Several committees intended to increase student liaison with the faculty and administration were created; moreover, students were seated on several important faculty committees and given voting membership on the Academic Council, the college's delegate legislative body. (3) The number of courses of instruction concerned with blacks and Mexican-Americans was increased. (4) Additional staff members from minority groups were appointed. (5) The college's program for disadvantaged and technically inadmissible but promising minority students was enlarged from thirty-seven students in 1967 to approximately four hundred in the fall of 1968. (6) On the basis of committee deliberations begun in the previous year, a new statement of student rights and responsibilities was adopted. This document included a code of conduct and carefully developed procedures for student and student-faculty courts.

As an embattled college president "leading" the way in these reforms, I have felt somewhat like Eric Goldman's description of Senator Vandenburg: "He had taken the immemorial path of effective leadership in a democracy: he led where the people were going anyhow." Yet the witticism is only half true—as every student activist or any reformer who has faced an obstructionist old guard can tell you. I find much that is hopeful in the two papers under consideration, not only in the basic attitudes expressed but also in the action taken by the two institutions concerned.

The first such hopeful sign is the assumption on which both Dean Magrath and Professor Sindler base their arguments: that students are going to participate in the governance of the university. That being the case, "the problem for American colleges and universities," as Dr. Magrath succinctly puts it, "is to move toward more formal, more institutionalized modes of student participation." College authorities ought not regard such a move as a retreat, as an abject surrender of administrative or faculty prerogatives, but as an advance in the practice of democratic principles.

Our remarkable technological society has brought with it the paradoxes of affluence and poverty; of freedom from enslaving manual labor and oppression of the spirit through the machine and the bureaucracy; of preparing the student at an early age to participate in democratic governance and denying him the right to practice what he has learned; of opening the doors of higher education to the masses but failing to redesign the curriculum and the methods of instruction to meet the needs of the society which has demanded the mass education (a new curriculum, I might add, which would avoid the higher learning for conspicuous leisure and vocational education, both scorned by Veblen). And above all, we are faced with the paradox that has resulted in a paralysis of will: a nation that has not only the power to annihilate but also practices a moral restraint or has a prudent regard for its own future that inhibits the exercise of that power—but within these constraints, permits a wanton waste of human lives, our own and the enemy's.

The students are right. We are not faced simply with a generation gap, with the rise of the young Turks to whom we must yield the old power: our society is faced with a crisis in values, and the student generation, more than ours, will suffer or profit from the manner in which we resolve the conflict.

I am not sympathetic with the view that we must destroy before we can build, nor am I ready to abandon Paul's admonition to hold fast to that which is good. But the students can help us to define the good, and the best means is for us "to move toward more formal, more institutionalized modes of student participation."

The second item I note and applaud in the two papers is the disposition to give students a greater voice in areas they regard as particularly their province: the relaxation of parietal rules at Brown, the greater responsibility for their own conduct at Cornell. Students demand abandonment of parietal rules, and some even ask for complete autonomy in establishing and administering general codes of conduct. Much of the public responds with shocked surprise, some of it with the wry complaint of the old boys in the Wowser Club of the cartoon "Grin and Bear It": says one of them, from behind his puffing cigar: "What I most resent about the new morality is that we didn't get in on it." I believe that law and order and morality are a product of the community and not, in a democratic society, the result of imposition by external authority.

So long as the students accepted the law (college and university regulations) as appropriate to their interests and welfare, order prevailed, save for sporadic outbreaks or individual aberrations of which the students themselves did not approve. But when a large segment of the society, including the student society, finds the governing regulations oppressive, alien, or inimical to its values, the regulations must be examined and possibly changed, and those most affected must participate in the examination and the change. I do not agree, however, that the students should have complete control. They are not an autonomous community, but part of a larger whole that includes the faculty and administration, the trustees and, particularly in public higher education, the constituents whom the trustees represent.

I should like to commend particularly the statesmanship demonstrated by the Cornell committee in defining relationships between the university and the community law-enforcing agencies. As Sidney Hook has observed, the cry of "double jeopardy" is a call to the university to abandon its responsibilities, but the calculated imposition of "dual" punishment or the university's assumption of the community's law-enforcement responsibilities are, as the Cornell committee pointed out, certain means to evoke student distrust of the university community. The Cornell declaration will be a model for many colleges and universities; I have already referred it to the Student and Academic Councils at San Jose State.

Both papers treat cases of student participation in the governance of their own conduct. Students aspire to much more. I shall not comment on their extensive demands other than to say that I believe in student participation. The degree must be carefully defined, and in the several functions of the university, participation should range from advice or expression of opinion to major responsibility for management. Both defining the degree and determining the manner of participation are fraught with difficulty and potential conflict. The students who demand power *in good faith* may not yet have accustomed themselves to dealing with those of their fellows who reject all authority, including student authority. Unhappily, we have taught our students to believe in panaceas, easy solutions. "Our name for problems is significant," said Dean Acheson. "We call them headaches. You take a powder and they are gone." Student participation will not remove the headache, and at this point in time it may even intensify the pain. But it may also provide the incentive and the means to achieve more quickly a healthier academic community.

Between Policy and Practice

MARTHA PETERSON

MAGRATH AND SINDLER, in their case studies in student participation, recognize that students do participate in campus decision making, and I assume from their papers that they believe this participation is good. Such student participation is not new. Students, by what they chose to learn and by the way they lived their lives on campus, have always influenced college policy, negatively or positively, as soon as those in charge figured out what students were saying. We may call it "delayed participation" when a staff member makes decisions based on "how it was when he was in college." In recent years (certainly after World War II and possibly since World War I), student participation has been formalized and institutionalized through student government, committee assignments, and the expansion of student personnel services.

Why then is there such active concern over the role of students in decision making now? If they do participate and have always done so, what has changed to make reconsideration necessary? Why do we need case studies to tell us what happens? Are there new factors in the students' requests, or is what we have claimed to be doing a sham? In my comments, I shall suggest several new realities and raise the question of the applicability of the examples in these case studies to the suggested new realities.

Is the heart of the present concern an insistent request from students for instant and direct influence, not twenty years later, as faculty members, not two years later when others begin to believe what they say, not six months later when the recommendations of the student government have received the necessary approvals, but now, by five o'clock this afternoon, with suitable supporting action to assure untrusting individuals that promises will be kept? If this requirement for instant and direct influence is a part of the present campus mood, then the cases described by Dean Magrath and Professor Sindler provide useful models for the process and problems of decision making. On the other hand, the orderly procedures described may seem to some to be delaying tactics or "cooling-off periods," designed to support the status quo. As we read the Brown-Pembroke and Cornell cases, we must ask whether, on our particular campus, we have "the time for such careful and time-consuming consideration."

Is the reality of the new urgency for student participation temporary, lasting only until structure and attitude catch up with the changes that the campus majority (qualitative or quantitative) agree must come? We may have said *in loco parentis* is not a useful concept to describe a college's relationship to its students; we may agree that teaching and learning must be improved; we know we must end the war in Vietnam. Do we support these convictions in action? When practices catch up with conviction, will the present campus crises be resolved; will students, faculty and administrators begin again to live in nonviolent respect for each other's competencies? If the present crises are, indeed, issue-oriented, then a direct attack on issues may be the efficient solution. Why not appoint ad hoc issue-oriented committees, convene a town meeting of the college community, or hold a referendum to establish the college's position and then get on with the important concerns of a college? The present cases do address pressing issues, but they illustrate a more useful concept. The present crises may be an immediate result of lag between policy and practice, but there are important considerations beyond the immediate crises. There is the hope of establishing a way of living together on campus that will be equal to cultural change and will decrease the possibility of a recurrence of defeating divisiveness.

Or is the new reality of student participation beyond current issues, instant answers, and the absence of trust? "The rules of social decorum," described as "petty" by President Eliot of Harvard in 1869, may not be the issue. The issue may be the right of a student to live his private life privately or publicly as he chooses, as Mr. Schwartz has indicated in his paper. The issue may not be Dow recruiters but the college's use of its political influence. The issue may be the kind of college and university governance that is viable for the next five or ten years. Committees can be useful at one stage in this evolutionary development. But if the issues are fundamental to the nature of a college community, then a committee—however perceptive and wise—will not have control over the final decisions. One of the keys to the effectiveness of the Brown-Pembroke and Cornell studies is the committees' understanding from the beginning of their limitations and, at the end, their knowledge, that their solutions would be modified to meet new problems. Committees or procedures set up without open acknowledgment of limitations may be useful for a time, but in the long run they will only provoke greater frustrations.

The final question I wish to raise is a simple one: Is it worth it? Dean Magrath and Professor Sindler have taken time from their own fields of scholarly competency or from their teaching or administrative responsibilities, but what are the alternatives? If students and faculty are thwarted in their search for opportunities to teach and learn, they need to join in the search for ways out of their dilemmas. The process will be wasteful of talents, of time, of energies and may postpone personal achievements. The case studies seem to say that the other alternatives are less attractive.

*He that wrestles with us strengthens our nerves and sharpens
our skill. Our antagonist is our helper.*

Edmund Burke, *Reflections on the Revolution in France*

BERTRAND DE JOUVENEL*

Academic Youth and Social Revolution

A SERIES OF STUDENT OUTBREAKS on American campuses runs from Berkeley in 1964 to Columbia University in 1968. Highly justified therefore is
the call of behavioralists for an over-all study of such events; surprisingly
parochial, however, is their intent to set it "on a national level." [1] Can
this mean that the major occurrences in Western Europe are deemed irrelevant? Is it not obvious that we are witnessing a general process of
eruption taking place in a great variety of countries, whose academic institutions present notable contrasts of character? Does it not follow that
an international investigation is required to sort out those factors common to all cases from those upon which a purely national study might
lay excessive stress?

---

* *Editor's note: Baron de Jouvenel accompanied his manuscript with a letter
that serves so aptly as an introduction to his paper that an abridgement of it is
included here:*

Anserville par Bornel, Oise
August 2, 1968

DEAR MR. CAFFREY:

I have responded more to what your letter suggested than to what was
asked for. It put in my mind the problem of the academic manager, which
you had so sensitively stated. Then came the events through which such communication was established with our students, which no amount of trying to
open conversation can achieve, which requires the heat of extreme situations.
It seemed to me then that the best contribution I could make to your meeting
would be to convey what this intensive experience superadded upon previous
information allowed me, nay urged me, to say about that transnational
populus in formation, the students. Whatever the faults of this paper, I have

[1] *Science*, July 5, 1968, pp. 20–25.

What is needed more is a systematic study based upon intensive case studies from which conclusions of extensive validity might be drawn. But events do not wait upon the findings of scholars. Thus, it seems to me an evasion to deny an expression of opinion on grounds of inadequate information, even though the inadequacy clearly makes such expression mere opinion.

My feeling is that instances of student agitation cannot be explained away as arising solely or mainly from conflict situations within the university but rather are signs of a conflict between academic youth and society, and that we are witnessing the birth pangs of a new political element that is arising in unexpected quarters, autonomous and prone to manifestations eccentric to the accepted political process.

The quarters are unexpected, because we tend to associate manifestations of discontent with positions of privation; yet students are in a favored position. When I say that the element is autonomous, I do not mean—which would be absurd—that it is insensitive to external influences, but I do mean that student movements are not the youth section of any senior political movement. Great worry is caused by the forms of action assumed by student movements; it is here that international comparison is of special importance, for it can show how far such forms depart from the usual, and to what degree and on what conditions they can be integrated.

---

poured into it my greatest efforts at understanding, and, if I may say so, I am hopeful that, though it may shock some readers, they will not find it useless.

I wish your conference every success. Circumstances make it a very important conference indeed. I would learn greatly from it were it possible to come, but we have undertaken here such a complete reconstruction that even those of us who are so fortunate as to be free of any organizational responsibility. . . As I write this disclaimer it strikes me that it has become a practical untruth. What has occurred can turn our Faculty into the sorriest mess or something extraordinarily vital. But each of us must be totally dedicated to success on behalf of the whole institution.

Kindly believe me   sincerely yours,
                                               /s/ Jouvenel

Students and the Social Climate

In France as well as in the United States the student body has increased tenfold or more since my day (the morrow of World War I). Taking such a long perspective is, however, not advisable as it obscures the great spurt that has occurred since the last war.[2]

Now, what is the social meaning of this spurt? Does it signify that our societies have become more sensitive to the enrichment of human personality by such exercise of our faculties as is afforded by higher learning, and have therefore felt impelled to impart such benefits more largely? Let us hope that some such concern has played a role in the widening of access to the universities. But surely this has not been the main motivation.

It is within a framework of enthusiasm for economic growth that higher learning facilities have been enlarged, in the conviction that the higher the education, the greater the potential contribution to such growth. Therefore the universities have been seen as essential to a fast-progressing society.

Little attention was paid to the psychological dispositions that might develop within these institutions, dispositions the more important as these institutions came to contain a larger proportion of the population.

These dispositions were bound to be affected by the over-all social climate. No society ever before has been so determined to move and to move fast. Characteristic of this determination is the enormous currency achieved by the adjectives "obsolete" and "obsolescent." Have they been put into circulation by revolutionaries, raising their voices against the existing social elites, sometimes termed "the Establishment"? Not at all! Denunciations of obsolescence come from within the Establishment; they rain down from places of authority. Such adjectives stud the speeches of General de Gaulle; they figure even in decisions of your Supreme Court.

Nor is this to be wondered at, since the authorities of our time, be they political or social authorities, are not committed to the conservation of a static order but see themselves as stimulators of change.

Business executives are generally regarded as a conservative element in our society. But what a misreading! Does a business executive propose to go on producing the same things, by the same processes, with the same machines and the same manpower? Quite the contrary! He is ceaselessly

---

[2] According to Unesco, the student population in Europe has grown at a yearly rate approaching 5 percent in the 1950s but approaching 9 percent in the first half of the 1960s.

concerned to develop new practices and new products. Faster and faster he rejects his existing machinery as obsolete; more and more frequently he shakes up the structure of his organization lest it settle into obsolescence. Indeed, he extends the notion of obsolescence to his very engineers, whose aging is said to impair their adaptability and creativeness. Thus the business community, especially in the United States, is the very source of concern with obsolescence which has come to pervade the whole of our society.

This concern with obsolescence is, as far as I know, an entirely new phenomenon in the history of civilizations. Leaders of civilizations have ever been concerned to build enduring monuments and enduring institutions. We, however, do not build to last, but in our every building project include a date for abandoning what is being set up.

Now consider the natural impact upon the formation of student judgments of this prevailing emphasis upon obsolescence. If it be true that length of experience makes engineers less useful—makes them, it is thought, cling to practices increasingly out of date—why should this not hold true of managers, professors, and statesmen? Is seniority then also not to be distrusted? If structures should be suspected of becoming inadequate to the march of progress, why should such suspicion spare the academic structures within which students find themselves and, indeed, the social structures wherein they will be called to take their places? Thus, the very social climate that induces the quantitative growth of the student population at the same time induces in that population a mood increasingly critical of existing authorities and organizations.

Another element of the social climate deserves mention, though it is less singular than that which I have just stressed. An interesting variable in the history of cultures is the rise which occurs at long intervals in the qualitative appreciation of youth. I am unaware of any studies of this phenomenon, but the merest retrospective glance suggests that each period of such rise is correlated with a turning point in the prevailing culture or institutions, which is logical enough as the greater favor accorded youth gives freer play to its character, spontaneity, ardor, enthusiasm, and dissatisfaction with things as they are. Such a rise has unquestionably occurred in the last half-century. Symbolic thereof is that epoch-making televised appearance of J. F. Kennedy, who, looking a young hero, spelt out his "I am not satisfied."

Such a period induces the young to call into question not merely the validity of existing authorities and institutions in terms of the kind of collective progress we are making, but also the very nature of this progress, the very values by which it is both impelled and constrained.

Students and the Future

And here is a quite major point that was strongly driven into my consciousness by the ten weeks of almost ceaseless discussions I had with the students of my institution during the student crisis in France. What was expressed with great intensity of feeling was their distaste for the direction in which our civilization is moving, associated with their dislike of the "promising" careers they would be called to within that future.

I say "promising" careers because, in my personal experience, those militant students were outstandingly brilliant as scholars. Of quite a few I had measured the ability before the event; of those I came to know within that time I obtained from fellow professors commendations most favorable to their scholastic standing. These are young people who could take for granted outstanding personal futures within the structure of our present society. (It may be otherwise elsewhere, and that is one of the interesting points to consider.) Further, it came to my mind that I had met much the same mood of distaste for the collective future-in-the-making, and for their personal futures therein, among some of the best students I had when I taught at Berkeley in 1960. In short, students differ from their seniors in that they are interested not only in change but in changing the direction of change, that is, in "second order" change.

I shall now leave this important theme of the inner impulse of students and hasten to compare it with the impatience-generating character of student life.

Students Are Adults

"Students are adults." This I do not mean as a normative proclamation but as a statement of fact, a fact the more to be stressed because it is recent.

Traditionally, legally, adulthood is set at twenty-one. It is to this definition that I am referring. I find great masses of people above twenty-one in the universities of today. It was not so in my day, or indeed well beyond my day; undergraduates were what Americans call "teen-agers"; graduation normally came at twenty but could be achieved much earlier, say at eighteen. Thus not only the undergraduates in general but also many of the graduates were under twenty-one.

As against this I now see few graduate students under twenty-one and many undergraduates above that age. In short, we are facing a substantially older student population than that to which we belonged. How much older, and why? I have been unable to lay hands on statistics displaying for each of several nations the change in the age distribution of its entire student population over time. Nor again have I found contemporary statistics stating age distribution, establishment by establishment, that would permit comparison of the age structure of different establishments within one country with that of similar establishments in other countries. For want of such data we cannot check any hypothesis concerning the factors contributing to such aging.[3] But never mind the causes, what matters here is the situation arising.

The older the student body, the greater the accumulation of frustrations. There is a natural progress of urges in the development of the human being: this progression impels him to break out of the protective shell which the family afforded his weakness and to try out his new-found strength in the wide world. Student life delays this breaking-out and venturing forth. It does so in the form of restraints that are specific to Anglo-American institutions and of deficiencies that affect students everywhere.

Of the restraints I shall speak but briefly, being in this respect a visitor from another planet. The European is amazed and delighted by the beauty and amenities of the American campus; puzzled at first by the extraordinary value set by students upon the automobile, in time he understands that it is to them a means of escape from Shangri-La, and this draws the visitor's attention to the disciplining of private lives, which is a necessary condition of a residential institution. Being nonresidents, our French students are subject to no such discipline, and the recent introduction of residence at Nanterre gave rise to violent revolts against the mildest rules.

But for all their freedom from university rules, our students lack the independence that is the natural attribute of adulthood. They are not

---

[3] It is patent that the institutions most immune from such aging have been those faithful to *numerus clausus* policy. But as such cannot, of course, be the general attitude of our educational system, it is in comparisons between the more accessible institutions that we must look for enlightenment.

self-supporting, an obvious source of irritation, and they are not *doers*, a point I wish to stress.

If you are so indiscreet as to ask a young man: "What do you do?" and he answers, "I am a student," you will then slip into asking: "And what is it that you propose to do?" And this points up his distance from *doing*, which he experiences, however unconsciously, as an inferiority.

This inner worry was suddenly brought out in May (1968), displayed by those French students who went to the factories occupied by strikers. Fraternization was the purpose, and the students sought out their age peers whom they approached in a mood for which the words "respect" and "envy" seem hardly excessive: these, their contemporaries, they regarded as veterans in the joust of life—on the sidelines of which they, as students, felt themselves to stand.

If, as is here suggested, students feel somewhat balked of normal expressions of adulthood, what is more natural than that an obscure but nagging impression of deficiency should impel them to some forms of self-assertion?

Students Are Uneconomic Men

Further food for thought can be drawn from the meeting of students with workers.

Impressive to the students was the great calm prevailing in the struck factories. Most workers did not come; those on union duty sat around quietly, playing cards or chatting. By merely stopping their activity, workers posed to the Government a vastly greater problem than that set by the spectacular agitation of students. And why? Because these people are providers of goods and services, which students are not. And thus they have power to deny, which is enormously effective.

Impressive also was the care taken by the workers to minimize disruption of domestic life—thus no interruption in the provision of electricity to households—and the attention paid to keeping everything tidy for prompt resumption.

Students were somewhat dismayed to be told: "Your strike costs you nothing. Ours loses us pay and brings hardship on our homes."

Finally the most extreme of the students, who had hoped that some brave new society would arise out of the turmoil, were disappointed to find the workers willing to go back to work on financial terms.

Thus were brought into relief the distinguishing attributes of economic man pertaining to the worker—bargaining power, immediate responsibility, and cost and benefit concerns. These marks are lacking in the student, who is not a supplier of goods or services and whose material status does not depend upon his work, which is not addressed to the market.

Typically students have no "jobs" in our economic structure; this condition they share with the "unemployed," but with a quite opposite social meaning. As it happens, the student population and the unemployed population are approximately equivalent fractions of what we characteristically describe as "the population of working age." But the proportion of the jobless is a measure of failure of our system, whereas the proportion of students is a measure of progress.

Thus within our "society of bees" we find a category which it is understood should not (and should not need to) hold jobs. Its members stand aloof from our economic system, and they enjoy freedom from the daily timetable of employment. Here are people who enjoy an exceptional mastery of their time, indeed far more pronounced in the case of the European than in that of the American students, our own being bound to show up only twice a week for sessions with teaching assistants. It is worth noting that such mastery of one's time was deemed by Aristotle the basic requirement for active citizenship.

Independence of one's material conditions (however mediocre) from one's activities and free disposal of one's time—these have been, throughout the history of civilizations, the conditions afforded to "freemen," "gentlemen," members of the political society, beneath which strove the economic men providing its substratum.[4] It is then hardly surprising that this stratum of students should have a potential disposition to reproduce the traits of these past political strata.

Within such layers, politics have always been a function of psychological dispositions, not of economic interests. Their themes have been war or peace, a hard or soft line in diplomacy, this alliance or that, repressiveness or permissiveness in mores, conservation or innovation in ritual and institutions, concentration or sharing of decision-making, submission to authority or standing upon personal rights, and so forth. These issues are emotion-laden as against those arising from conflicts of material interests; issues that do not readily lend themselves to compromise as they are not

---

[4] As American orthodoxy classifies people by income strata and as American radicalism applies the terms of "privileged" and (somewhat bizarrely) "underprivileged" to the richest and poorest, it may be proper to stress that "privileges" have a quite different meaning: they are the rules applying to those whose business is not business.

couched in terms of more or less; issues that, arising out of psychological differences, can be brought to a boil by gestures or words that offend feelings.

As the student population has some characteristics common with the political societies of the past, it is not unnatural that it should have the same political potential, that it should be available for emotion on similar issues. It has indeed manifested such a potential throughout European history; but earlier it was minute in numbers.

If no manifestations of such a potential had occurred in the United States before 1964, then it might be well to investigate the causes which up to then prevented such manifestations rather than to concentrate on those which have intervened since.

University and Society

A clash between the university and society has long been in the making, and I hope you will bear with me while I place it in historical perspective.

The chief contrast between modern and traditional societies lies in placing productivity ahead of personal worth as the supreme social concern, which involves the ranking of production managers as our social elites. Such changes, first foreseen by Saint-Simon early in the nineteenth century, have materialized faster in the United States than in Europe, but they now prevail in all advanced countries.

They are recent by comparison with the antiquity of universities. And let me point out that however new a university may be, it partakes of university tradition.

Medieval universities focused on theology, to which philosophy and rhetoric were auxiliaries, and of which canon law was an application. On leaving the *studium*, one did not leave its concerns: one belonged to the clerisy, set far above society as its moral teacher, and coupled further research with preaching. Such persons were exempt from material cares; indeed they were strongly forbidden to involve themselves in any management of temporal interests.

The character of Renascence universities was different and is well expressed in the title of Vergerio's famous treatise, *On the Manners of a Gentleman and on Liberal Studies*. The idea was to bring to the highest possible pitch of civility those called by birth to the upper walks of life, to imbue their minds with such worthy examples and to cultivate their feelings so that they would behave with dignity, discrimination, and delicacy. This of course forestalled any disjunction between university life and social role. Students of that time went into a social stratum wholly unconcerned with material cares. As is well known, Oxford and Cambridge have long remained the repositories of this Renascence character.

Thumbing through the centuries, I come to the foundation of Berlin University in 1808. Its founder, Humboldt, made it clear that the purpose of learning is to produce men of learning: "The State should not look to the universities for anything that directly concerns its own interests, but should rather cherish a conviction that in fulfilling their real function, they will not only serve its purposes but serve them on an infinitely higher plane. . ." Note the expression "an *infinitely* higher plane." This unmistakably signifies that Learning is thought of as standing quite outside the workaday pursuits of society, that its function is not to fuel new energy into those pursuits but to shed light. This view is of great importance, since German Learning has been the major influence upon academia throughout the Western world in the nineteenth and twentieth centuries.

Now we live in societies whose excellence is measured in material achievements. Just as a society essentially addicted to war would be rational in assessing its institutions according to their war-worthiness, so is a modern society assessing them according to their production-worthiness. Research in universities may be as pure as you will, but it should give rise to useful developments. Similarly, teaching may be as pure as you will, but it should bring forth men and women fitted for useful employment. These requirements gain emphasis, not only as more is spent on universities but also—and mainly—as a greater proportion of youth is inducted into higher education.

These requirements press upon universities, coming not only from above but also from below, from the many students to whom graduation is a necessary step up the social ladder. What stands against these pressures? Is it only outmoded traditions that can and should be swept away? It is more than that.

The Product-oriented University

The very nature of a university precludes its integration into an economic society. The main tenet of an economic society is to maximize payoff; that is, to minimize costs or to attain a given result with the least possible effort. Now this tenet in the university would make bad teachers and bad students. It is the bad student who, faced with a problem, wants to be told what technique should be used for its solution, while the good student is eager to work it out for himself, to invent anew what is trite to others. And no one is a good teacher who does not arouse in students the enjoyment of such seeking. A professor feels that he has a good class when its members outstay the time allotted, press their inquiries beyond the frontiers of the course, in short spend more energy than is required.

It is well recognized by all that such must be the climate of a university, but too little, I think, has been made of the difference of climate with society. On every occasion I have had, over the years, of conversing with students in various institutions and different countries, I have found in the most brilliant students a reluctance to take the plunge from the stimulating climate of the university to what they regarded as the dull and confining climate of economic life. Possibly they quite misjudged this climate, and it may be that many of those who foresaw it as such now appreciate it. What I am testifying to is their anticipation.

And I must here state that in my view the most powerful influence toward generating their distaste has not come from this or that philosopher but has been the work of the advertising community. The imbecile smugness of the sleek, alert junior executive who is to be seen on every glossy page, smoking this brand of cigarette, or drinking that brand of whisky, or driving some car, is enough to disgust any young man in his senses, enough to keep him from wanting to step into such shoes.

I argued with the students that we are a society of workers, proud to be "servants of one another," and that, having enjoyed the privilege of superior education, it behooved them to take their place among the workers, with the more zeal since they could expect to be called to relatively high places. To which the answer commonly was, "Useful employment, yes, but is this useful?" And they would go on to denounce public relations, advertising, salesmanship, and generally, as they put it, the stimulation of artificial needs for profit.

I need not enlarge upon the well-known indictment of "the consumer society." But, if I may use old-fashioned expressions, it is entirely natural that people who are being induced to internal adornment should frown upon pressing inducement and increasing addiction to external adornment.

In short, students, formerly few, at one time found in society roles wholly consonant with university values; now students are a large and increasing proportion of their age group and, on coming into society, are called to a diversity of roles which have in common their discrepancy with university values. That minority of them that has been most responsive to university values feels least at home in the outer society.

Conflict within the University

The emphasis of my exposition has been on the conflict between university and society. To my mind, the great problem lies here, and not in a conflict between academic authorities and students. The inflammatory factor in the latter relationship arises, as it seems to me, from the political activities of students and the eventual reactions of academic authorities.

I do not mean thereby to play down the difficulties which are indigenous to the life of the university. But the intense experience afforded by the French crisis, of which I have given a full account elsewhere,[5] has provided me with two object lessons. On the one hand, a huge "nation-quake" has been brought on by the clumsy handling of initially unimportant political activities of some students; on the other hand, in the very midst of this "quake" an unprecedented experiment in constructive cooperation between academic authorities and militant students was brought to a successful conclusion.

As to the first lesson, it suffices to concentrate on a single day, May 3. That morning the students attending the suburban institution at Nanterre found no less than five hundred policemen forbidding access to the lecture halls. Such was the extreme answer of the local academic authorities to the incidents of the previous day. What incidents? At Nanterre the charismatic personality of Cohn-Bendit had brought integration of a variety of extremist groups elsewhere divided. All such groups throughout France had set May 2 and May 3 as days of "sympathy for Vietnam." The Nanterre group wished to manifest such sympathy by showing films, and had asked the authorities for use of a large amphitheater. When they were refused, the students seized the amphitheater and refused to give it up to the professor whose lecture was scheduled to be given there. Noises and alarums followed. The episode was not very serious in itself but was made serious by the heavy reaction of the academic authorities.

Finding their institution closed, the activist students of Nanterre, perhaps two hundred strong, went to the Sorbonne to stage a protest and were reinforced by an equal or somewhat larger number of Parisian ac-

[5] See the September 1968 issue of *Analyse & Prévision*.

tivists. They entered the Sorbonne, as anyone normally can, and held a meeting in its courtyard. As to the tone of this meeting, witnesses differ. Whatever it may have been, the supreme academic authority, the Rector of the Paris Academy, decided to call the police. The demonstrators were pushed out and, by all accounts, went quietly. But, to their surprise, they were pushed very slowly, and why? Because as they reached the street they were packed into police cars. This, then, was a slow process, occurring in full view of sympathetic student groups that in the meanwhile had been alerted. This of course generated a street disturbance which proceeded far into the night.

On the following morning, the Quartier Latin awoke to find the Sorbonne shut down, heavily guarded by forces which, moreover, were also to be seen everywhere about. It shocked not only the students but the whole academic community as well that forces had been called into the Sorbonne, an unprecedented invasion, that the Sorbonne was closed down, again an unprecedented event, and that forces were ostensibly deployed throughout the Quartier Latin. A revolt was thus set on its way, which rapidly gained in extent and intensity, feeding on increasing repression. Repression was such, on the night of May 10, as to evoke national sympathy for the students, which the unions materialized by organizing a huge march on May 13, out of which came the mood for workers' strikes. The student crisis had escalated into a national crisis.

My second exhibit is far more pleasing. It refers to what occurred during this student and national crisis within one of our major academic institutions, the Paris Faculty of Law and Economics, which numbers 36,000 students.[6] Its students were called upon to strike in sympathy with their comrades of the Sorbonne, and the Executive of the Faculty [7] made no objection to the use of the lecture rooms for relaying these calls.[8] Further, the Strike Committee also appealed to the sympathy of the professors. After the night of May 10, the Executive voiced a strong public protest against police violence.

[6] In France, "The University," in the singular, denotes the whole system of higher education; a regional division is an "Academy" (thus the Paris Academy has 160,000 students). "Faculty" is the name of a specific institution.

[7] The Executive of a Faculty consists of its Dean and Assessors, of which there are three in our case. This Executive is answerable to the Assembly of Professors, of whom there are 120 in our Faculty.

[8] It is here relevant to recall that traditionally in France we have no campuses, that our Faculty, in physical terms, reduces to the structures where teaching is performed, and that therefore there is no other place where the students may assemble. From this physical situation it also follows that student demonstrations naturally deploy in the streets.

On his return from an untimely visit to Asia, the Prime Minister, on the 11th, took cognizance of the public emotion and decided to reopen the Sorbonne. Thus its students, together with others, could march into it on the evening of the 13th, after the gigantic street demonstration, in the mood of conquerors. The other Faculties were equally taken over by the students, including ours, with the difference however that it had never been closed against them.

"Student power" was thus established. Some academic authorities saw this as a dreadful episode, to be dealt with by the Government. Not so our own authorities. Our Executive thought that if it left such "power" to be swept away in due time by political authority, the students would experience a feeling of deep resentment. It felt that the solution to the situation should be reached directly with the students. Therefore, it encouraged those professors whose impulse it was to go into the occupied building to enter into discussions with the students. I, among others, did so from May 14 onward, for practically every day of two months. Those of us who thus mixed with the students from the outset could testify that they were engaging in enthusiastic but meaningful discussion of social and academic problems.

On May 21 the Dean opened the formal meeting of the Assembly of Professors by inviting in a delegation of the Strike Committee. This was unprecedented in the history of the French University. But more was to follow. When the delegation had left, the dean, M. Alain Barrère, submitted to the Assembly a resolution which stated that a new constitutional structure should be set up in the Faculty on the general principle of the students having an equal voice in its government, and which proposed that a commission of professors be named to discuss this future structure with an equal number of students. This resolution was accepted by a huge majority though it implied that the Assembly of Professors would be superseded by a General Assembly, half of whose members would be students. The members of the commission were immediately named, and the joint commission went to work. It was made clear that its function was not consultative; it had a mandate to decide. On the basis of its mandate it came to its conclusions on June 6. Elections took place on June 18, on a basis of proportional representation; the lists of the Strike Committee obtained an absolute majority. The General Assembly then met on July 3, divided into commissions, and concluded its work on July 12.

The conclusions reached bore upon every aspect of the learning process and its organization. Impressive were the earnestness and thoughtfulness of the students. In fact, the professors were often driven to remark that the changes the students called for would demand very much more personal effort on the part of the students than do present practices.

Obviously, I cannot go into details, however interesting. But the point to be made is that waves of irritation arose whenever students were reminded that a great deal of what was being agreed upon required the sanction of the political authorities, an obvious result of our educational system, which is wholly state-owned and state-supported. Further, it was apparent that the political liberties claimed by the students within the Faculty might be so used as to stimulate conflict with the political authorities.

I am happy to say, in concluding this section, that the present Minister of Education has chosen as his chief assistant one of the professors who had been most active in the process here sketched, M. Alliot.

Student Politics and Academic Authorities

I have here shown, on the one hand, disastrous failure in dealing with the outward-addressed activities of students and, on the other hand, great promise in dealing with inward-addressed demands for reform.

The lesson clearly emerges that academic authorities should avoid coming into conflict with students' outward-addressed activities. Such avoidance must be regarded as the more necessary the more one believes, as I do, that student political activity is only beginning, that this is a developing phenomenon. Arresting such development is surely beyond the power of academic authorities; I fail to see that it is even in any way within their duty.

Doubtless, everybody would agree with this insofar as student political activities fall within the established pattern of politics, that is, consist in rallying to and canvassing for well-established political parties. Upon such activities we shed a benign smile which can be thus interpreted: "It warms the heart to see these young people learning to play our grand old game."

The fact is, however, that "these young people" are not enthusiastic about a game which they recognize as "old" and do not think of as "grand." In general terms they regard the existing political system as incapable of effecting the kind of reforms they wish, and in this they may be wrong. But surely they are right in feeling that, within the regular processes of the system, they have no sort of hold upon it that affords them any chance of moving it their way. Imbalance between the strength of their wishes and the ineffectiveness of their voting power moves them naturally to disregard regular procedures. Moreover, the intensity of their feelings calls for a stronger mode of expression than the casting of a vote. And finally, experience shows that a small minority may achieve major results by the ardor and frequency of its demonstrations.

Thus, everything impels student activists to run off the rails of regular political activities. And last, but not least, even repression is a promising risk, because it must bring them, by arousing solidarity, a wave of support far beyond the backing previously enlisted by their goals.

I am far indeed from underestimating the problems set by activist minorities. I have indeed pointed it out earlier as the great political problem of our time.[9] But as a factual problem it is a problem for the political authorities, while as a scientific problem it is one for political scientists.[10]

It is not a problem for the academic authorities; it is one indeed wherein they cannot meddle without taking on the character of watchdogs for the social order.

But, it can be objected, is it possible for academic authorities to wash their hands of the disturbances caused in academic life if such demonstrations take place *in situ?* To this my answer would be that disturbances are the problem of those who are being disturbed. As I see things, those who suffer from the disturbances are the students. Surely the place of learning is a place to which students repair to increase their knowledge and develop their minds. It is the function of professors to serve the students therein. The losers from a disturbance which impairs the service are the students; it is for them to assess the costs and benefits of the disturbance. It is for them to keep these disturbances from inflicting excessive losses upon them. Although students who feel injured by the disturbance are apt to demand action from the academic authorities, they should be made to understand that this is nonadult behavior, in its essence "running to mother." Such behavior is, of course, encouraged if the academic authorities represent themselves as responsible for "law and order" within the university. It is obviously absurd to claim this responsibility and not to exercise it, to develop no responsibility upon

[9] Especially in my *Pure Theory of Politics* (Part VI, chap. 2 and elsewhere).
[10] In the above-mentioned work I complained that factual studies have been addressed to weak political behavior such as voting (Part I, chap. 3).

the students and yet expect them to behave responsibly. I for one would willingly make a complete devolution of the "law and order" function to the elected representatives of students. But however we act, we shall not easily waft away the problems raised by student activism.

There is no more natural place for the exercise of democratic self-government than in a university, with a citizen body limited in number, of the same order as that of ancient Greek cities, and higher in intellectual development than any ever before seen. Moreover, these citizens can, if they wish, turn for advice to professors standing on the sidelines. These are ideal conditions for democratic self-government. If we do not trust it under such conditions, this must mean that we do not believe in it at all.

Afterword

Denver, Colorado
October 10, 1968

I mention the success of the policies recently inaugurated by the Faculty of Law and Economics at the University of Paris. Meetings with students gave rise to absolutely no incidents. On the contrary, it was an affair of good fellowship between students and professors.

In the medical school, where examinations started somewhat before ours, there had been incidents. Students saw ushers (proctors) who were suspect in their eyes; they thought they were policemen in civilian clothes, and I don't think they were wrong.

Each of our establishments is governed by a dean who is a professor elected by other professors. Our dean called on us to act as ushers. From early morning, we checked the outer and inner doors and were with the students taking examinations. Only the full professors did this. Some of our faces were not known to students, who are not obliged to attend classes, but some of them knew us and were rather sensitive to this. They rather liked it. They asked us why we did this. We said, "Because we think your examinations are important." And so there was a good atmosphere.

The main thought of the students was not a quarrel with the university—though they might have had one if they knew the difference in conditions between French and American universities. For example, there is not enough room in our libraries for students to sit down, and books are hard to obtain. We have 126 professors for 36,000 students!

The concern of students who are advanced in their political views was the connection of the university with society. Their quarrel was with society. "We do not want a university which merely fits people for jobs, however rewarding, however promising. We want a university that is critical of society as it is."

To make the university a center critical of society can be good or bad. We chose to think that it is a stimulus to intellectual excitement and that young people who think society is imperfect (and they should think so, and it is) should concern themselves. We decided to develop our teaching on the basis of the changes that can be made in society in the future. What values, what goals, what means, and what studies and experiences of reality should lead to these changes?

There is in France the problem of fitting courses to careers. Students were against this fitting. They decided this was making learning conform to the functions to be performed afterwards. Perhaps they were too contemptuous of the functions in the economic system that are of service to the government. Their whole idea was to refute the university system, which does not allow them to understand the reasons for their place in society. They contest a society which would wish to forbid them to penetrate the conflictual nature of social relations.

In the French university the only general idea taught is that of marks in school. The French university does not converse efficiently with the tools of research *and* understanding. (It is perhaps notable that in our faculty, which teaches the rather exact disciplines of law and economics, things went better than in the faculties of letters, where precision of thought was perhaps less taut.)

The moral urge is essential, but the intellectual discipline to know what to do about it is also essential. It is easy to lead people who are confident that you are sympathetic to their feelings. It is not too difficult to lead them to realize that they must acquire intellectual skills which allow them to serve these moral ends. It is easy to tell them, "Look, if you are going to act only upon your passions, it is no use at all coming to the university, because you can have these passions without coming here. Therefore, if you do come here, it is in order to act rationally on the basis of your value judgments."

The real value of the university is scientific neutrality. You cannot depart from it, certainly, but it can pose problems to students. We say, "You want these changes, and this is your work. We do not have to associate with this want. We do not have to become partisan, as you are, but we can help you find out how to advance these values." Discussing the future is a good ingress to it, because there is a diversity of futures, with some limits to what is feasible. Each may be achieved on its specific condition. "As an intellectual, a scholar, an educated man, you must understand the relationship between the results and the causes, between the goals and their means of achievement." This sort of language is quite easy to speak to students.

The year 1968 will go down in history as a year as important as 1848. Being a Frenchman, of course, I attach great importance to events in France. This is our national failing. But I also attach the utmost importance to what has happened in Czechoslovakia, where there was an effort to have liberal institutions. Note the demands of the Czechs. The crushing of these demands follows a pattern well-known between 1815 and 1848. Compare the 1821 intervention of Austria at Naples. Exactly the same words were used, and the same aspiration was represented in Naples as in Prague.

We have all believed that political problems derive from social regimes. Here we see two utterly different regimes. Naples was pre-industrial, Czechoslovakia communist. Under two utterly different regimes the same political problems stem from the simple, basic concept of liberty. I think students throughout the world are moved by this feeling for liberty. I think it is extremely important, a very good phenomenon, and it should lead us to encourage the idea of liberty to take precedence over many things of which we think we may disapprove.

We must keep to the essentials of political guidance—to liberty, equality, and the effort to *promote* fraternity; this last is always the forgotten term.

This struck me deeply when we had an occupied building. Ours was occupied for ten weeks. In this occupation, there was first of all among the students an atmosphere of active cooperation which had been unknown before—much more unknown than it is in the United States, because you have student houses, and we don't. Second, the professors who immediately went there and talked with the students were filled with a warmth of feeling which had been unknown before, and links were forged between students and professors which were unimagined before.

I remember a professor who was very shocked by everything which had happened and yet who said, "You know, it is a new climate, it is a new atmosphere—and I like it."

JOUVENEL

COMMENTARIES ON

Academic Youth and Social Revolution

GRESHAM M. SYKES, GLENN E. BROOKS,

HUGH W. LANE, MALCOLM MOOS,

ROBERT BOGUSLAW

The Unspoken Conflict
GRESHAM M. SYKES

PROFESSOR DE JOUVENEL's paper, "Academic Youth and Social Revolution," provides an extremely worthwhile comparative note on the present crisis of the university. It is all too easy, sometimes, for us to forget that the problems of particular universities—with all their specifics of time, place, and people—are part of a large-scale historical movement embracing all modern industrial societies. The relationship between education and society is being transformed, and in that process, with all its straining and upheaval, we are often unable to see the larger pattern of which we are a segment.

It is interesting, however, that in most attempts to understand the social revolution now taking place in education, much of the analysis has been directed to the causes and the nature of student protest. Changes in the age structure of the student population, the vast increase in the size of the student body, the rejection of a consumption-oriented society that allows or encourages gross injustice—these are typical of the factors examined as sources of many of the present dilemmas in colleges and universities; and typically these factors are seen as the driving force behind student demonstrations, student dissatisfaction, and so on. If a university suddenly explodes into violence and disorder, the administration and the community ask, "Why do they act that way?" and *they* refers to graduate and undergraduate students.

What's odd is that we seldom ask why the university acts the way it

169

does. The most simple models of social behavior suggest that any social situation is the result of a number of interacting forces. But this obvious fact is frequently ignored, and in trying to analyze the revolts of students we are prone to concentrate on only one side of the picture—the student side—and think that if we understand that, we understand everything.

This approach, I suggest, is seriously in error, and, instead, we must begin to try to understand why the university responds to demands of students as it does. A student revolt is a situation in which students have made certain demands on the administration that have not been granted. If we are to understand that situation, it is not enough to ask why the demands were made; we must also ask why the demands were not met. In other words, the response of the university administration is problematical in the sense that it needs to be explained. Our imagery of the university reacting to student rebellion is often that of a brave, intelligent, and civilized garrison defending a fort against the onslaught of a wave of barbarians. We have paid a good deal of attention to the motives of the barbarians—we have seldom examined the motives of the soldiers within the fort and asked why they fight as they do.

The reactions of universities to demands for student power have, of course, shown a great deal of variation, as have the specifics of the student demands. In many places, however, the demands have been refused, met only partially in token gestures, or granted only with the greatest reluctance. This negative response of the universities, if we can call it that, is what I would like to examine. Many of the reasons commonly given by the administration and the faculty for the negative responses are undoubtedly believed, at least in part: Students are transients and not permanent members of the institution—although it is true that students are sometimes more "permanent" than some of the faculty and administrative staff. Charters and constitutions must be changed before new policies can be adopted, and this sometimes is a long process. Students do resort to violent tactics which can bring much of the educational function of the university to a halt. If students are given an important voice in determining the content of the curriculum, they may substitute trivial and momentary concerns for the reality of worthwhile aspects of a liberal arts education.

The Economic Aspect of the University

These reasons have some validity, and they certainly are the conscious motives, in many cases, of university resistance to student protest. I would like to argue here, however, that they are by no means the whole story. I must disagree with one major idea in Professor de Jouvenel's paper. He argues that the real quarrel of the students is not with the university, its faculty and its administrative staff, but with the larger society. The university, he says in effect, is organized for knowledge, for the development in the students of a desire for learning and creativity. The society is organized for monetary profit and consumption. That, he argues, provides the basic fight, and the faculty and the students are natural allies in a struggle against a materialistic and inhumane social order. Professor de Jouvenel may indeed be right about the Sorbonne or other European universities, but I don't think he is right about a great many American universities. Rather than being a scholarly enclave in a crass world, the university in the United States often turns out to be a rather close reflection of the larger society. We live in a business culture, and I think it deception to believe that our universities do not partake of that culture in a very pervasive fashion.

Now if the university is more like a business enterprise than a monastery in many ways—and I think it is—it becomes relevant to ask who owns it, what is the nature of its product and its pricing policy, what determines its costs, its market? That is, the economic aspect of the university is a crucial factor in understanding the nature of the university, its actions and its reactions; yet it is an aspect of the current situation involving the struggle for student power that is seldom mentioned.

Although descriptions of the present conflicts with students are often couched in terms of educational philosophy, professional concerns, the wisdom of mature experience versus callow thoughtlessness of youth, and so on, I suggest there is an underlying economic struggle which is of fundamental importance but which is unrecognized or is disguised. That is not to say that economic motives are the true motives, the basic motives, and that all the rest is a smoke screen. It simply suggests that there is an economic element in the university's resistance to demands for student power which needs to be taken into account.

A nice legal question is who really "owns" the university, be it public or private, and just what rights are part of that ownership. Regardless of the legalities of strict ownership, the university resembles many other business enterprises in that the management exercises most of the control and has a major economic stake in the enterprise in the form of salaries and careers. And if we follow the argument of Riesman and Jencks that the so-called academic revolution has brought the faculty to a position of dominant influence in the university, then the faculty is a major part of management, and its stake in the educational enterprise is of central importance.

Student Protest as an Economic Threat to Faculty

Demands for student power may pose something of an economic threat for the university administration. If the demands are accepted, there is at least the possibility that alumni gifts will decline, an angry legislature may withhold funds, and so on. If controls over the private lives of students are abandoned, both parents and the community may attempt to impose all sorts of sanctions. It is actually the faculty, however, which I believe is most threatened by the student revolts, for the demands of the students frequently come to bear directly on the occupational arrangements the faculty has worked out within the university.

Some of these demands are quite obviously a challenge to the managerial position of the faculty and their economic status. The right of students to participate in the selection of new faculty members sets up the future conditions of competition among the faculty and disrupts the elaborate system of influence of older faculty members. Similarly, a demand for participation in promotion and tenure decisions exposes the faculty to new criteria of ability and performance which will be reflected in salaries, security, and career advancement. Again, well-designed course evaluations by students which are made public could mean that many faculty members would feel threatened in their jobs. The redesign of the curriculum—whether done in the name of relevance, new fields of inquiry, or what have you—must mean at least in part the redesign of the faculty, and the scholar—no less than the clerk whose job is about to be computerized out of existence—is faced with an economic threat. Student attacks on the grading system mean a re-examination of student performance, which raises again the question of faculty performance and faculty competence. And the student demand that students should truly be taught, and not simply processed in an educational bureaucracy, raises one of the most disturbing questions of all. It threatens the intricate, delicate scheme that has been worked out to reward research rather than teaching and that lies behind the faculty's climb to power within the university. The diversion of the faculty's time from teaching to research has been labeled the major form of academic white-collar crime. Many might find the phrase offensive, but I suppose embezzlers prefer not to be called embezzlers.

There are other ways in which the student protest that has developed in the last several years threatens to disturb the faculty's position as salaried management, such as the opposition to some—or even all—Federal grants, and so on. My main point, however, is simply this: Students' demands for changes in the organization of higher education are not simply questions of the best ways to teach, of proper curriculum content, of the student's right to participate in the government of the university. These demands also involve profound questions about the occupational role of the teacher and the whole system of hiring, firing, promotion, working conditions, standards of competence, and pay schedules which make up the intrinsic rewards of the professor's job.

If this argument is correct and if the student demands for changes in the university do pose a serious threat to the economic status of the faculty, why has the faculty not taken a more active role in opposing student revolts? Is it because the faculty is not stirred by economic motives? Does an ideological agreement with the students override economic considerations? Do individual faculty members think they will come out ahead and it will be their colleagues who will suffer?

The answers are not clear, inasmuch as the faculty position in the present crisis of university administration has not been much explored. It is clear, however, that up to now, with a few exceptions, the faculty has left most of the battles to the administration. I suggest that if major changes in the organization of the university are to be made, the unspoken conflict between faculty and students will have to be brought out into the open and resolved. The faculty will not give up its economic privileges easily, in my opinion, any more than any other occupational group. It is a barrier to significant change which has been largely ignored.

In the Developing World
GLENN E. BROOKS

M. DE JOUVENEL invites international comparisons of academic youth to determine whether the present tension is indeed a global phenomenon. Having just returned from a year at the University of East Africa, I have the impression that M. de Jouvenel's generalizations are only partially applicable to newly independent and developing nations. His gen-

eralizations seem most appropriate to societies with (1) a highly indus-
trialized, mass-consumption economy, (2) old and rather unresponsive
universities, and (3) a hard core of student revolutionaries who have
enough strength to affect the society at large as well as the internal
operation of the university. These conditions do not prevail in the
developing world, at least in East Africa.

To be sure, there are some important similarities. On the three campuses of the University of East Africa—in Kenya, Uganda, and Tanzania—it is not difficult to find students who are at odds with their
society and unhappy with the existing structure of the university. Some
protest the direction as well as the rate of change. They are keenly
aware of the complexities that arise from obsolescence—planned or
otherwise—in their new society. The students are relatively old; they are
not doers; they are uneconomic men. But these similarities have not produced a revolutionary situation because the combination of ingredients
is not the same.

First, students in East Africa have not encountered the industrializa-
tion and mass consumption that seem to generate so much student discontent in the United States and France. My students came from
progressive peasant families. As university students, they were living on
government scholarships which permitted them a higher standard of
living than they had ever known before. Most were preoccupied with
getting their university degree and taking their place in the new elite.
Most were driven by a heavy sense of obligation to their families—and,
as you know, the African extended family covers a multitude of cousins
and nephews. Therefore they felt that they must get a professional position that would enable them to help their families and still live at least
a modestly affluent middle-class life. Here, I think, is one of the critical
points of difference. Increasingly, Western students see affluence as a
form of slavery. For most African students that I know, being free is
virtually synonymous with having a house, a car, and a little money in
the bank. (Once in a conversation with a group of African students I
argued that a man was not free unless he was capable of turning down a
job that paid twice his present salary. Most of them thought I was
crazy.) When M. de Jouvenel says, "The imbecile smugness of the sleek,
alert junior executive who is to be seen on every glossy page, smoking
this brand of cigarette, or drinking that brand of whisky, or driving some
car, is enough to disgust any young man in his senses, enough to keep
him from wanting to step into such shoes," he is not talking about very
many students in the University of East Africa.

This preoccupation with becoming a member of the elite, however, does not mean that African students are uniformly in favor of the existing government or the social structure. The students I knew tended to fall into three groups:

1. Those who more or less uncritically support the present leaders and constitution of their country.

2. Those who are incipient revolutionaries, disenchanted, skeptical, worried. But I met no overt revolutionaries. They lack organization among themselves. They have no ties to revolutionary groups outside the universities. Completely dependent on the government for financial support, they have no alternative means of attending the university. East African governments are rather vigorous in suppressing antigovernment movements before they get very far. And finally, much of the hostility of the incipient revolutionary is directed against the former colonial powers rather than against the national government. When something goes wrong in Kenya, the CIA is likely to get as much blame as the Kenya government.

3. Those—the mass of students—who are just waiting to see if the present government will succeed in building the nation and maintaining political stability. If it falters, many of them will be drawn to revolutionary causes. If the government sustains its power, they will become loyal and uncritical members of the establishment. The very newness of independence makes it difficult for students to know which people to bet on.

In East Africa, the mix of uncritical supporters, incipient revolutionaries, and "wait-and-sees" varies from country to country. I would say that Kenyan students are the most highly critical of their government, Ugandans are about in the middle, and Tanzanians are the most enthusiastic in their support of the existing regime. The reason may very well be that Tanzania, under the leadership of President Julius Nyerere, is unquestionably the most radical of the three countries. The government is deeply committed to doctrines of socialist self-reliance, extensive nationalization of the means of production, and severe restrictions on the accumulation of personal wealth. In Kenya and Uganda, which have rather impressive records of economic growth, the governments have been more inclined to welcome foreign corporations and to avoid drastic moves in the economy.

Perhaps I will be proved wrong by events, but I would suggest that a genuinely revolutionary government can command the loyalties of its youth and extract considerable sacrifice from them. A pragmatic, evolutionary government—even if it is producing better material results than its radical neighbors—can command the loyalties of its youth only so long as it can give them secure and rewarding positions in its elite corps. Even though the government of Tanzania places Draconian limitations on its public servants (for example, they cannot own stocks or rental property or be directors of private companies), my Tanzanian students were much more eager to pursue a government career than were their Kenyan and Ugandan brothers, who regarded the public service mainly as a place to get a secure job.

It is still too early to tell whether students in East Africa will turn against their governments. For the moment, there are still some openings in the elite corps. But the situation is changing rapidly. Just after independence, university graduates were moved swiftly into top government positions. Now those positions are filled by fairly young men who have no intention of retiring. The present university students can still look forward to reasonably good positions in the elite. In another four years or so, however, the ranks of the elite may be substantially closed off, and a new generation of frustrated African students may carry a revolutionary potential.

Not much student hostility seems to be directed at the University of East Africa itself, at least not at present. Student demands for changes within the institution have been confined, as far as I know, to such matters as better food or improved campus walkways. But as university education becomes less a privilege and more a right and as students acquire the means of supporting themselves, African universities may well be struck by major unrest. Even though the campuses are relatively new, especially in Kenya and Tanzania, the curriculum, calendar, and academic structure suffer from serious problems of irrelevance and obsolescence. Students are beginning to question a system that was transplanted from England. The Africanization of the faculties has not proceeded as rapidly as many students consider desirable. Three-quarters of the faculty in East Africa are still European, and black students are troubled, if not demoralized, because they continue to be taught by white men. So far, however, students have not been sufficiently organized or sufficiently interested to play a significant part in university reform.

A Single, Stark Statistic

HUGH W. LANE

THE CENTRAL FEATURE of the student unrest which is of concern to us today as we view the American scene is that it is essentially moral. It is concerned primarily with the disparity between our teachings and our actions, between our preachments and the example we set, between the conclusions we reach through thinking and reasoning and our actual behavior.

It is a mistake, I believe, to think of the unrest as starting this year or in this decade. Many of us trace its origins to the sit-ins of the civil rights movement which on the surface were concerned with a cup of coffee at a department store or some similar issue, but on a deeper plane represented a striving to see the American Creed made manifest in American society and culture. Thus campus unrest—student activism—sparked the civil rights movement and led to general social activism on behalf of the weak and the downtrodden in a society of affluence and power. Nor is it accidental that the origins of campus activism dealt with the concerns of black people as students and citizens. For some time now the mistreatment of the American black has stood out like a sore thumb as an example of American inhumanity to American, and as a black eye to the nation, in general rendering incredible our moral posture on the world scene.

It is of some concern that the continuing failure of American institutions to come totally to grips with the problems of the American black man (white racism is the face by which the problem is known) is not represented formally and as a separate area on this program. For the American institutions of higher learning have certainly and clearly failed to date to put their house in order.

Title VI of the Civil Rights Act of 1964 clearly bars discrimination based on race, color, or national origin "under any program or activity receiving federal financial assistance." The law of the land clearly calls for recruitment, admissions, and financial aid practices that will ensure that the benefits of the higher learning will obtain for these groups in proportions which represent their proportion of the population. And yet the figures on compliance with the Civil Rights Act gathered last year by the Office for Civil Rights showed that less than 1 percent of those enrolled in undergraduate, postsecondary institutions in the fall of 1967 were black.

I suggest that this single stark statistic is the major source of fuel for the moral unrest which manifests itself as campus activism. This clear instance of illegality which is also immorality cannot possibly be explained away to students—neither to black students nor white—nor to the various minority segments of the American population who play the game and call for an end to deceit and to chicane.

Clearly the American institutions of higher learning have failed to make and to carry out those policy decisions that are necessary to reshape practice into conformity with law and morality. At a 1968 meeting in New York, the chief executive officer of a great state university charged admissions officers with the task of making those policy decisions necessary to bring American colleges into more relevant service to the non-white middle class. Certainly this was at the least an evasion of responsibility, for such policy decisions must be laid down at the levels of presidents and chancellors and boards of trustees. Faculties and professional staff must indeed implement them, but the guidelines must be laid down at the level of ultimate legal responsibility.

This is not a matter of light concern. I could cite many instances of the crucial failure of leadership in this area. A letter actually crossed my desk in which the president of another great state university wrote that "only because of incessant pressure from NSSFNS are these Negro students on our campus in the first place." In the face of such demonstrated failure in commitment and understanding, campus unrest and student activism come as no surprise to me. The students dare not leave to us decisions of such ultimate concern to their future and the future of their country and the world.

Unless you, unless we, get serious about Our Father's business, I predict that the unrest will not be quieted, and I say a solemn "Amen."

The Walking University

MALCOLM MOOS

BERTRAND DE JOUVENEL's paper has both depth and scope. So saying, I hasten to add that the main purpose of my critique is to draw out additional implications from several of his topics. My difficulty in responding to his paper arises from its compression of diverse levels of analysis into a brief statement. Its quick range from the broadest theoretical interpretation of student activism to consideration of the practical and immediate issues of academic governance tends to obscure some excellent ideas that merit greater ventilation.

Essentially, M. de Jouvenel's thesis is that the primary conflict for college students is with society rather than with the university. Student activists in Europe, as well as America, are challenging the direction of change in our societies and the implicit value systems that define the social roles for which university preparation is supposedly relevant. Therefore, student activism cannot be thought of as only an internal university problem. Rather, the phenomenon calls for fundamental reconsideration of the role of the university within society.

The analysis is both important and accurate. But it suggests that universities cannot function simply as systems that prepare students to serve existing social structures and value systems; they must also permit and encourage the re-examination of directions of change in society. This is a most delicate task, but M. de Jouvenel does not tell us how it is to be accomplished without endangering the traditional intellectual autonomy of universities. Yet reconstructing the role of the university is the problem that bedevils all of us.

I believe that to attack the problem, we must first refurbish the land-grant concept. The land-grant college's traditional willingness to solve the real problems of rural communities must be extended to the full range of social problems facing society. Recently at the University of Minnesota, I received two visitors from Brazil. They were much intrigued with the word "communiversity," which we sometimes use there to describe the interlocking relationship between the community and the institution of higher education. One of the visitors told me that this term translates into Portuguese as the "walking university"—a most appropriate phrase to describe our mission. The university should work side by side with the community leaders to rid our cities of noise, dirt, poverty, racism, and a host of other problems. More and more, students demand that the university accept and work toward the same goals. If the university does not move in this direction, the primary conflict suggested by Jouvenel cannot be resolved.

A second but related observation by Jouvenel is that change moves at a faster pace in society than it does within the university. Change in our technological society is so staggering that the university has been ineffective in directing its capacity for inquiry into the issues of value that inevitably accompany such developments. Jouvenel might well have added that the university must provide the student with a framework in which he can seek out a system of values for a world he perceives as valueless. The paradox is that the university cannot properly propagandize for values other than those essential to the processes of inquiry. It must achieve the infinitely more difficult role of serving as a place where values may be discovered. The irony is that, through its massive research efforts, the university itself has fueled the fires of rapid technological change. But now it must mount a similarly massive thrust on the lagging value system. To fail to do so is to guarantee a permanent and growing disaffection in our society which can result only in disaster, for the university as well as society.

Jouvenel says also that society perceives students as in a state of becoming, while students perceive themselves as in a state of doing. In consequence, the student feels removed from the society, with the inevitable result that he has a strong feeling of inferiority and rejection.

All of these responses hurl the student into a conflict with the social system. Moreover, university authorities often intensify this conflict by using methods that students perceive as rejection. When this happens, students are divorced from their base of operations. The institution further accelerates the turmoil if it stiff-arms student activity directed at changes outside the university.

On one matter that Jouvenel raises, however, I feel most uneasy: I feel quite uncomfortable with his apparent belief that the university could effectively exist by assigning directly and wholly to students the problem of maintaining law and order within the university community. He tends to treat students as a single community which, for reasons of self-interest, would protect the university from inordinate levels of political disruption. I see students as members of plural communities, with some groups quite willing to abrogate the interests of other students, and of the faculty, for purposes of personal or political gratification.

The institutional functions of accumulating, ordering, disseminating, and adding to knowledge cannot be sustained without attention to the social conditions under which faculty members, as well as students, may carry out their tasks. To be sure, students should participate in defining and sustaining these conditions. But it is not tenable to assume that faculty members can tolerate conditions of governance that might deny them orderly access to laboratory, library, or classroom.

In my view, arrangements for internal governance of the university should be rigorously reviewed to provide the maximum interaction between students and other members of the academic community. Maximum interaction, and its accompanying opportunities for personal and intellectual growth for students, should be the focus of our efforts. New forums, new frameworks, new combinations, and new arenas are needed. In the end, it is the provision of new levels of interaction on the campus on which we must rest our new concept of the university.

Forms and Trappings

ROBERT BOGUSLAW

BARON DE JOUVENEL fears his paper will shock some readers. For a distinguished, conservative scholar to conclude that "I for one would willingly make a complete devolution of the 'law and order' function to the elected representatives of students" must indeed appear shocking to some. To others, however, it will appear as a woefully inadequate concession to the demands of students throughout the world. To see this in somewhat clearer perspective, it is necessary to examine more closely the forms, fictions, and substance of democracy on the university campus.

Jouvenel specifies three ideal conditions for democratic self-government, all of which are present in the university: (1) a relatively small number of citizens, (2) a relatively intelligent body of citizens, (3) wise men standing on the sidelines (i.e., professors).

In my own view, an indispensable precondition for democracy is a requirement that citizens be allowed to participate in the democratic process without fear of threats, reprisals, or sanctions of any description. This condition does not exist in the American universities I know, and I would doubt very much that it exists even in French universities. Students in Western societies are largely, Jouvenel states, "uneconomic men." They are dismayed to be told by workers that "Your strike costs you nothing. Ours loses us pay and brings hardship on our homes." The distinguishing attributes of economic man—bargaining power, immediate responsibility, and cost-benefit concerns—we are told, are lacking in the student. Within our "society of bees" the students presumably form a category whose members should not hold jobs and who "stand aloof from our economic system."

I don't read the facts of student and university life quite this way. Most of the students I know are very much economic men and cost-benefit analysts. They worry about the terms as well as the conditions of employment in Western society. They compete for scholarships, for admission to professional or graduate schools, and for future full-time jobs. It is precisely in contemplation of the future that their sense of alienation becomes most acute and their desire to change the rules of the economic and political games becomes climactic. They are very much a part of the world outside as well as inside the university. The larger world is waiting for them to complete their studies or drop out of school so they can be impressed into service for Vietnam or some other idiocy. Visions of probable alternative futures make the present intolerable. Even for those who successfully elude the clutches of the draft board or the recruiting sergeant, the prospect of a future dedicated to tinsel, tedium, and trivia has become terrifying. The benefits of mechanical comforts and cute gadgets apparently do not begin to compensate for the costs to individuals. These costs may crudely be described as psychic. They probably ultimately derive from a sense that the needs of human beings in our increasingly technological society must be secondary to the needs of our technological systems, whether these be military or industrial.

Thus the indispensable precondition for democracy does not exist for students in our universities. They cannot participate in a democratic process as free men or even as "uneconomic men." The wise men sitting on the sidelines too often are not free either. Their own ambitions, fears, and vulnerabilities too often convert their wisdom into little more than artful strategems for obtaining support for their own narrow ends. They are the guards who control the entrance gates into our larger society through which students must ultimately pass. Student democracy under such conditions can readily lead to little more than legitimation of oligarchic controls.

It is only in a broad philosophical sense that I can agree with Jouvenel's feeling that "Research in universities may be as pure as you will, but it should give rise to useful developments" and that "teaching may be as pure as you will, but it should bring forth men and women fitted for useful employment." There are many institutions in Western society which perform these functions. Virtually every large industrial corporation has its own training program for socializing employees and shaping them to meet the demands of the organization process. Private and government research organizations are specifically equipped to carry on the research which will lead to new product development or policy implementation. Every society needs, for its own sanity and continued existence, a set of institutions which can specifically challenge its fundamental premises and ultimately help it decide what developments and employments are indeed useful and for what purpose. I see the university as the most important of these vital institutions.

But no university can serve these indispensable societal needs if its faculty and administration are faced with the choice of co-optation or extinction.

I could not agree more with Jouvenel when he insists that the great problem lies in the conflict between the university and society rather than in a conflict between academic authorities and students. But my view of the nature of this conflict probably differs considerably from his. And the consequence of this difference is seen most clearly in the conclusions it is possible for us each to reach. Baron de Jouvenel seems to feel that the problem can essentially be settled by what to some will appear to be the "shocking" solution of turning over the law and order function to the elected representatives of students. I am not opposed to democracy. Indeed, it is because I feel so deeply about the need for democracy on all levels of political and economic life that I become so deeply concerned about sham solutions that provide the forms and trappings of democracy while corrupting its spirit. Democracy involves participation in the choice of alternative courses of action. Will the larger society allow student participation in those decisions which relate to the allocation of resources to provide economic support for universities? Does a choice exist between acceptance of corrupting forms of economic support and institutional death? If we are to talk of democracy, let us consider it on this level. Otherwise we have simply succumbed to the temptation to use unwary students to handle our own hot potatoes. This is not democracy; it is tyranny of the most subtle and vicious sort.

Spider-web autocracy is no less despotic than steel-fettered democracy. It is precisely this mechanism of social control that has become so universal in contemporary Western society.

JOHN W. GARDNER

The University and the Cities

THE UNITED STATES is experiencing domestic troubles that surely rank among the most serious in the history of this country. We have fought several wars in which the external threat to the nation was inconsequential compared to the internal crisis before us now. At such a moment, every segment of society and every significant institution must do its part.

But in our advanced and complicated society, all the major categories of institutions have developed a high degree of specialization, and this has become an obstacle they must surmount before they can serve the common good. Recently a businessman made the specialist argument to me in eloquent terms. He said, "You must not make me into something I am not. I am a businessman and I serve the nation best when I function strictly in that mode. When you draw me into other kinds of activities, you run the risk of impairing my effectiveness and, therefore, impairing the vitality of the economy."

With the substitution of certain key words this argument can be transformed into the one used by some universities. Or by some labor unions. And in using that argument business, the universities, and the unions are joined by many of the other specialized segments of our society. The arguments are sound, but at a certain point in the unfolding of a national crisis, a new set of priorities must take hold.

The only alternative would be for the nation to build into government at all levels the full capability of dealing with any and all crises. Then business, the universities, and all the other segments of the private sector could pursue their specialized missions with unruffled calm. For them the alarm bell would never ring.

184

But that would be a very, very different kind of society.

The colleges and universities of this country have not responded impressively to the urban crisis. They have been notably laggard. There is, of course, a great amount of activity going on in higher education that has the word "urban" attached. But many college leaders are not satisfied with the quality of those activities, and I share their view. Many of the urban affairs centers that have sprung up on college campuses are not to be taken seriously. Much of what they are doing today can only be described as dabbling. Many are reinventing the wheel and not doing a very good job of it. Very few have pursued any aspect of the urban crisis with the intellectual rigor it requires. Even fewer have accepted the real world of the city on their doorstep as a laboratory in which they can advance those intellectual pursuits.

Difficulties and Possibilities in Institutional Involvement

College leaders point out that there are real difficulties in the way of more active participation in urban affairs. First, the colleges and universities are deeply preoccupied with their own problems at the moment; and institutions, like people and nations, turn inward under stress. Second, colleges and universities are so organized that the only way they can take on a new interest is by accretion. Everything is an add-on. They have no way of eliminating less relevant commitments in order to meet new challenges. Third, the people who have firsthand acquaintance with city problems, for example, public officials, are rarely able to state the problems in ways that are sufficiently fundamental or intellectually challenging to give a faculty member something to chew on. And the faculty member often doesn't know enough about the city to formulate the problems for himself. Fourth, the university administration cannot, of course, commit the faculty to any particular interest, new or old. Fifth, most urban problems are social in nature, and the strong tradition of small-scale individual research projects in the social sciences does not lend itself to the large systems problems one encounters in urban affairs.

These difficulties are real, but they can be surmounted. I am convinced that the colleges and universities will benefit from active participation in urban affairs. Every human institution stands in need of continuous renewal—not least the colleges and universities; and crises, rightly viewed, are instruments of such renewal. It is chiefly through the continued effort to be relevant that an institution renews itself, but that is a difficult effort to make in placid times. Any institution that cares about renewal will seize the moment of crisis as the appropriate instant to break the settled mold of life and create fresh patterns.

The problems involved in the urban crisis are enormously varied. There are the problems of government, of taxation and the allocation of resources, of law enforcement and the administration of justice. There are the problems of education, health, income maintenance, social services, recreation. There are the problems of city planning and architecture, transportation, land use, pollution control, solid waste disposal, and renewal of the city's physical plant. There are the problems of economic development, jobs, housing, black entrepreneurship, consumer protection. There are some fascinating issues centering on the question of population distribution—issues relating to dispersal of the ghetto, patterns of migration, and new towns. These are but some of the points where the intellectual interests of the university intersect the agonizing difficulties of the city.

What are some of the ways in which the colleges and universities can be useful in these matters? First of all, the significant intellectual questions involved in urban affairs can be dealt with in a variety of undergraduate courses, so that *every student* will have some exposure to matters that should concern him deeply as a citizen. Students complain, with reason, that their undergraduate experience does not prepare them to become involved with or to understand contemporary urban life; and they do not see the university establishment as providing them with opportunities to do so.

At a more advanced level the colleges and universities can prepare students to work professionally in urban affairs or to teach one or another of the subjects relevant to the field. There is hardly an area of professional training where the interests of the university and the needs of the city do not overlap. Renewal and relevance in the professional schools, whether the field is medicine, education, law, management, architecture. or engineering, demand that we think in terms of "neglected" client groups, in terms of the needs of citizens now unserved by the system.

In addition there are important contributions to be made by university extension work. One university is undertaking to train ghetto leaders. Another is providing mid-career courses for city officials.

The research that needs to be done extends from the most fundamental problems, for example, the nature of human prejudice, to action research, for example, the means of solving the city's current transportation problems.

Every city, partly because of deficiencies of municipal personnel, partly because of the sheer complexity of the problems being faced, is gravely in need of technical assistance. The colleges and universities have proven their capacity to render such technical assistance in Nigeria, Indonesia, and scores of other foreign countries. But most colleges and universities have not yet brought themselves to render the same service to the communities of which they are a part.

Another set of problems arises from the fact that colleges and universities are not only educational institutions, they are also corporate citizens of their communities. Sometimes a university is so large in relation to its community that it plays a genuinely commanding role. The university has not always asked itself with sufficient force what this implies in the way of obligations. The most obvious obligation is to examine employment practices with respect to equal employment opportunity. I need not stress that further. If academic leaders do not get to work on that, the students are likely to get to work on them.

Finally, we must re-examine the role of colleges and universities with respect to those groups in the population that do not now derive any benefit from higher educational institutions. Many of those who do not benefit are taxed for the maintenance of the higher educational facilities they never use. The colleges and universities, by making this a technological and highly professionalized society, have made it increasingly difficult for noncollege men and women to play an effective role.

Approaches to Involvement

I could suggest that if you approach this subject prudently you will surely find a piece of the problem that suits you and your institution. But rather than dipping your toes into the water, I suggest that you plunge.

There is on every campus an ample supply of analytical talent, knowledge, and skill that the city needs. There is on every campus a reservoir of concern among faculty and students—concern for social justice, for human decency, for an enhanced quality of life for all Americans.

That reservoir of human concern on the campuses has burst to the surface on many occasions and in many ways. The manifestations have not always been productive; often they have been counterproductive.

So I say to students, faculty, administrators, and trustees: Here is a battle on which you can expend every useful energy that you have. Here is a task of redesigning human institutions that will demand the freshness of vision of the students, the skills of the faculty, the executive gifts of the administrators, and the influence of the trustees. And you will be working on the most fateful domestic problems of your generation.

Since our institutions of higher learning are so diverse, each will have to define its own response to the urban crisis. But here is one step that most could take at once: create urban task forces consisting of representatives of students, faculty, trustees, and administration, together with neighborhood representatives from the immediate vicinity of the campus.

Such collaboration of all segments of the university community could in itself have a beneficial effect on the health of your institutions. And in that collaboration, I would emphasize the great resource represented by the students. Academic leaders are accustomed to thinking of students' educational potentialities as a resource, but rarely think of their activist inclinations in the same light. For the nation and for the local community, however, they are such a resource. Many thousands of students have participated in constructive projects in the ghetto. More recently many have participated constructively in political campaigns. They are seeking an outlet for their idealism. They have the impatience that makes for social renewal. They have a role to play.

The urban task force might begin by making inventories, (*a*) of what is already being done within the university and (*b*) of capabilities within the university community to tackle one or another urban problem. Things are already being done that would benefit greatly by more community support. There are individuals or groups who have excellent ideas or even well-developed plans and who need only support to get started. The League of American Cities has received a Federal grant to assist the universities in relating themselves to urban affairs. Any university that undertakes to create an urban task force might find it worthwhile to be in touch with the League.

Urban Coalition

If an urban coalition has already been founded locally, the university urban task force should, of course, relate to the coalition in some formal way. If no such coalition has been formed, the university may want to join with other community groups to create one.

For those who may be uncertain as to what an urban coalition is, I will say a few words: After the riots in the summer of 1967, a group of outstanding leaders in American life came together to form the Urban Coalition. The members of the Steering Committee included mayors such as John Lindsay of New York and Jerome Cavanagh of Detroit, business leaders such as Henry Ford and David Rockefeller, labor leaders, leaders from the black community, and religious leaders.

I would emphasize the importance of the coalition principle. Some people think of the Coalition as just another organization tackling the tough urban problems of the day. But it is unique. Our distinction is that we bring together leadership elements that do not normally collaborate in the solution of public problems. In fact, we bring together segments of American life that often have been utterly out of touch with one another and, in many cities, are still out of touch.

Because of the need for such collaboration at the local level, the national organization set out immediately to form local coalitions. We now have thirty-six and we hope to double that number very soon. Like the national organization, each local organization includes representatives from a variety of leadership segments in the community—the mayor, business, labor, minority groups, and religion. The participation of other relevant elements—the universities, the schools, the press, the professions—is encouraged.

As the university, through its urban task force, brings itself into relation with the local urban coalition—or helps to form a local coalition—it will necessarily enter into relationship with all of these other elements. Because universities have traditionally kept to themselves, they may find this a difficult barrier to cross. They may have a strong impulse simply to go to work on the problems by themselves without relating to other elements. If so, they will not be the only ones to feel that impulse. It is quite common among the leading members of the business community, who, with the best will in the world, often say, "Why should we get involved in a lot of bickering with other elements in the community? Let us identify the problems and go to work on them quietly on our own."

It is a reasonable suggestion, but a hopelessly old-fashioned one. Anyone who isn't willing to engage in open dialogue with other segments of the community had better not get into the game at all. The university community, as well as all the others, must learn to sit down with people who do not speak the same language, people whose style of discourse is different, people with whom it does not feel particularly comfortable, and it must learn to solve problems collaboratively with those people. There isn't any other way.

Now it would seem that if academic institutions take my advice and enter into such relationships, I should at least offer them surcease of tension and conflict. But I cannot. There aren't any tranquilizers for this trouble. Nor am I offering a public relations gimmick. Institutions, by this course of action, will not magically become more popular in the community.

In short, I can't offer a happy short-run future. The best I can offer is a *constructive* future, a future in which the tension and conflict flow into creative outcomes.

Some may say that I am proposing a diversion of attention from the true concerns of an academic institution. That is a serviceable argument in tranquil times. But attention to the gravest domestic problem of our generation is not a diversion. It is the main show.

If academic institutions plunge into this task with enthusiasm, they can help pull this fragmented society together again. They can help to create an America in which men speak to one another in trust and mutual respect, sharing common objectives, working toward common goals. They can help to return this nation to a path of confidence and well-being, a path that we shall never regain until we resolve the bitter human problems of the city today.

Revolutions are not made; they come. A revolution is as natural a growth
as an oak. It comes out of the past. Its foundations are laid far back.
Wendell Phillips, in a speech, January 28, 1852

JAMES FARMER

To Be Black and American

ANYTHING THAT ONE WRITES today that deals with people and an attempt
to understand people and what is happening to them in our country is
political. College and university campuses reflect the changes that are
taking place in the national community. Changing demands are being
made both by those who were demanding years ago and by those who
were not demanding because they were invisible and had no voice. But
now they are finding their voices.

The ferment is greater on the university and college campuses than
it is elsewhere in the country, and that is to be expected. The old
answers which many of us had, which a few years ago seemed adequate,
now appear to be archaic. The answers are changing as fast as the
questions.

I had a call from an old friend of mine recently. I had not seen him
for a number of years, and he said, "Jim, I am baffled, I am puzzled,
I am confused." I wanted to know what the problem was.

He said, "A few years ago you so-called civil rights leaders told us
that the most meaningful, progressive, and militant thing we could do
was to integrate a lily-white suburb. Well, Jim, we took you at your
word. My wife and I took the bull by the horns, and we moved out into
Lovely Lane, next door to Gorgeous Gardens, and we bought a split-
level house and we mowed the lawn. We faced all of the garbage, the
hurled rocks, the obscenities, the burning crosses, and the isolation."
And he said, "Now we have overcome. We are accepted by our neighbors. They invite us over for cocktails, and we have them over for tea.
And so now we are called Uncle Toms for living out there with all
those white folks."

This is indicative of some of the changes that are taking place. In Los Angeles I attended a series of seminars sponsored by the Board of Education. Some of the members of the board informed me that very shortly they would announce a total desegregation plan, which would by fiat eliminate *de facto* school segregation. Ten or twelve years ago, when the movement began against *de facto* school segregation in Los Angeles and elsewhere, the Board of Education did not even acknowledge that it had a problem! It said, "This must be a case of mistaken identity. This isn't Mississippi, this is Los Angeles. There is no segregation here."

Several years later the Board of Education grew a bit and said, "Well, of course, we have a problem. There is segregation here, *de facto* segregation, but it is *de facto* and not *de jure*, and that puts it outside of our field of competence, outside of our sphere of jurisdiction. After all, it is tied up with housing, and we are not the housing authority. We are the education authority. So there is nothing we can do about it."

Some time later the board said, "Well, of course, it is our problem. We must do something about it." But they were not sure what to do. Now they have a plan which would, in one fell swoop, wipe out *de facto* school segregation!

Somewhat sadly and perhaps nostalgically, I had to inform them that when they do, even if the plan is all that they say it will be, they must expect that it will meet with a lukewarm reception in the black community and, from large segments of the black community, outright hostility because the agenda has changed—and changed so rapidly and so completely.

One among many reasons for this changing agenda is that the movement toward integration has failed. I am pointed out as a successful civil rights leader. I quarrel with that a bit. None of us has been successful. In fact, from 1954 to 1965, while we were battling against segregation, segregation was increasing in meaningful areas of the nation's life. There is more residential segregation now than there was in 1954 and, consequently, more *de facto* segregation. Those school boards which have sought to eliminate such segregation, under the civil rights movement, have in reality only slowed down the rate of increase. They have not reversed the trend, much less halted it. The failure of the efforts of all of us has necessitated a change in the agenda. Any tactician worth his salt who finds that he is winning battles and yet losing a war must reassess and re-evaluate, try to find out what went wrong and what changes in strategy and tactics are required. That process is now taking place throughout the black community. We see it on our campuses. Black students who heretofore have fought to be included in the dormitories without segregation are now saying, in many cases, "We want our separate dormitory or our separate segment of it."

Today there is a great debate on the campuses and in the black communities throughout the nation, and the debate is not about segregation versus integration, though that obscurantism has been stimulated by headlines. It is not a debate about age versus youth, though the majority of folk on one side tend to be young, at least in mind, while those on the other, who have not accepted the changing agenda, tend to be older. Nor is it fundamentally a struggle between militancy and moderation. That, too, is a headline formulation, because there are militants and there are moderates on both sides of the present debate.

What Course for Black America?

The basic debate is: Which course for Black America? Dispersion or ethnic cohesiveness? This is not a new debate. All ethnic groups that have come to this country have been involved in it. They have been in turmoil, especially during their first generation here. They have been torn asunder. Some forces said, "We must forget any ties with the past, forget that we are members of an ethnic group, and seek to disperse and to be assimilated and to be just Americans, not hyphenated Americans."

Other forces have said, "We must honor and celebrate those ties that bind us, those ethnic ties, and then work out a rapprochement in our new life, our new home."

This is essentially the debate which the black community is having now. It was long in coming in the black community. Most of the ethnic groups in America were involved in this debate during their first generation, but it is not the black man's first generation here, obviously. Though we didn't come on the Mayflower, we met the boat. But in one sense it is our first generation—as urban dwellers. More than 70 percent of Black Americans now live in the cities. That was not true prior to this generation. As urban dwellers we are forced closer together. Communication is quicker and easier. Identity is simpler, and cohesiveness is not so difficult to achieve. Because it is our first generation, this is the time when the debate has become fierce within the black community.

In the past our motto was *color blindness*. To understand what is happening on the campuses and throughout our land, we must understand this particular change. Color blindness has not worked. We must reorient our thinking to grasp the intellectual changes in the black community.

We said to the Black American, until quite recently (if I may oversimplify and summarize it), "Forget you are a member of a group. Forget you are black. Think of yourself as an individual, and if as an individual you can gain a little money and a little education, then as an individual you will be acculturated, and as an individual you can be assimilated and will become, in effect, a white man with an invisible black skin."

That was the dream and aspiration held out to Black Americans.

In the early days of CORE we were a color-blind organization. We told ourselves a story which has become a classic, of the little white child who went to the first grade when school opened and came home telling his mother about the wonderful little friend he had just met. Every day he raved about his young friend Johnnie, also in the first grade.

Finally, something that he said caused his mother to wonder whether Johnnie was black or white, and she asked him, "Phillip, you talk about little Johnnie. Is he colored or he is white?" And Phillip's answer was, "I don't know, I didn't notice. I'll have to go back tomorrow and look, and then I will tell you."

We used to tell ourselves this story. It was symbolic of the kind of color blindness that we expected in our nation.

But that didn't work, either. America is not color-blind, cannot be color-blind.

We used to say to employers, "Be just absolutely color-blind and do not see the color of the job applicant. Merely hire the most qualified person who happens to apply for the job, and be blind to his color."

It didn't work. We would go back to him several years later and ask him, "How many black people did you hire?" His answer would be, "How in the world should I know? I am color-blind." We would make a visual check and find that he had none. His answer would be, "So what? I am color-blind. I can't see the color."

When color blindness was the motif of the movement, it was even written into the laws. It was written into the rules of many colleges and universities. They would not ask the color of an applicant—no pictures, no indication of race.

One college president some time ago received a questionnaire to fill out, asking him, "How many minority group students do you have?" He said he refused to answer that, because this was in violation of color blindness, which was his philosophy. Why should he know how many black or Puerto Rican students? That would suggest that he somehow was discriminating. This was nonsense. It made sense a few years ago but does not make sense now because color blindness does not serve a useful function any more.

The fair housing laws, the fair employment practice laws were all color-blind. To show you how absurd it became at times, CORE a few years ago mounted a campaign against job discrimination in a chain of hamburger joints in the Bronx. We picketed, sat in, and demonstrated, and we had rotten vegetables thrown at us, and some crosses were burned. Finally, the management agreed to sit down and talk. Management said, "Why, Mr. Farmer, you're right. We have discriminated in the past. We have no black employees above the level of janitors, and that's wrong. We would like to change that. We would like to hire black people up and down our work force. Indeed, we will need 50 sales personnel within the next three months." (That is a euphemism for counter people.) "We would like to hire black people for those posts in order to repair the imbalance created by past discrimination. However," they said, "we cannot do it."

"Why not?" I asked.

"Because we get our employees from the State Employment Service, and if we call them up and say, 'Send us 50 black sales personnel,' they will immediately charge us with violation of the State Fair Employment Practices Act, which says you must be color-blind and may not seek for or look for or ask for employees on the basis of color."

I then called up a friend of mine who worked for the State Employment Service and said, "You realize the law is archaic." He said, "Of course; it is one of the old color-blind laws that we fought for."

I said, "Well, now, what shall we do?"

He thought for a while and said, "Jim, have this fellow call me and tell me his needs. I will then call our office on 125th Street in Harlem and have them send him 50 qualified applicants regardless of race, color, creed, or religion."

Now we say, "Be color conscious for the sake of wiping out color discrimination ultimately." But color consciousness is required at this stage. Black people are now finding their blackness. In the past they

196 POSSIBILITIES . . .

have rejected it. They are trying to answer that question, "What does it mean to be black and American?"

That is a very difficult question, similar to the question that the immigrant groups from Europe asked themselves in the first generation. "What does it mean to be what I was *and* what I am?" They found one answer in being hyphenated, being Irish-American, Italian-American, Polish-American, and so on, at least for a period of time.

What Does It Mean To Be Black and American?

The Black American is now wrestling with that question: What does it mean to be black and American? And we are both, though there are those who deny we are American.

(The late Malcolm X used to argue, "The black man is not an American, he is a black man. He should not call himself an American, he should call himself a black man." One day Malcolm debated someone, also black, and Malcolm asked, "Why do you call yourself an American?" The answer was, "Because I was *born* in this country." Malcolm smiled and said, "Now, if a cat has kittens in the oven, does that make them biscuits?")

Obviously, our Americanism must be based on something more than the accident of birth. I think it is based on something cultural. Our subculture, which may be the only indigenous American culture, except for that of the American Indian, grew out of our life experiences in this country, and if anything can make us anything definable, then that does make us Americans. But we are also black, which sets us apart, and we have been taught to reject the blackness.

I had the occasion to look at a stack of preschool books several years ago when my little girl had received gifts of large numbers of them, and I wanted to see what kind of a self-image she would get as a black child. I found that in most of those books she would not see herself at all unless she was carrying somebody else's bag, cleaning someone else's house, or in some absurd position with a string tied around her toe and other kids poking fun at her and laughing—clearly not an acceptable self-image. But all of the instruments which have disseminated culture have said that, not only to the whites but to the blacks, and we thus have been taught to reject ourselves and to indulge in self-hate.

Imagine a man whose skin is black and whose hair is kinky referring to kinky hair as "bad hair" and straight hair as "good hair"—every black person knows what I'm talking about. One used to hear that frequently in the black community. Within the past two or three years he hears it less frequently because of the new emphasis on ethnic pride and identity and esteem. But the old rejection was there.

We rejected Africa, too. We were the only people who had no roots in the past. Until the new nations of Africa began to emerge, we had the Hollywood image of Africa. We had no umbilical cord to that, because it was a picture which we wished to reject. Our picture of Africa was of a few half-naked black savages dancing around a boiling pot with a missionary in it, and the common saying in the black community was, "Man, I ain't lost nothin' in Africa."

We used to watch Tarzan on the screen in the movies, a different Tarzan from the one on TV now. They have cleaned it up a lot in the past years to make it acceptable. In those days Tarzan was killing black savages and saving missionaries from the pot, and we would sit there watching the missionary in the pot with the heat building up as he awaited the timely and inevitable arrival of his hero and ours. We identified with Tarzan. "Kill him, Tarzan, kill that savage!" And we were watching anxiously for Tarzan to come swinging through the trees, and they would show the Africans dancing around the pot to the tom-tom beat, and they would flash on the screen a close-up of the face of an African, all painted and fierce. Then I would elbow my buddy and say, "Irving, that's you."

Irving's reaction was negative. "No, that ain't me, I didn't come from no Africa. I ain't no African."

Well, Irving and twenty million Irvings were indulging in self-rejection, which was self-hate.

As the new nations of Africa began to emerge, many black people, especially the young, began to identify more with Africa. They saw a different image, a prouder black image, a Chief Adabo debating some fine point of international law in the U.N. They said, "Hey, wait a minute, is that Africa or is the boiling pot Africa?"

As the new image spread, it tended to eclipse the old. Many people who in the past had denied their blackness now asserted it. Twenty years ago, even fifteen years ago, if you had walked through one of the Harlems of the country and called a man black it would have been an insult. He would have argued, "I'm not black, I'm brown or bronze or tan," because he had been told that blackness was a deformity and had come, to a great extent, to believe it. Now that same man would walk up to you and say with pride, "I am a black man."

This is extremely positive to me. One must learn to love himself. As Shakespeare said, "Self-love, my King, is far less vile a sin than self-neglecting." And for all these generations, for four centuries, we have been indulging in the grossest kind of self-neglect.

Black people now, especially young black people, are hyphenated, calling themselves Afro-Americans. This, too, is quite new and promising and hopeful, and people should not be so terrified by it. Perhaps we discover that hyphen in order eventually to lose it; I am not sure about that. It will be more difficult for us to lose than it was for others. The ancestors of white persons who were hyphenated in their first generation looked pretty much like the people who were outside their ghettos, and it was easy for them to be assimilated, to merge, to disappear in the outside world.

It is not so easy for us because of our visibility. We can run but can't hide. In fact, it doesn't even help us to change our names. So at least it will be much more difficult for us to lose that hyphen, but we are discovering the hyphen, and that is important—black people honoring Africa, learning of African history and culture and art and insisting upon being taught more about it in the colleges and universities, just as they insist, rightly, on being taught more about their own culture and history —Afro-American culture and history.

All this is great, but it is not extraordinary. Others went through the same thing. The Irish, for instance, came to this land en masse, a century ago, at the time of the potato crop failure in Ireland. They were pushed around, told they were nothing but dirt, spat upon. Signs in windows said, "Man Wanted. No Irish Need Apply." Sometimes they didn't even spell out those signs, "Man Wanted. N.I.N.A." Everyone knew what it meant.

They had riots in those days. They had some riots that would make what has happened in the past few summers look like child's play. In New York they blew up an armory, in the 1860s, and passed out all the guns—to the Irishmen, of course—and they burned down a children's home. They had a plan to burn down the whole city of New York. At that time, the professional police department in our major cities was founded, because the vigilantes, made up of people who had already been there for a while, couldn't deal with the Irish. They said, "We have got to have professionals," and the professional police departments were set up. The Irish figured, "If you can't beat 'em, join 'em."

After being pushed around, the Irish banded together. They sang songs. I heard one of their songs sung recently by Joe Glazer, the labor bard, and it shouted, "It's an honor to be born an Irishman." When people are told they are nothing but dirt, it is essential that they assert, "You're wrong. We are something of infinite importance and worth."

It is an honor to be born an Irishman. It is an honor to be born whatever one is born, as long as there is no dishonor in being born something else. And what's the difference between saying, "It is an honor to be born an Irishman" and saying, "Black is beautiful; it's wonderful to be black"?

It is the same concept, the same human reaction to a similar set of circumstances and problems. Some say, "Yes, but you shout it too loudly. Can't you whisper it?"

We can't whisper it. We must shout it precisely because we are trying to drown out those millions of voices outside in the society which tell us the opposite, which tell us black is ugly and that it is vile to be black. We are trying to drown out those many voices inside ourselves, because of our conditioning through a racist culture, which tell us that "Black is ugly and it is vile to be black." So now we are trying to de-program ourselves and to develop pride.

This is not separationism. America has not been a melting pot in the usual sense of the word, where you pour people into a pot and shake them up and pour out a common solution. That has not been America at all. America has been a pluralistic culture.

In New York, every time I turn on the radio and hear them say "Where eight million people live together in peace and harmony," I roar with laughter. They live together most often in mutual hostility and tension, which is kept from surfacing by power blocs and alliances and coalitions, economic and political. In New York, and in many other cities, I find there is no real polyglot; I see a community that is essentially Irish, or Italian, or German, or Polish, or Scandinavian, or Puerto Rican, or black. This has been America.

Now in trying to discover the hyphen which once we sought to evade or skip, we are following a course that is thoroughly American, as American—not as cherry pie, as Rap Brown once said—but as American as gefüllte fish or pizza pie or sauerbraten. We are seeking to fit into that American equation of pluralistic culture.

There is not unanimous agreement among black militants on this, obviously, on the college campus or off. We are debating it. I state my position, and I believe that it is a majority position. There are some who are still all wrapped up in the "Let's get Whitey" bag, or the "I'm more militant than you are" bag, both of which bags are essentially dysfunctional. But the majority, even of the young militants, under the umbrella of black power, are thinking constructively in terms of programs—cultural, educational, economic, and political programs—which would empower the powerless.

I hope we can ultimately destroy racism in the country. That is a massive educational task, probably spanning many generations, using all of the instruments which have disseminated racism *into* the culture in the first place, using them now, instead, to eliminate racism. We would have to use comic books, preschool books, textbooks, Hollywood, television, radio, national magazines, newspapers, Madison Avenue advertising, industry, trade unions, civic organizations, fraternal groups, and all. Though that would be a long, long road, I hope we will embark upon it.

In the meantime, however, we must seek to short-circuit racism and to prevent its damaging people, to minimize the extent to which it can damage people, to checkmate it. How? By allowing people who have been outside the decision-making process, who have been invisible and nonvocal, who have been powerless, part of a colony or an economic or political plantation, to have a share in the decision-making process of the nation, to empower the powerless. And then we can sit there and negotiate at a common table with all the other Americans who are proud and who have some semblance of economic and political power.

This does not mean that we will be loved, but it is not necessary that people be loved in order to be respected and dealt with as equals. Black people now would much prefer to be respected than to be loved if there is a choice. In fact, many care little about being loved. They want to be respected as eyeball-to-eyeball equals and sit down at the table and negotiate as others negotiate.

Many today who are anti-Semitic will negotiate with Jews because power will deal with power, economic and political power. And we would like to share that power now.

The first step toward the sharing is to discover ourselves, to honor ourselves, and to understand that humanity transcends color. I will not give up, I will never give up the ultimate ideal of a color-blind society, where color is put in proper perspective as an irrelevancy and loses its power to divide and to intimidate. But that time is not now. That will come perhaps at the millennium or in the Kingdom of God. In the meantime we must live in the real world, and the real world is not the world of universal love. Ultimately, we hope it will come.

Humanity, I say, transcends color, but remember, man cannot love humanity until he first learns to love himself. If one hates himself, how in the world can he love mankind of which he is a part?

As Hillel put it, "If I am not for myself, who will be for me? If I am for myself alone, what am I? And if not now, when?"

PART 3

... AND PROSPECTS

The reasonable man adapts himself to the world;
the unreasonable one persists in trying to adapt the world to himself.
Therefore all progress depends on the unreasonable man.

George Bernard Shaw, *Maxims for Revolutionists*

Vorwärts! Avanti! Onward! Full speed ahead!
without asking whether directly before you was
a bottomless pit.

Santayana, *My Host the World*

HOWARD R. BOWEN

The Financing of Higher Education:
Issues and Prospects

IN THE EARLY 1950s, American higher education was in the doldrums. Enrollments were low following the departure of the GI's, salaries were meagre, capital plant run-down, programs static, and the mood one of discouragement. Following 1955, however, the nation was jolted into a new appreciation of higher education by the cold war, reported educational progress in the U.S.S.R., and especially by the dramatic launching of Sputnik. At that time, also, it became obvious that enrollments would soar after 1962 when the first postwar babies reached age eighteen.

With this background, a new era of support for higher education was ushered in, with rapidly mounting state appropriations, much more in private gifts, massive Federal aid programs, and higher fees. From 1950 to 1968, both general operating income and plant funds increased by more than six times.

In 1950, institutional expenditures (operating and capital combined) were about 0.8 percent of GNP; I estimate that in 1968–69 they will be about 1.9 percent of GNP. Thus, the rate of growth in resources for higher education has been twice as fast as the growth rate of the national economy. But the percentage of the GNP devoted to higher education is still surprisingly small.

Many observers of higher education fear that the rapid and steady financial progress of the past thirteen years may taper off. It is often said that state and local governments cannot continue to increase appropriations at recent rates, that parents and students cannot stand continued escalation of tuitions, that private gifts are approaching practical limits, and that the Federal government—busy in Vietnam and facing numerous demands at home—cannot continue to provide additional funds for higher education at recent rates of increase. When educators project past cost increases into the future, and compare these cost projections with their estimates of feasible revenues, they almost invariably predict a widening gap. And they usually conclude that new approaches to the finance of higher education are needed if a crisis is to be averted.

I agree that financial problems loom ahead, and that new financial solutions are called for. However, I think that "crisis" is not the apt word to describe the situation. I doubt if there was ever a time in the history of higher education when educators could project past cost trends into the future and count confidently on finding the necessary funds. "Crisis" in this sense is a normal situation for higher education; we are always faced with the necessity of securing a progressively increasing share of the national income. In this paper I shall try to outline some of the choices and issues related to the finance of American higher education in the next decade. I shall consider both the finance of institutions and the finance of students. The discussion throughout will be based on the assumption of a stable general price level.

The Future of Institutional Costs

Enrollments are likely to increase from about 6.5 million in 1967–68 to perhaps 11 million in 1979–80. The precise size of this enrollment increase will depend in part on the kinds of financial aids made available and in part on the accessibility of colleges and universities (their location, admissions standards, and part-time programs). In any event, no one seriously doubts that substantial expansion lies ahead.

The cost per student is also almost certain to rise. Faculty salaries and nonacademic wages and salaries are likely to increase at least in proportion to the rise in earnings of other workers. The advancement of technology and the proliferation of information will call for ever-increasing outlays for equipment and for libraries, just to keep up with the times. Electron microscopes will appear where Bunsen burners used to be, computers will largely supplant adding machines, and library acquisitions will grow by geometrical progression. The relative expansion of expensive vocational-technical education and graduate and professional education will also increase average costs. And so on.

The resultant of higher enrollments and increasing cost per student will surely lead to rising institutional cost—even to maintain the present quality of education and the present range of services. At the same time, society will undoubtedly demand new services in such areas as continuing education, extension programs for the inner city, research on environmental pollution, special educational programs for disadvantaged minorities, and the like. Also, changes in the prevailing standard of living in the community will be reflected on the campus by more air conditioning, better lighting, and more private offices that are more spacious, etc. And society will also expect improvements in quality and effectiveness of instruction and research.

Ways may be found to increase the efficiency of higher education, that is, to accomplish a given amount and quality of education with a lesser use of resources. If this could be accomplished, some of the factors producing cost increases would be offset. Among possible means of improving efficiency would be: better utilization of plant; expansion of average class size; other increases in faculty teaching loads; substitution of lower-cost personnel for some highly trained and expensive faculty members; expansion of independent study programs; use of teaching machines; reduction of overhead through enlarging the scale of operations; simplification of the curriculum; elimination of nonessential services and functions; interinstitutional cooperation; avoidance of duplication.

Many sectors of the economy, especially manufacturing, retailing, and finance, have been able to offset rising labor and other costs by improving efficiency. So far, higher education has been unable (some would say, has been unwilling) to achieve significant improvements in efficiency, and rising labor and other costs have produced steadily advancing costs per student.

Most educators, I among them, have grave doubts about the feasibility of improving efficiency very much without sacrificing quality of performance. It is not ineptitude on conservatism or stubbornness that prevents higher education from achieving greater efficiency. Education, and the scholarly work associated with it, is a highly personal, or labor intensive, process which inherently requires large amounts of human time. Nevertheless, though educators have a heavy obligation to find whatever ways are practicable to cut costs, the results are likely to be miniscule in comparison with the forces pushing costs upward. Hence, higher education will require a steadily increasing share of the GNP, as it has in the past. This fact of educational life is a major source of financial stress and strain. It means that educators will be constantly and increasingly pressed financially—as they have always been. Legislators and donors often ask: "When will the end be in sight?" The answer is: Not in the foreseeable future.

On the basis of experience, one might guess that cost per student will increase over the next decade at the rate of 4–5 percent a year. Enrollment is estimated to increase at the rate of 4–5 percent a year. Combining the two, the total cost of higher education may increase by 9 percent a year. At this rate the operating cost will increase from about $12 billions in 1967–68 to perhaps $33 billions in 1979–80. To this must be added substantial capital costs, to bring the total bill in 1979–80 to at least $40 billions. This amount is embarrassingly large. However, it will probably represent only about 2.6 percent of the GNP; but this 2.6 percent compares with only 1 percent of the GNP as recently as ten years ago.

Will Society Foot the Bill?

Projecting the future bill for higher education from past trends, as I have done, is easy. However, cost is the obverse of income. The costs of higher education are limited to the amount of money society provides for it. The only reason costs increased so rapidly in recent years—salaries raised, faculty expanded, buildings built, and equipment added—is that government, donors, parents, and students were willing to increase their support. Any estimate of future cost must be based not only on a projection of past trends but also on an estimate of the willingness of society to foot the bill. If society, through its various decision-makers, decides to reduce the rate of increase in education funds, our projections of future costs will prove to be too high. Or if society decides to demand more services from higher education than it has in the past decade, costs will rise even higher. Cost is not an independent variable but, rather, a very dependent one.

The nation can afford to support higher education on the scale suggested by the projections if it so chooses. In rich America, there is ample discretionary income so that another one or two percent of the GNP *could* be devoted to higher education, *given the will to do so.* However, as the percentage of the GNP required rises, persuasion could become progressively more difficult.

The political climate in which education is operating today is less favorable than it was a decade ago. Then, the system of higher education was clearly impoverished and the need to do something dramatic was demonstrable—especially in view of the cold war and scientific competition with the U.S.S.R. The scandalously low level of faculty salaries was by itself a persuasive argument for action. Today, in contrast, higher education presents an appearance of success and even affluence. Faculty salaries may not be at the ideal level, and buildings, equipment, size of staff, and the like may not be fully adequate. But it is hard to make out a case for widespread, abject poverty. Meanwhile, student unrest, and especially faculty participation in it, has produced negative public reactions. And I suspect that the academic community sometimes conveys to the outside world an air of arrogance that evokes a negative response. The increased visibility and influence of higher education have brought it under closer political scrutiny through the new state coordinating agencies and various public investigations, and it is becoming an issue in partisan politics. Public officials, worried about budgets, are searching for ways to retard the rapid escalation of all education costs. For all these reasons, the political climate has become less favorable. On the other hand, higher education enjoys an enormous fund of public good will. It is widely understood that many of the hopes for our children and our nation rest with the colleges and universities. Responsible leaders know that they must not allow deterioration to set in.

Perhaps more important than the political climate is the increasing competition of new claimants for public and philanthropic dollars. Among these claimants are poverty programs, environmental pollution and restoration, urban renewal, housing, improved elementary and secondary education, health care, space exploration, and economic development of emerging nations. The competition may well be keener in the next decade than it has been in the past ten to twelve years. The universities will, of course, be involved in many of the new and expanding programs and can expect to share in the monies apportioned for research and training grants. Nevertheless, the competition for funds to support the basic teaching and research functions of higher education will probably intensify.

Optimistic speculation has it that the end of the Vietnam war will release vast amounts of money and bring early financial relief to higher education. An end to the war would almost surely help. Realistically, however, the pullback from Vietnam will likely be slow, and potential trouble spots elsewhere will likely cause the nation to continue a sizable military establishment. The experience during and after the Korean War may be instructive. Below are the budget expenditures for national defense during that period, with comparative figures for the corresponding stages of the Vietnam war (in billions):

1949	$12.9	1964	$97.7
1950	13.0	1965	96.5
1951	22.5	1966	107.0
1952	44.0	1967	126.7
1953	50.4	1968	135.0
1954	47.0	1969	?
1955	40.7	1970	?
1956	40.7		
1957	43.3		
1958	44.2		
1959	46.5		

After Korea, military spending leveled off and the GNP increased. As a result, nondefense spending expanded, and education became a major beneficiary. But after Korea, the competition for the tax dollar was not as keen as it probably will be after Vietnam.

My conclusion is that because of certain adverse features of the political climate, competing claims for public and philanthropic funds, and likely continued high defense expenditures, higher education faces a genuine financial problem. To sustain the rates of progress to which higher education has become accustomed in recent years may be difficult. Nevertheless, I expect progress to continue. Public understanding of higher education, public good will toward it, and the obvious dependence of the nation on it, should be sufficient to prevent deterioration and to ensure at least modest progress. But educators are justified in showing concern.

Future Pattern of Financial Support

The principal sources of support for colleges and universities are:
  Appropriations from state and local governments;
  Appropriations from the Federal government;
  Student fees;
  Private gifts and grants from individuals, foundations, and corporations;
  Other (income from endowments, profits from the sale of services and commodities, and miscellaneous).

The problem is to combine the support from these sources into a pattern of financing that is adequate and consistent with the basic objectives of higher education. Table 1 shows the pattern of support for

TABLE 1: *Current Income of Higher Educational Institutions,
Public and Private*

Year	State and Local Government	Federal Government	Student Fees	Private Gifts and Grants	Other	Total
	Amounts (millions of dollars)					
1949–50......	$ 562	$ 527	$ 396	$119	$ 257	$ 1,861
1951–52......	693	453	448	150	303	2,047
1953–54......	840	420	554	191	352	2,357
1955–56......	998	494	726	246	418	2,882
1957–58......	1,286	712	939	325	500	3,762
1959–60......	1,541	1,041	1,162	383	586	4,713
1961–62......	1,880	1,542	1,505	451	694	6,072
1963–64......	2,368	2,142	1,881	562	837	7,790
1965–66*......	3,050	2,950	2,500	620	970	10,090
1967–68*......	3,600	3,700	3,300	690	1,060	12,350
	Percentage					
1949–50......	30	28	21	6	14	100
1951–52......	34	22	22	7	15	100
1953–54......	36	18	23	8	15	100
1955–56......	35	17	25	8	15	100
1957–58......	34	19	25	9	13	100
1959–60......	33	22	25	8	12	100
1961–62......	31	25	25	7	11	100
1963–64......	30	27	24	7	11	100
1965–66*......	30	29	25	6	10	100
1967–68*......	29	30	26	5	9	100

* Estimated.

Source: American Council on Education, *A Fact Book on Higher Education*, p. 73. These figures do not include capital funds, income to auxiliary enterprises, or student aid. "Other" includes endowment earnings, sales and services of educational departments, and related activities. Estimates for 1965–66 and 1967–68 were made by the author projecting on the basis of data from a variety of sources, for example, U.S. Office of Education, *Projection of Educational Statistics to 1975–76* (1966 ed.), pp. 9, 59, 73, 82–84; *Fact Book on Higher Education*, pp. 216–23; *Statistical Abstract of the United States* (1967), pp. 133, 391, 421.

current operating funds for the last two decades. Throughout, the amount derived from each financial source has been growing,[1] although the relative amounts from the several sources have been changing.

The percentage received from gifts and grants has been declining. The reasons for this decline are, partly, that private institutions, which depend heavily on this source, are becoming a progressively smaller segment of higher education, and, partly, that gifts and grants, even in the private sector, are probably not growing as rapidly as other sources. This downward trend in share will, I suspect, continue. William G. Bowen has cited several reasons for a probable slowing down in the rate of increase

[1] The Federal government's contribution declined during the period 1950–54 as its commitments for the GI bill declined. The growth trend was re-established after 1953–54.

from gifts and grants, among them: (1) announced cutbacks in support of higher education by some foundations, (2) a leveling-off of long-term upward trends in total philanthropic giving as a percent of personal income, (3) increasing competition for philanthropic funds, and (4) diminishing returns from fund-raising activities.[2]

The percentage from "Other," which includes endowment income, has also been declining. Though endowment income will continue to be important to particular institutions, like gifts and grants, it will probably provide a progressively smaller share of the total and for the same reasons. The decline may be partially arrested by the recent rise in interest rates, by changes in accounting practices with respect to capital gains, and by improvements in investment practices.

The percentage of income from student fees has been relatively constant even though fees have been pushed up about 7 percent a year. This experience suggests that rapid increases in fees will be needed in the future simply to maintain the present percentage. Such increases would be possible only with a massive expansion of financial aid to students. One of the major policy issues before the country is whether to attempt to shift a larger share of costs to student fees by providing a system of generous long-term loans to students. I do not know whether this plan will receive public acceptance to the extent that fees can continue to produce a quarter of higher education's operating income. My guess is that it will not, and that the percentage from fees will trend slowly downward.[3]

The percentage from state and local government has been slowly declining since 1953–54, and I would expect this decline to continue. Both state and local governments have shown remarkable capacity to expand their revenues and expenditures, and, in fact, their fiscal expansion has exceeded that of the Federal government. However, there are limits to the financial capacity of both state and local authorities, and both are faced with a multiplicity of competing claims for their funds. So while

[2] William G. Bowen, "The Economics of Major Private Universities," to be published by Carnegie Commission on the Future of Higher Education.

[3] If the student aid were in the form of grants or loans to be financed by the government, the system of high fees would be largely a device for shifting the load to the government. Only if the high-fee plan were financed by long-term loans derived from private lenders would it represent a new source of funds for higher education. In another paper, I have explained why I believe the method of finance that calls for high fees coupled with student loans is not in the public interest. See my essay, "The Finance of Higher Education," to be published by the Carnegie Commission on the Future of Higher Education.

one may expect substantial increases in amounts appropriated for higher education, the relative percentage is likely to drift slowly downward.

With the shares of all other sources declining, the share of the Federal government must increase, as it has been doing since 1955–56. The Federal government, with its powerful revenue system, including the graduated personal income tax that automatically generates an increasing percentage of the GNP as the economy grows, is clearly called upon to bear a greater share of the cost burden of higher education.

By 1979–80, I would expect the percentages and absolute amounts from the various sources, as compared with those in 1967–68, to be as shown in Table 2 (compare with Table 1). Here, again, the projected

TABLE 2: *Current Income for Higher Education,*
by Source, 1967–68 and 1979–80

Source	Percentage		Amount (millions of dollars)	
	1979–80	1967–68	1979–80	1967–68
State and local government..........	25	29	$8,250	$ 3,600
Federal government................	40	30	13,200	3,700
Student fees......................	24	26	7,920	3,300
Private gifts and grants............	4	5	1,320	690
Other............................	7	9	2,310	1,060
Total..........................	100	100	$33,000	$12,350

percentages imply that over the next decade the amount from each source will increase but the rates of increase will vary among the sources. With the vast amount of discretionary income in our society, each source has the capacity to push ahead, at least in proportion to the rise in the GNP, if the will to do so is there. However, the rate of progress suggested by these estimates will not be attained unless the Federal government actually raises its contribution to something like 40 percent of the total by 1980. Also, this rate will not be attained unless each of the other sources expands its contribution.

One danger is that increases in Federal support will cause a slackening of effort by state and local governments and private donors. To avoid this tendency, the additional Federal aid should be distributed in ways that encourage or require other sources to increase their effort. For example, the Federal government might make unrestricted grants to institutions to meet increased costs on the condition that other sources share in meeting these increased costs. Without some such provision, increased Federal aid might well merely replace other forms of support, and needs would not be met.

Finance and the Goals of Higher Education

The financial system should not only yield adequate funds, it should also contribute toward certain important qualitative goals of higher education, among them, (*a*) reasonable autonomy of institutions and academic freedom for their students and faculty; (*b*) reasonable balance among the functions of teaching, research, and public service and among the various disciplines; (*c*) excellence of performance; and (*d*) openness of educational opportunity for students and free choice by students of institutions and programs of study.

Colleges and universities need substantial autonomy if they are to be able to adapt to the needs of their students and of their local communities, if they are to be able to experiment and innovate, if they are to be able to ensure academic freedom for their faculties and students, and if they are to be able to achieve unity and coherence as institutions. From the financial standpoint, autonomy requires support from diverse sources so that no one agency or group can dominate, and it also requires substantial unrestricted monies which are then allocated by the institutions and not by outsiders.

In recent decades a broadening in the diversity of sources has occurred because of the entry of the Federal government, the large foundations, and the corporations into the finance of higher education. In my judgment, there have been gains in basic academic freedom (in the sense of freedom of thought and speech). I cannot say to what extent these gains may be ascribed to financial changes, but I am fairly sure the financial changes of recent years have not diminished academic freedom. On the other hand, I have the firm (but undocumented) impression that the proportion of funds that are restricted as to use has been growing. Foundations and the Federal government have given primarily restricted funds, and many state governments have increased their budget powers not so much through providing detailed appropriations or conditional grants as through establishing coordinating agencies to supervise institutional budgets. The categorical grants have resulted in serious imbalances between teaching and research and equally serious imbalances between the natural sciences and the humanistic disciplines. The state coordinating agencies may be having the effect of reducing the initiative, the flexibility, and the innovative power of institutions. I believe that, on the whole, ground has been lost in the past decade or two in the self-determination of institutions. In future financial plans, it is important that some of the freedom be recaptured. What is called for is not only restraint in the operations of the state coordinating agencies but also the entry of the Federal government into programs of substantial unrestricted grants to institutions.

A striking feature of contemporary higher education is a struggle for power over the colleges and universities. This is manifested in the efforts of faculty and students to gain greater influence in decision-making, it is seen in the unionization of both faculty and nonacademic employees, and it is evidenced by the increasing attention given to higher education by politicians and by the establishment of state coordinating agencies. Modifications of the financial system are part of the process by which the power structure is changing. From current trends in finance, it would appear that the states and private donors are losing power and that the Federal government is gaining power. Those who would increase tuitions to be financed by students would be placing increased power in the hands of the students and their families. I do not know precisely what constitutes an ideal balance of power among the contenders, but I suspect that higher education will serve society best if there is a reasonable diffusion of power, as represented by diversity of support, by substantial unrestricted funds, and by participation of various interest groups in decision-making.

Though institutions of higher education need a high degree of autonomy, they are servants of society and should be impelled by strong incentives to strive for excellence and to direct their work toward urgent social purposes. Colleges and universities are, it must be admitted, tradition-bound institutions and are slow to respond to changing conditions and needs. There is indeed a place for categorical grants which are intended to raise aspirations and effort and to stimulate development in directions suggested by the needs of local regions or of the nation. The problem is to achieve a good balance between institutional autonomy, as represented by unrestricted funds from diverse sources, and response to social needs as represented by various kinds of categorical and conditional aid. From time to time, as the categorical grants proliferate, they need to be consolidated into unrestricted block grants. Meanwhile, new categorical programs that are designed to meet new conditions and needs should be added to the base of growing unrestricted support. Without periodic consolidation of categorical grants, the finance of higher education would become a veritable jungle of conditional grants, and institutions would lose their coherence.

The system of finance must provide open opportunity for students.

By open opportunity, I mean freedom of qualified young men and women, regardless of socioeconomic backgrounds, to attend colleges and universities of their choice and to enter fields of study of their choice within these institutions.

With other things equal, openness of opportunity will vary inversely with the level of student fees. The lower the fees, the greater the opportunity. Similarly, other things equal, openness of opportunity will vary directly with the level of financial aid. The greater the aid, the greater the opportunity. Openness of opportunity will also be affected by the *form* of the financial aid—the proportions given in the form of work, loans, and grants. The problem is to achieve a suitable combination of fees and of three forms of aid.

Most people agree, in theory at least, on the desirability of open opportunity, but there is sharp disagreement on the financial method of achieving it and on who bears the responsibility.

At one extreme are those who would finance institutions predominantly with student fees and finance students entirely by parental contribution, work, and long-term *loans*.[4] An extension of this position is that the fee for each field of study should be set according to the cost of that program; for example, the student fee for chemistry would be greater than that for English or economics. The loan system under this plan might be a variant of the proposed Educational Opportunity Bank suggested by Milton Friedman, Jerrold Zacharias, and others.

At the opposite extreme are those who would eliminate student fees in public institutions, hold them to a minimum in private institutions, and finance students primarily by parental contributions, work, and *grants*—using loans only as an incidental form of aid. An extension of this position is that student fees should be the same for all fields of study so that choice of program would be unaffected by cost to the student. Between the two extremes is a host of combinations.[5]

---

[4] See Milton Friedman, "The Higher Schooling in America," *The Public Interest*, Spring 1968, pp. 108–12.

[5] I have recently made a proposal which represents a middle position; see "The Finance of Higher Education." My plan calls for: (1) a slowing or preferably a cessation of the escalation of student fees in both public and private institutions; (2) an increase in public funds for the support of institutions in the form of unrestricted grants from the Federal government; (3) finance of students primarily through parental contributions, work, and grants; (4) the grants to be set, according to individual needs, to enable students to attend low-fee institutions without incurring heavy debts; (5) supplemental loans to enable students to attend high-fee institutions and meet special problems and needs.

In my opinion, neither extreme is desirable or politically feasible. To rely heavily on fees to finance institutions and on loans to finance students would confer upon students excessive power over institutions and would tend to limit opportunity for many students, especially women and minority groups, who would be reluctant to go heavily into debt. On the other hand, to eliminate student fees in public institutions would reduce the autonomy of institutions by narrowing the base of support and would prevent students and their families from contributing toward an activity from which they receive undoubted personal benefits. Moreover, such a plan is politically impossible. It seems that some middle ground is both desirable and practically necessary.

Under present conditions, however, a strong case can be made for very low (or zero) student fees in the community colleges. These institutions are intended primarily to broaden opportunity for those who may not have the means, the motivation, or the preparation to attend conventional four-year institutions. There is need for some point of entry to the higher educational system for which the barriers are at an absolute minimum. However, even in community colleges catering to local students, financial aid to students will be necessary if there is to be true openness of opportunity. Many students can attend these institutions only if costs of attendance, including in some cases foregone earnings, can be financed.

A special issue relating to free choice of institutions is the widespread and increasing differentials between resident and nonresident fees in public institutions. In view of the high mobility of the population, the out-of-state fee differentials are anachronistic. And in view of the unevenness of educational facilities among the various states, these differentials inhibit free choice of institutions and of educational programs. These differentials are as improper as tariffs on the movement of commodities over state lines, specifically prohibited by the Constitution. The problem is that each state legislature is understandably reluctant to appropriate funds to educate students from other states. However, as Federal contributions to institutions of higher education grow, it should be possible to reduce these interstate barriers. Specific action by the Federal government is probably needed, beginning perhaps with the more specialized and advanced fields of study.

A closely related issue is whether any substantial part of Federal support to higher education should be distributed to the state governments for further distribution to the institutions or should be distributed by the Federal government directly to the institutions. This issue boils down to the question of "states rights" and governmental decentralization. I lean toward direct Federal administration mainly on the ground that institutional autonomy will be advanced if the states and the Federal government share control—especially if there are many Federal agencies involved. It can be argued in favor of direct administration of Federal grants that higher education is increasingly of national concern and that the Federal government is likely to command a more effective staff than the states for dealing discerningly with the complex issues of higher education. On the other hand, it can be argued in favor of state administration that the state governments would be more sensitive to local needs and aspirations, that the state governments should be supported and strengthened to preserve our Federal system, and that geographical "equity" would be more fully attained if Federal grants were apportioned among the states. The likely compromise is that some programs will be administered nationally (especially those involving research, graduate study, and professional education) and some will be administered by the states (especially those relating to undergraduate education).

This paper has been designed, not as a "plan" for the finance of higher education, but as an outline of some of the major issues and choices.

I have attempted to estimate the size of the future bill. It is clear that the colleges and universities will need a progressively larger share of the GNP—the share increasing from the present 1.9 percent to perhaps 2.6 percent by 1980. For a variety of reasons, mainly the increasing competition for public funds, it may be more difficult than in the past decade to secure the necessary annual increments for higher education.

The pattern of support for higher education is likely to change in the next decade. All sources will produce increased absolute amounts, but a smaller share will be derived from private gifts and grants and from state and local governments and a larger share from the Federal government. The future role of student fees is still uncertain. In my opinion, the percentage from this source will decline slowly.

The system of finance—both the diversity of sources and the attached conditions and restrictions on use of the funds—will influence the extent to which higher education will be able to achieve basic objectives such as institutional autonomy, balanced programs, excellence of performance, and openness of opportunity for students. In recent decades, the diversity of sources has been widened, but the proportion received with restrictions and conditions has also probably increased. Thus, higher education has, in some respects, gained and, in others, lost ground in degree of autonomy. There is a place for categorical aid to encourage the development of higher education in directions required by the national interest and by local needs. But in the future planning for the finance of higher education, a reasonable compromise should be sought between institutional autonomy, as represented by unrestricted funds from diverse sources, and response to social needs, as represented by various kinds of categorical aid.

COMMENTARIES ON

The Financing of Higher Education

H. THOMAS JAMES, CLARENCE SCHEPS,

ALICE M. RIVLIN, JOHN W. LEDERLE

Future Costs and Benefits

H. THOMAS JAMES

PRESIDENT BOWEN's paper constitutes a carefully reasoned estimate of the increases to be anticipated in demand for education and of the revenues required to meet the costs of those demands, together with a well-balanced review of some of the major issues to be considered in financing higher education in the years ahead. While the magnitude of the fiscal needs may seem appalling, the increase as a percentage of the gross national product is modest, and may well be acceptable, given continuation of the remarkable and rising enthusiasm of our people for extending educational opportunities.

In addition to the perennial hope expressed by Mr. Bowen that the trend line of military expenditures may one day turn down again, I see another development ahead that is propitious for higher education: Elementary and secondary enrollments have stabilized, perhaps even begun to decline, after twenty years of remarkable increases. The annual birth rate declined steadily after it peaked in 1959, so that a million fewer children are now being born each year than in that year. Consequently, elementary and secondary enrollments probably will decline by perhaps ten million pupils in the next twelve to fifteen years, and thus free resources not available had birth rates remained high. The decline in number of births also sets boundaries for one of the factors that has caused the costs of higher education to rise, for the annual student input into colleges and universities should begin its decline also after 1977.

220

I share with President Bowen the anticipation that government, particularly the Federal government, will play a larger part in financing higher education; but I wish to voice a small doubt about his proposal for periodic consolidation of payments into unrestricted grants. This course, I fear, would lead to further governmental meddling with the processes of determining educational policy. We are now debating the aims of higher education, and most especially we are divided whether the task is to be the education of man or the training of manpower. I have more faith in the free market as a means of settling this historic argument than I have in government. Hence, I urge that we consider most carefully the development and broadening of a system of grants to individuals that can be used to purchase educational services. Perhaps we should also encourage corporations, both private and governmental, to develop new institutions to provide vocational education services oriented to their needs. Both individual and corporate income could then be expected to flow into and supplement government grants in purchasing the highest level of that kind of education to which the individual aspires. The advantages gained through specialized institutional arrangements would also help the individual clarify aims if pursued in different kinds of institutions. The conflict now apparent among faculty and clientele pursuing very different aims would also be reduced.

My third comment goes quite outside Bowen's frame of reference, but it needs stating to hedge our estimate of the future, which always turns out to be surprising. The extension of education is always a revolutionary act for, if properly done, it leads the educated man to question the culture and the institutions that served his ancestors and to ask whether they are right for his times. The social institutions serving our times are aging and have developed an unhappy rigidity that resists such examinations; even the colleges and universities stiffen before the winds of change, though they, above all others of our social institutions, should lead and encourage the continuing assessment and redirection of social purposes in the interests of individual liberty.

The evils of our time, particularly as reflected in interracial conflict and in the pollution of our environment, appear to be growing at a pace so rapid as to defy control by government, an omen that, if present trends continue, almost certainly portends social revolution. Consequently when we estimate the future costs of higher education, we can also, I hope, come to weigh its benefits measured in increased understanding of man in relation to his environment and in our continuing search for the meaning of human existence and for viable rules for governing ourselves. If colleges and universities cannot contribute more to those objectives than they have in the recent past, they will not be supported, nor will they be worth supporting.

Competing Claims for Funds

CLARENCE SCHEPS

I AM IN SUBSTANTIAL AGREEMENT with President Bowen's analysis of the financial dilemma facing higher education in the decade ahead. Therefore, I shall attempt to underscore rather than to take issue with what he has said.

In the opinion of many observers, including this one, both state and private institutions—but especially private—are already in serious financial difficulties which are bound to intensify in the years immediately ahead. Ample evidence is available, if one looks around, to support the contention that higher education is in serious financial trouble:

1. An article in *Fortune* magazine for February 1967 asserted that a group of 20 colleges—reputed to have the largest endowments in the nation—showed combined deficits of $3 million in 1966–67; the figure was predicted to rise to $40 million by 1973, and $110 million by 1978. According to the article, the presidents of these institutions said they had no idea where money to offset these deficits was to come from.

2. An increasing number of private institutions are becoming tax-supported. To name some, but not all: Pittsburgh, Houston, Seton Hall Medical School, Buffalo, Chattanooga, Kansas City, and Loyola Dental School.

3. A recent issue of *The Chronicle of Higher Education* reported that ten of the nation's 50 dental schools are facing the real possibility of going out of business because of the unparalleled financial crisis.

4. Although most state universities are prohibited by law from operating at deficit levels, some observers believe that a quality deficit has already begun to develop because of inadequate state allocations.

5. A recently published report of the American Alumni Council, entitled "The Plain Fact Is," describes the responses of 500 college and university presidents to a question about the financial future of their institutions. With a few exceptions they agreed on this answer: "The

money is not now in sight to meet the rising costs of higher education . . . to serve the growing numbers of bright, qualified students . . . and to pay for the myriad activities that Americans now demand of their colleges and universities."

The seriousness and immediacy of the financial problem varies greatly among institutions. Some institutions that I know about have already reached the crisis state in their financial affairs. Others are concerned about the immediate future for they cannot see how the rising curve of expenditures can be met out of predictable resources.

Why, after several decades of almost miraculous growth and remarkable improvement, is higher education—never in higher esteem nationally—suddenly in financial difficulty? Here are some of the causes:

1. Progress was great, expansion was rampant, but many institutions expanded without any thought of future costs.

2. Many of the programs added during this period were expensive programs in graduate and professional education. Many were added with the assistance of foundation or government support, which was subsequently withdrawn or reduced, forcing the institution to find other sources of support. Federal research programs and foundation programs implanted into the operating budgets of institutions are almost automatic cost-acceleration factors.

3. While industry has expanded the volume of its operations many times during the past several decades, the *unit* costs of higher education have continued to rise rather than go down. Although part of the increase can be attributed to the nature of educational institutions, some of it results from our failure to operate on principles of sound academic and business management. A portion of the rising costs stem from the inevitable proliferation of courses, ever-decreasing teaching loads, decreased class sizes—in short, decreasing productivity.

4. There has been no national planning for the development of higher education in this country, regional planning has been spotty, state planning frequently inadequate, and interinstitutional cooperation scant, even on a local level. This lack of planning has led to duplication and inefficiencies.

5. The steady inflation since World War II has forced up the cost of everything the college has to pay for.

6. Higher education, in a sense, has used up some of its line of credit. This is one of the major reasons why the prospective picture is not as bright, looking ahead from 1968 to 1978, as it may have been from

1950 to 1960, or even 1960 to 1970. In the case of private institutions, the tremendously successful efforts at fund-raising have increased operating-cost levels and have encouraged the initiation of new programs for which new and continuing support constantly must be found. The major national foundations, a bulwark of assistance to private institutions since World War II, are tending to withdraw support from higher education in favor of the other dominant needs of society. In the case of public institutions, state appropriations for higher education, which have doubled in the last decade or so, are now threatened by competing claims for funds by other public programs.

In examining the possibilities of increases in resources in the years ahead, President Bowen analyzes the situation with respect to tuition and fees, state and local appropriations, private gifts, income from endowments and Federal support. I share his concern about the ever-increasing cost of tuition and fees, especially in the private institutions. In the case of my own institution, for example, tuition was $750 in 1958; in 1968–69, it was $1,900—an increase of more than 150 percent. If the trend continues at the same rate, by 1979 annual tuition at my university will be about $4,700. If financial aid to students does not keep pace with such increases in tuition, the composition of many student bodies will change drastically.

I share President Bowen's view that appropriations from state and local governments will not rise at the same rate as in the past decade. Moreover, gifts from private philanthropy, since 1965, have tended to level off.

Where, then, do we turn for the solution to our problem? Many people, including President Bowen and myself, think that vastly increased Federal support is the principal answer. President Bowen estimates that by 1978 Federal support will have to increase by nearly four times over the 1967–68 level—and, significantly, most of this increase will have to be in the form of general support for higher education. Competition from the war and from other pressing national needs may retard or usurp some of the support otherwise anticipated from this source.

I would emphasize, perhaps a bit more than has President Bowen, the absolute necessity for those of us in academic administration to find ways to exercise better academic management. New programs should be added only with full knowledge of what the programs are going to cost and how the funds to finance them are to be obtained. Too often in the past academic administrators were either unwilling to find out about costs or perhaps did not want to face facts about the added burdens of maintaining new programs.

In my judgment, most institutions will not be able to conduct their affairs on a business-as-usual basis. I recognize increased efficiency might be achieved at the expense of quality, and this danger we will have to guard against at all times. On the other hand, reduction in the number of courses offered, reduction in the number of degree programs, perhaps even modest increases in class sizes, do not necessarily lead to a decrease in quality. In any event, there will have to be better planning, more intelligent cost analysis, more facing up to and dependence on facts, more fundamental innovations than we have been willing to undertake in the years immediately past.

I am convinced, as is President Bowen, that new approaches will have to be developed for financing higher education. Although I may perhaps be a little more pessimistic than President Bowen, I too feel that, even though the financing problems of the years immediately ahead will be difficult, bordering on crisis in many institutions, somehow or other the importance of higher education to this nation and to its people will continue to be recognized and that ways will be found to solve the problems.

Choices Must Be Made

ALICE M. RIVLIN

I do not suppose that I was invited to this distinguished meeting of educators because I am a nice girl or even because I am a card-carrying economist who once wrote a book on financing higher education. The gentlemen who made up the program must have had two things in mind in inviting me to Denver. First, I am a high-level Federal official, sometimes known to the opposition as a tired bureaucrat. As such, I might be expected to bring a Federal perspective to the discussion of financing higher education. Second, I am not now and never have been a university president—not even a vice-president or a dean or a department chairman. I might, therefore, be expected to liven up the proceedings by suggesting some alternatives to President Bowen's well-stated position that the Federal government ought to be giving university presidents more money. In order not to disappoint the gentlemen on the program committee, I am going to attempt to play these two roles.

First, let me say that I see no reason to quarrel with President Bowen's admittedly rough estimate of the magnitude of resources that might reasonably be devoted to higher education by the end of the decade of the 1970s. More and more young people aspire to an education beyond high school. If these aspirations are to be fulfilled, enrollments will rise rapidly. Moreover, students aspire to a "good" education. Barring some unforeseen revolution in educational technology, providing future students with education of even present quality will imply continued increases in cost per student. President Bowen's estimate that the total bill for higher education by the end of the decade of the 1970s might run around $40 billion certainly does not seem unreasonable to me. Surely, a rich nation can devote 2.6 percent of its GNP to the higher education of its citizens if it so desires.

The question is *not:* Can the nation afford that much for higher education? Clearly we can. Assuming that we wish to devote about $40 billion to higher education a decade from now, the real questions are: (1) How should the bill be shared between taxpayers and the consumers of higher education (since Bowen rightly points out other sources of support are minor and unlikely to increase)? (2) What should be the relative roles of state, local, and Federal government? (3) Should Federal funds go increasingly to students, or should they go directly to institutions, and, if so, for what purposes?

On these three points, Bowen's position is clear. He feels that taxpayers should pay an increasing share of the cost of higher education. He believes that the Federal government should bear an increasing share of the burden (relative to state and local government). He also feels that the Federal aid should emphasize funds channeled directly to institutions to be spent at their discretion. Let me assure you that if I were a university president I would also hold this last position very strongly.

What perspective can I give you in my role of Federal official? I am afraid I can only remind you that the choices to be made about how to spend the Federal dollar are very hard ones. More for higher education means less for preschool education, neighborhood health centers, rehabilitation of the handicapped, rebuilding of urban slums, and a lot of other things that most of us regard as essential. To the university president the need for replacing the antiquated chemistry building or raising faculty salaries may seem urgent and self-evident. But the Federal official is constantly reminded that welfare payments for children in Mississippi are $8.00 a month; that infant mortality in some ghetto areas is three times the national level; that the tuberculosis rate among Indians is tragically high. These are only a few of the claims against the Federal tax dollar with which that chemistry building has to compete.

I share Professor Bowen's view that even when the Vietnamese war is over, the choices at the Federal level will not be much easier. Military spending will certainly not drop precipitously. Pressures for a Federal tax cut will be great, and the claims against the Federal dollar for meeting vast social needs will be just beginning. If we are to move from the demonstration and model stage to real implementation of promised programs to rebuild neighborhoods and make high-quality education and health care available to all, many tens of billions of dollars will be necessary.

Incidentally, I am not sure I entirely share President Bowen's pessimism about state and local government support for higher education. The record of the last decade is one of remarkable increases in support. It does not seem obvious to me that the state and local share of higher education support will fall, especially now that enrollment increases in elementary and secondary education are slowing up, thus easing the pressure on this major item in state and local budgets.

Not long ago, I read an interesting statement about state and local support. "There is a further complication to the whole question of desirable level of student charges. There is undoubtedly a growing concern with the tax burden of government at all levels in our country. A threatened revolt against the cost of government is especially evident in our states." The speaker was John D. Millett, president of Miami University. The time was 1959.

If Federal resources are likely to be scarce, it is necessary to ask: What is the most effective way of spending them? How do we get the biggest bang per billion of additional Federal dollars for higher education? The answer, of course, depends on what we are trying to accomplish. I think President Bowen and I and many other people are agreed on at least three objectives of future Federal aid to higher education. One is increasing opportunities for students of all income levels to participate in higher education. The second is maintaining and improving the quality of instruction in higher education. (None of us know how to define "quality," but we do know that, whatever it is, it costs money—money for books and buildings and equipment, and, above all, faculty salaries.) Finally, we all want to protect institutional autonomy; at least, none of us wants the Federal government dictating how colleges and universities should spend their funds.

President Bowen is proposing that we move toward these objectives by giving institutions of higher education direct and unrestricted Federal support distributed on the basis of a formula. Suppose we spent a billion dollars a year this way, what would it buy? It would buy about a 10 percent increase in the current funds available to the average college or university for educational and general purposes (exclusive of organized research). Now, 10 percent in free funds may increase university self-determination significantly, it can't help but aid in the maintenance of quality, but it clearly is not going to produce any significant changes in what President Bowen calls "openness of opportunity." Reverting to the jargon of my bureaucrat role, such formula aid would be "equal opportunity inefficient."

An alternative strategy for the deployment of our imaginary (I make no promises) billion dollars of Federal support, might be to expand and concentrate these funds on scholarship grants based on need. Of all the varying reasons for government support of higher education, none is more clearly a Federal responsibility than the assurance of equal opportunity. Moreover, a billion dollars in expanded student aid will make a really substantial contribution toward attainment of that goal. On grounds then of emphasizing the unique Federal responsibility for correcting the unequal education chances of low-income youth and on the grounds of effectiveness, a broad expansion of Federal student aid might be a suitable use of expanded Federal funding.

Does such a program address itself properly to President Bowen's, and my, concern for institutional self-determination? It seems to me that such a program would greatly enhance the university's ability to obtain discretionary funds. It would, first, set free some of the one quarter of a billion dollars in funds now expended for student aid out of state and private sources. More important, a massive program of student aid would remove a major impediment to increased tuition fees at both private and public universities. If each hundred dollar grant to students from needy families induces institutions to raise tuition by $50, the impact on college finances will be substantial. For this is, indeed, an affluent society: there are many, many more college students willing and able to pay the extra $50 than there are potential Federal grant recipients. Thus, in keeping with President Bowen's caveat that additional Federal aid be distributed in ways that encourage other sources to increase their effort, the plan I have outlined here promises to stimulate new and general-purpose funds from the private sector.

To those of you who find the prospect of large increases in student fees dismaying or impossible, it is sobering to remind ourselves of the one basic truth in higher education finance: there is only one gross national product and there are lots of ways of tapping it. Each of us who exercises some control over a part of the pie emphasizes his own difficult budget choices. This is true of parents, state legislators, donors. But it is also true that choices must be made at the Federal government level, and we cannot expect full Federal funding of every "needs gap" in every sector of the economy. Especially not when non-Federal sources have not been fully and efficiently utilized.

In closing, I must say that none of my roles really permit me to speak with any authority on the question of the power balance in the modern university and how this balance will be affected by greater dependence on student fees. Perhaps, if we looked very hard, we could find someone who was an able president of a private college, heavily dependent on student fees, and also later a very excellent president of a public university, less dependent on tuition funds. If such a person could be found, he could contrast for us the transformation of his power in the two institutions. Barring finding such a person, we may have to revert to disparate references to Columbias and Berkeleys for our clues as to how student fees affect the power of the college administrator.

A Climate of Willingness

JOHN W. LEDERLE

PRESIDENT BOWEN's paper is an excellent summary of the financial scene in higher education today and a perceptive view of the future as well. Using the approach of an economist, he has ably addressed himself to the decision-making process as it involves the distribution of limited resources in response to the various demands that are placed upon them.

In my view, what resources go to higher education in the future will depend heavily upon political considerations, not upon any inherent limitation on the public's ability to pay. It is more a question of the public's *willingness* to devote a greater (though, as Bowen demonstrates, a still small) percentage of the gross national product to higher education than of the public's *ability* to support and finance the rising costs of higher education.

President Bowen rightly emphasizes the increasing competition for the tax dollar. At the state level, in any year the governor and the legislature are besieged from all sides. For example, the conservation department will demand 100 more forest rangers, claiming that without them thousands of acres of forest land will be destroyed by fire, to the horror of all nature lovers. The state police, pointing to the mounting death toll on the highways, will call for many extra policemen to put an end to the holocaust. And next will come the well-intentioned representatives of the department of mental health, demanding, figuratively if not literally, that we forthwith construct at great expense a roof over the entire state, for we all appear on the verge of mental breakdowns, and a substantial percentage will need hospitalization. Given this competition for funds, the case for higher education will have to be articulated well if our expanding financial needs are to be met.

But the problem is not solely one of competition with other state services. In my view, the demands of all the claimants on the public and philanthropic dollar are legitimate. They should not be segregated so sharply. With respect to the future quality of society, all the claimants cited by President Bowen may be said to constitute elements of a single system: to wit, the "public sector," which itself is deserving of top priority. The response we make to any one element on the list will affect all the others. If adequate housing is lacking or if we have no effective urban transportation, we may not achieve anything in dealing with juvenile delinquency or with education. If higher education is inadequate, then the advances made with the other elements will impede preparation of the next generation. Rather than stressing the negative aspects of competition, we should acknowledge that higher education, both public and private, is an integral element in a whole complex of social issues.

If even the most conservative projections of economic growth are borne out, there will be ample per-capita income to meet the projected needs of higher education as well as those of the other claimants. Discretionary income will expand, and the problem will be the psychological and political one of inducing the citizen as philanthropist and as taxpayer to provide the needed funds. Outlays for education already make it the largest industry in the nation. Up to now, the public seems to have agreed with Plato that education is the single most important function of the state, since it is the transmitter of all our cultural values. However, one does note more and more lay criticism of higher education, more and more skepticism about its teaching methods and about its "managerial efficiency." It is only natural that the public wants to know what is going on. And, I might add parenthetically, private institutions which are now turning to the government for salvation should realize that with increased public funding will come the embarrassing questioning, auditing, and outside scrutiny that public institutions have come to accept as a fact of life. If we respond petulantly, if we view such questioning as interference with institutional autonomy, if we fail to communicate what higher education is all about, we will lose a measure of public support. Only by open and full disclosure can we create a climate of *willingness* to meet our needs.

We face at least two tasks in creating this climate. First, we must devote more effort to enhancing and demonstrating educational productivity. Second, we must conduct our campuses as scholarly communities and deal vigorously with those who would go beyond the limits of academic freedom and prevent orderly deliberation.

If we are to win financial support, we should demonstrate sincere concern about how the educational dollar is spent. It is hard to justify in economic terms an educational plant's remaining idle during the summer. In an affluent society, air conditioning, private offices with telephones, and other facilities have come to be accepted as a matter of course by the professor. But as he escapes from teaching, through a steadily decreasing course load, what improvements has he introduced into the teaching process itself? We need more research on learning theory and on student motivation. We need experimentation and innovation. To the extent the public is convinced that educational institutions are efficiently run and are constantly seeking ways to improve so as to enhance educational productivity, so far will the job of securing more financial support be eased.

Finally, I will comment briefly on the adverse effect of campus demonstrations and violence on financial support. I bring up this point with some reluctance, for I am likely to be misunderstood. Let me say at the outset that I believe it is the role of a university to provide an environment in which teachers and students may pursue the truth wherever it leads and no matter how palatable it is to society. In general, the American public has been sympathetic to the view that the academic community must be protected from outside interference with its search for the truth. The concepts of academic freedom and of tenure are supportive of this objective.

What a far cry from this concept have been the violent demonstrations, the hissing and booing, the disruptions of scholarly and classroom activities on some American campuses recently. Future financial support, the contributions of private philanthropy and of the tax-paying public, will depend on our conducting internal affairs in a businesslike, deliberative fashion that comports with the dignity of a community of scholars interested in hearing all points of view. I am not suggesting that we get control of ourselves simply as a matter of good public relations. Rather I suggest we do so in order to carry on as a community of scholars meriting continued and expanding financial support.

Tomorrow I purpose to regulate my room.
Samuel Johnson,
Prayers and Meditations

ALVIN C. EURICH

Managing the Future:
Some Practical Suggestions

PROBABLY SOME PEOPLE who hear about our discussion of how to manage the future in higher education will think we have our heads in the clouds. That is understandable: it is obvious that we are having one devil of a time managing the *present*. The college or university administrator who is pondering the prospect of higher learning in the year 1980 or the year 2000 may be jolted out of his reverie when a brick comes crashing through the window. To speculate on the problem of administration in the future is indeed a chancy business when, on many campuses, student activists and even some professors seem to want no administration at all.

Yet the very perils of the present make our scrutiny of the future not only defensible but absolutely necessary and long overdue. Americans, it has been said, often act as if they had no past and no future. In higher education, the mistakes and myopia of the past are catching up with us today. Our failure to define our goals with precision; our failure to examine critically and to revise imaginatively our ways of teaching; our failure to put our financial houses in order; our failure to participate in the management revolution that has swept American business and in-dustry—all these failures are haunting higher education today. If colleges and universities are to flourish—or even survive—in the years to come, we had better look into the future, and do what we can to manage its direction in the best interests of America's young people and American society.

Any coherent and intelligent attempt to manage the future of higher education includes certain essential ingredients:

· A candid recognition of past mistakes.

233

- A sensitive awareness of major current problems.
- An intense desire to eradicate obsolete attitudes and practices, and to make our institutions relevant to existing and emerging needs.
- Imagination and ingenuity in the search for better answers to pressing problems.
- Careful planning that takes full account of all major aspects of higher education—from educational goals and instructional techniques to finances and administration.
- Courage to act.
- Effective activation of plans, and constant evaluation and re-evaluation of the results.

Our own efforts at the Academy for Educational Development to come to terms with the future have involved us in many studies and projects over the past five years, including long-range programing and planning for higher education in California, Colorado, Connecticut, Delaware, Indiana, Kansas, Maine, New York, Ohio, and Pennsylvania. In addition, the Academy has surveyed and analyzed plans for the future in the nation's graduate and professional schools, for the National Institutes of Health, the U.S. Office of Education, and the Bureau of Health Manpower.

One example of our work is the volume *Campus 1980*,[1] which the American Council has provided in a special edition as supplementary background reading for the discussions of the future academic community. It includes probes into the future of higher education by such imaginative and experienced men as John Gardner, David Riesman, Nevitt Sanford, Logan Wilson, and Clark Kerr.

Their view of what we may expect by 1980 is encouraging and frightening at the same time. In fact, when we read the manuscript through for the final time before sending it to the publisher, the thought arose for some discussion that perhaps the title should be *Campus 2000*. To us, the changes which the contributors see occurring in a dozen years or so seemed too basic and diverse to come to pass by 1980. But then we realized that the value of the book—as of any truly penetrating speculation about the future—is its very power to line out potentials for good and evil. As Whitehead remarked, it is the business of the future to be dangerous. It is *our* business to look ahead as best we can—to avoid or minimize the evils, to foster and increase the good.

The aim of this paper is to describe some of the many things that every

---

[1] New York: Delacorte Press, 1968.

institution might be doing, right now, to prepare for the future. Obviously, this short paper cannot hope to be comprehensive, but it can outline many aspects of planning and the process of planning, and many fairly simple, straightforward techniques that a busy administrator may have overlooked or neglected. And it can point out a few current examples of farsighted and effective planning, not only by institutions themselves but also by agencies that assist colleges and universities in the planning task. In addition to the examples cited further on in this paper, others have been reported in the professional literature and discussed at the first meeting of the newly formed National Society of College and University Development Planners, held at the University of Michigan.

I shall confine myself to considering how we could better manage the future of higher education in four major areas: goals; the process of instruction; finances; and management itself. Finally, I shall offer a proposal to upgrade the process of planning for the future.

Goals

Clarifying goals and establishing priorities among them are the first order of business in managing the future.

Much of the work of academic administration is concerned with immediate, day-to-day problems. The systems analysts classify this necessary but rudimentary form of administration as "The Housewife's Principle": When you see a mess, clean it up. The resulting activity is useful and necessary, but limited in scope. Too many academic administrations tend to get completely bogged down at that level and to progress no further.

The long-range future of a major instution cannot be handled on a piecemeal, *ad hoc* basis.

A philosophy of education is required—a philosophy expressed in a set of clear-cut goals and priorities which go beyond platitudes of the catalogues: "Emphasis on academic excellence and the maximum maturity of the individual students. . . ." "Integrating all facets of a student's education. . . ." "Receiving the student into the community of scholars and teachers in the tradition of university education as broadly conceived. . . ." "Dedication to the highest standards of learning. . . ." "To produce broadly educated men and women with mental horizons beyond the limits of specific professional interest. . . ." "To establish an ideal community governed by high yet reasonable codes of conduct and dedicated to things of the mind."

The moral to be drawn from these samples of catalogue prose is that no one—prospective students, parents, academics themselves—any longer accepts such rhetoric, if they ever did. At a time like the present, when values are changing so fast, no college or university can set forth its goals in such windy and unexceptional generalities. To continue to do so is to invite degeneration into irrelevance.

Hard questions need to be asked about which distinctive jobs each institution can do best, and about the most important jobs each is most aptly fitted to tackle. Not many institutions in the country today, for example, have adjusted their basic goals to deal adequately with the crisis in our cities. Surely there are a large number of urban institutions that should and could move this complex concern—so critical to the nation's welfare—much higher in their priorities, perhaps in some cases even restructuring the entire academic organization and program to this end.[2]

My practical suggestion regarding goals, then, is that each academic community, led by its administration, accept the responsibility to define its aims and functions precisely and with particular regard for emerging needs. Goals should be so developed that they can be translated into actual policies and programs. The goals must be specific enough to indicate the action required and the programs needed. And the goals must change as rapidly and as fundamentally as do the needs of man and the society to which the institutions are supposedly responsive. How can this difficult task be accomplished?

To begin, each institution of higher learning requires not only leadership but a continuing mechanism for discerning and expressing appropriate objectives. The administration, headed by the president, must supply the leadership; otherwise confusion, discord and petty bickering, turmoil, and ultimately, riots will result. Colleges and universities, no less than any other social institutions, governments, or business organizations, must have a clear sense of direction, must know where they are going and why, and must have maps showing how to get there.

As for a mechanism, there is obviously no single solution that would meet the need of all the nation's colleges and universities, in their diversity, to revitalize their sense of purpose and direction. All we can be sure of, in view of widespread student and faculty unrest, is that the institutions must undertake the task or perish, and each must evolve its own pattern, based on its own history and hoped-for destiny in modern society.

[2] See *Campus in the City*, Annual Report of the Educational Facilities Laboratories, 1968.

Whatever the pattern, if goals are to be realized, all important elements of the college—in its broadest context—must take part: trustees, administration, faculty, students, ancillary staff, constituents, alumni, community, and cooperating institutions.

A basic and flexible mechanism might have, as its first element, an institutionwide committee on goals, chaired by the president, the academic vice-president, or the dean of faculty. The committee should be relatively small, certainly no more than fifteen at the outset, including representatives of all the groups named above.

The efforts of this group should be directed toward a definitive statement of the particular kind of institution that the committee envisions ten to twenty-five years hence. Unlike the high-sounding generalities of the typical catalogue, the statement would pinpoint the place of the institution in society as defined by its particular setting and orientation (rural, suburban, urban, regional, national). It would identify the institution's constituents; characterize the students; establish the emphasis to be placed on teaching, research, and service, and, in some cases, the balance among them; analyze the local community (residential, industrial, commuting populations, economic and class structure, degree of integration or segregation, and so on); clarify relationships with the community and with other institutions; and gauge the full range of expected financial support.

These are a few of the requisites for a clear statement of institutional goals. They are merely illustrative of the precision required to make these goals meaningful. Each college or university must state them so precisely that they can serve as signposts against which the institution can check its year-by-year progress toward the proclaimed goals. With goals specified thus, the making of a map to guide the way to achievement becomes easier. When goals are ambiguous or ambivalent or conflicting, the map constructed would have to be surrealistic—like a road map showing how to go from Chicago to New York and San Francisco simultaneously.

The Process of Instruction

Setting instructional goals that are relevant and precise—which say clearly, for example, what the student should know when he graduates that he didn't know when he arrived on campus—is an activity which must involve the whole institution. It is not enough to have a top-level committee pondering the aims of the institution as a whole. Every part of the university community should be constantly at work to clarify the particular aims of instruction in every course. In some of the experimental college programs around the country, the student's registration for a course is complete only after he and the teacher have come to a personal agreement on the goals to be achieved. Again, institutions may focus extensive orientation programs on clarifying, through free discussion between students and professors, the purposes of college education and of particular courses. Although some of these devices are unduly cumbersome, they derive from a genuine need: to understand the purposes of instruction before teaching and learning commence.

Thus the setting of instructional goals, if carried out thoroughly, leads directly to a consideration of the process of instruction. Once we have grasped a conception of what we really want the university as a whole to achieve, as well as particular courses, it becomes clear that college teaching as currently organized is grossly inefficient and shockingly unimaginative. For there are more effective means available for accomplishing our instructional goals than those we now use.

Much of teaching is communication. Yet in the era that has produced the most powerful communication media ever known to man, books aside, our chief means of conveying information in college instruction is still the human larynx. We seem to feel that what a student needs to learn is somehow increased in value through being processed by a hundred and seventy pounds of flesh. The presence of a warm body at the front of the classroom has seemed so important that we have often chosen to maintain the conventional ratio of students to professors, even at a cost of lowering the quality of instruction.

Fortunately, this view is now being seriously questioned. The AAUP, in a recent policy statement, recommended urgent consideration of use of instructional technology to increase the fruitfulness of college teaching and to keep costs down. The alternatives—lower quality of instruction and an even greater squeeze on the funds available to recompense faculty—are decidedly unattractive. The AAUP statement reflects an aphorism expressed years ago by the late Charles Johnson of Fisk University: to maintain the small-class ideal at a cost of using poor teachers is merely to transmit mediocrity in an intimate environment.

But this is the *negative* reason for harnessing new technology to the process of instruction. The positive reasons are more compelling to me: The new media can help us achieve the most important goals of instruction and therefore improve higher education. It is in the interests of better *learning* that we should reconsider our penchant for small classes, our myth of the potency of the lecturer, and our assumption that technology and freedom are incompatible.

Students can learn by various means—from lectures, from motion pictures and television presentations, from audiotapes and records, from books, from discussion with their peers, or alone or in small groups. There are many media of communication that can be used to enrich students' education, many ways in which the faculty's knowledge and wisdom can be placed at the student's disposal, many opportunities for tailoring each student's program to his individual needs and aspirations. Some things are best learned through independent study, some through field work, some through foreign travel. Different students learn different things in different ways. Our approach should be to use the full range of available options to permit and encourage each student to learn in the way best suited to the purpose at hand. This means using television to bring outstanding lecturers to all students who can benefit from hearing them. It means tapping the reservoir of superb instructional films that are already available. It means using the long-distance telephone to bring outside lecturers to the campus. It means harnessing every modern medium of communication to expand and strengthen the process of instruction. And each of these must be used with a clear purpose in mind: to inspire, inform, guide, stimulate, drill, test, or otherwise advance the student's learning toward the instructional goals he and the university have agreed on in advance.

The emerging technology of college teaching actually provides unprecedented opportunities for individualized instruction. After all, everything a student learns he must learn himself; no one can learn for him—other people can only help. The new media of instruction can help, too. Language laboratories can enable students to master foreign tongues with new ease and accuracy. Programed learning can allow them to proceed at their own rate, with constant reinforcement and testing. A wide variety of audio-visual materials can stimulate students to independent study that may be more effective than classroom instruction.[3] We will soon discover that the more technology we introduce on our campuses, the

---

[3] The most up-to-date survey of the use of these and other new technologies is in James W. Brown and James W. Thornton, Jr., *New Media on Campus* (Washington: Division of Educational Technology, National Education Association, September, 1968).

more we will increase the individuality, flexibility, and effectiveness of our total programs. Far from dehumanizing the student and professor, modern teaching tools and techniques can liberate them from the constraints of conventional instruction.

Of course, technology can have a dehumanizing effect if we use it for the wrong purposes. That is why clarity of goals is so important. The students who have protested on campus after campus recently, against the dehumanization of the "multiversity," were right in feeling that they were not being treated with sufficient sensitivity and respect as human beings. But they were wrong in blaming this on the new technology, by carrying signs reading "I Am A Human Being—Do Not Fold, Spindle, or Mutilate." What they should have protested—and what in many cases they have now come to recognize as their real enemy—is a set of goals and priorities and attitudes insufficiently committed to using technology and every other available means to humanize and individualize instruction.

As a practical proposal in this area, I suggest that each institution reconsider the possibilities of using modern technological and organizational skills to bring education to the students wherever they are, rather than relying exclusively on bringing students to the campus. Just as the land-grant colleges brought, through county agents, new knowledge to the farmers, we can now use state-wide educational television networks, correspondence study, portable teaching machines, and the computer in all its infinite combinations, as well as the good-old-fashioned book, to spread opportunities for higher learning much more widely than at present. I believe that the new communications technology affords the opportunity for a radical decentralization of higher education through a renaissance of home study. *Communication* of information and learning aids can more and more replace *transportation* of bodies to provide much wider access to learning for mature people. Such a development could do much to ease the demand for more buildings and bigger (even if less effective) faculties, and the pressure of spiraling costs.[4]

Finances

In no area does managing the higher education future look more ominous than it does in financing. Already, farsighted observers of the

---

[4] The Academy is currently undertaking the staff work for the Commission on Instructional Technology, appointed by the Federal government, but independent in its operation, to explore such questions as they apply to education at all levels.

academic scene—like McGeorge Bundy of the Ford Foundation and Alan Pifer of the Carnegie Corporation—have warned that America's private colleges and universities may be headed for a financial crisis. Universities like Pittsburgh, Temple, Buffalo, and Houston have been driven to the wall and necessarily become associated with public systems. There is little doubt that other institutions, big and small, will follow this pattern in the next ten years. As Allan Cartter, chancellor of New York University, has said, "Much of private higher education cannot survive until 1980 if the trends of the last decade continue." (See also Howard Bowen's paper, "Higher Education Finance: Issues and Prospects," in this volume.)

In the past ten years, thanks in considerable measure to the pioneering work of Sidney Tickton in conceiving, designing, and helping colleges actually develop long-range planning budgets, higher education has come far in adopting the proven business methods that some of our leading industrial concerns have long used. Tickton's *Needed: A Ten-Year College Budget* [5] has now been used as a guide by hundreds of institutions. It has helped them to meet their objectives by providing a tool in the area of financial planning.

But now more is required. As a practical matter we must bring processes of academic and fiscal planning *together*. Future program plans must be sorted out and costed out. When educational options are weighed, each option should have a price tag attached, and due consideration should be given to cutting back in some areas as well as advancing or expanding in others.

Moreover, the tendency to treat plans as static must be overcome. Too many institutions have undertaken the Herculean task of preparing a plan (or working with advisers or consultants to prepare one) only to rest back in the false assurance that the job has been done. Thereafter, whenever anyone asks where the institution is headed, the plan is taken off the shelf and leafed through. Such a procedure might have been suitable in quieter times. But today, events are moving so quickly that planning must be recognized as a continuing, corrective, asymptotic effort to maintain the fullest possible awareness and take the fullest possible account of a constantly changing set of future probabilities.

Model programs of this kind are now progressing at a few universities around the country, notably at the following, which have been supported recently by Ford Foundation grants:

[5] New York: Fund for the Advancement of Education, 1961.

· The University of California, which will use its new funds to press ahead with new applications of the systems-analysis techniques already adapted to university problems. President Charles Hitch, formerly with the Department of Defense, has been in the forefront of applying new management techniques to higher education since going to California two years ago as financial vice-president. Among projects under consideration are the adaptation of program budgeting to a large university; the development of planning models that will deal with academic, fiscal, and physical factors in a rapidly expanding university system; cost-effectiveness studies are alternative ways to utilize resources.

· Stanford—because of the Ford Foundation grant—will be able to complete in three years, instead of nine, an undertaking already begun to establish an integrated computerized system for all of its administrative activities. It will report on how the ability to order and call up data affects the decision-making process. Stanford now has seven different systems of information and records to integrate and program for computers. For example, files on the same student are kept by various school offices, alphabetized and cross-referenced in a variety of ways. The proposed integration would substitute teletype or television stations for all but one of these sets of files.

· Princeton will focus on the application of new analytical techniques and computer technology to academic issues, and will attempt to integrate financial and academic data. Activities planned include an extensive overhaul of the Princeton budget to reflect present and future consequences of alternative decisions; the scheduling of time and space in the academic program; and a systematic evaluation of teaching and teaching methods.

And it is gratifying to note that other, smaller, forward-looking institutions are moving boldly in this direction. An example is the planning at Wesleyan University, under the direction if its new president Edwin Etherington, former president of the American Stock Exchange. At Wesleyan, educational planning and cost analysis are going forward together, and the result may be a program-budgeting format suitable for other small universities.

Such approaches underline the importance of recognizing that finances cannot be divorced from the other aspects of the educational enterprise. For a good part of the economic squeeze which afflicts colleges and universities comes not just from the limited amount of money they get, but from the way they use those dollars. Proliferating courses and specialties, sacrosanct departmental fiefs, the penchant for small classes as an end in themselves, the aversion to technology, the reluctance to cooperate on an interinstitutional or an intrainstitutional basis, underutilization of the physical plant—all these contribute greatly to the cost-price squeeze, and, more important, they hold down the *quality* of learning.

Management

At the root of the problem of Mangaging the Future is the management of *management* in American higher learning. How can we bring about a higher level of performance in the management of all the aspects of the educational enterprise: formulation of goals, the process of instruction, finances, and other? "When you see the mounting pressures on our colleges and universities, better management may be their only way to sustain their academic freedom," says Marshall A. Robinson, the Ford Foundation's program officer in charge of higher education and research. "You don't take the vitality away from a dynamic institution merely because you know something about its component parts. You do not necessarily dehumanize a university when you try to take the measure of its problems."

One widely accepted way of tackling this problem is through employment of specialized consultants to examine and make recommendations about critical aspects of the institution's operations. Although many such studies have been made, with widespread benefits to the institutions studied, this is not the complete or final answer. Future planning and management improvement must be a continuing, intensive, internal function of every college or university.

Every major institution of higher learning in the United States should begin now to build its capacity to manage the future. Specifically, there should be established on every major campus an Office for Planning and Development, headed by one of the administrative vice-presidents.

The purpose of this office and of this officer would be to change the posture of the institution vis-à-vis the future. Instead of adjusting grudgingly to the momentous changes which are transforming American society, colleges and universities must aggressively plan for the future. Of all institutions in our society, universities should be the best equipped to face and master the changes which they themselves—through the knowledge explosion—are doing so much to bring about.

The mandate of the Office for Planning and Development would be to look to the future of the institution's philosophy and goals, in the context of community, region, state, and nation. It would maintain contact with others whose business it is to probe the future: planners in industry and government, as well as the many new agencies and organizations whose interests are specifically focused on the future, such as the centers recently established at Syracuse University and Stanford to develop descriptions of alternative futures for American education as a whole.

The office would feed information to the trustees, to the top administrators, to the students and faculty, and to the other constituencies of the institution. And it would, in turn, benefit from the views of all these groups as they articulated their needs and ideas.

In consultation with the other top administrative officers, the office would develop plans and cost them out as options for the consideration of those responsible for charting the institution's future. Moreover, it would maintain continuing surveillance over the execution of plans and over external developments which might change the expected future.

To fulfill his role effectively, this vice-president should report directly to the president of the institution, not through the dean or another official. And, in turn, the office in the college or university that handles institutional research should report to this vice-president, rather than to the business manager or another official. This vice-president should have no line duties other than the operation of his unit—he should not also be the registrar, bursar, or the librarian. For support of its activities, this office should command a small but reasonable percentage (say one-fourth of one percent) of the institution's budget. If these criteria are met, then I believe that a first-rate person can be recruited for such work, and that he could make a unique and profound contribution to the future health and growth of the institution. (This was certainly the experience at Stanford University in the mid-1940s, when the position of "director of planning" was established. First, the use of the then-existing resources were surveyed—so much land, so many buildings of such-and-such capacity, so many professors and students, so many (inadequate) dollars, and so on. By the time the survey and planning were completed, the entire development of the institution was changed: the enrollment was doubled in one year, plans were made for more productive use of land and buildings, and, among other things, the Stanford Research Institute was established.

The most important role for this office would be, not to predict the future, but to plan for it. *Predicting* the future in detail is impossible. *Shaping* the future so that it is closer to best hopes is a much more plausible and profitable undertaking. Rather than merely striving to discern what changes are coming in the society and in the institution, the office could and should try to analyze emerging needs and opportunities, and devise new ways to meet them.

For example, the better elementary and secondary schools are currently undergoing very substantial changes in their organization, curriculum, and emphases. Much more attention is given to individualized programs, independent study, use of technology and new ways of organizing for teaching, and the like. The students who are now coming out of the high schools and arriving on the campuses are clearly different from those in the past. It is even clearer that tomorrow's student will be different from today's. Yet only a few campuses are giving significant thought to devising programs to meet the needs of these students—and the very great opportunities they offer—as they come to the campus with quite different orientations to learning from those the institutions have encountered before.

Nor, to take another example, do I see much evidence of planning ahead for the multitude of youngsters from the inner-city black communities who must and will be brought into the mainstream of higher education in the next five years if we are to avoid social disaster.

An Office for Planning and Development, then, is a broad, practical approach to the problems of managing the future.

A Proposal To Upgrade Planning

But where will the people come from to staff such offices? Every administrator knows how difficult it is to find able, imaginative, adequately trained planning directors. Such offices as already exist are often poorly staffed or, in some instances, not staffed at all. And though institutions around the country are doing fine work, none of them is exploiting even what we know now about future planning for higher education.

To make this proposal really practical, then, requires an additional innovation. People capable of doing the job must be made available. From past experience we know how to go about this task. When other areas of higher education administration faced comparable manpower problems, the following programs were instituted:

1. *Admissions:* Recognizing the discrepancy between what was required in college admissions officers and what was currently being provided, the College Entrance Examination Board some years ago initiated a series of training programs and related activities to produce professional people to do this job the way it should be done. The result has been a

discernible improvement in performance of the admissions function in American higher education.

2. *Scholarship and financial aid:* Recognizing a similar situation in its area of concern, the College Scholarship Service initiated a program to provide training opportunities for able people who wanted to bring their abilities to this important task. The consequent professionalization of this role on many campuses has been commendable.

3. *Business management:* The National Association of College and University Business Officers has worked on helping college and university business managers to widen their concerns from physical plant to other aspects of program and services to the whole institution.

These successful precedents suggest that a professional agency should consider embarking on a program of internship-training in institutional planning. (Of course, an internship program is only as good as the experienced practitioners under whom the interns serve.) Such internships would have to go far beyond the one- or two-day sessions which the Ford Foundation has sponsored to acquaint administrators with the long-range planning budget. The internships might well be year-long programs, open to budding administrators of proven capacity and undoubted commitment, which would take them to a variety of campuses around the country, as well as to some of the noneducational agencies which have led the way in envisioning the future—the Rand Corporation, the Hudson Institute, and the planning offices of major corporations.

Along with the upgrading of individual and institutional performance, however, broader action is required. Our society is changing so fast, and new educational approaches and methods are developing so rapidly, that no one institution can possibly undertake studies of the future that are sufficiently broad and penetrating to serve all its needs. From the perspective of the individual institution, some societal trends defy anything approaching full comprehension. There are possibilities for improving education which entail regional or national arrangements. These prospects, problems, and possibilities transcend the level at which the future planning office of any single institution is likely to be working most of the time.

Awareness of this kind of situation has spurred the Department of Defense to create institutions like the Rand Corporation. More recently, it stimulated the U.S. Office of Education to establish the two centers, referred to above, at Stanford and at Syracuse to probe the future and articulate its implications for the nation's educational system as a whole.

Regional centers or a national center—or both—to do this job with the specific concerns of higher education in mind will become increasingly desirable. Associated with such centers might be selected institutions where a wide variety of new practices in the management and practice of higher education would be brought together and tried out.[6]

Managing the future in higher education—from establishing relevant and practical goals, through devising new instructional programs and making existing ones more effective and efficient, to finding the money and making it go as far as possible through rigorous analysis of alternative uses of resources, to creating and revising total plans for institutional advancement and the advancement of American education as a whole— all of this critical activity requires the full energies of highly able and thoroughly trained individuals. The future health of American higher education will depend in large measure on our capacity to identify, motivate, train, and use such men.

[6] Such a program of "model universities" might follow the pattern of the Ford Foundation's grants to selected school systems for "comprehensive school improvement," or the more recent grant of over one million dollars by the Danforth Foundation, for a six-year "model schools" program organized by the National Association of Secondary-School Principals.

COMMENTARIES ON

Managing the Future

MARTIN MEYERSON, MURRAY H. BLOCK,
THEODORE M. HESBURGH, C.S.C.,
THEODORE WALLER, FRANKLIN PATTERSON

Constantly Expanding Needs

MARTIN MEYERSON

Alvin Eurich has wisely advocated that universities try to shape their futures rather than merely predict them. Detailed prediction is passive; moreover, it is rarely possible. If university communities do not choose the directions in which they wish to go, they will either be swept along on the tide of past assumptions and practices, perhaps to a devastating conclusion, or be cast adrift and buffeted by immediate problems. Dr. Eurich places special emphasis on the reappraisal of organizational goals, on instructional methods, on finances, and on managerial techniques. I agree that these are among the highest priorities, and I applaud his position. My comments thus are essentially footnotes to his theme.

First, the present section on goals may overstate the need to keep redirecting the goals of an institution of higher learning. This may be a period of discontinuity. However, it might be harmful both to the university and to the society if the goals of the university were changed "as rapidly and as fundamentally as do the needs of man and the society to which the institutions are supposedly responsive." A university cannot leap into a new venture or a new program in response to a particular societal need, and then be forced to abandon it (for example, because of the scarcity of resources) and leap into the next seemingly urgent societal need, as defined by some vocal members of the community. Past overreactions to industrial fashions are a case in point.

As I see the question of the reappraisal of goals, the emphasis should

248

be less on shifting goals from the outmoded to the mode and more on having each member of the academic community constantly check his or her goals and activities and also those of colleagues. Many must participate in the reappraisal process; indeed, that should be part of the ongoing functions of faculty senates, of student governments, of administrative groups, and of presidents. Most questions will be raised when an activity irritates someone: fortunately or not, people on campuses have a low irritation threshold. Thus, prompted by questions on the ethics of Dow recruiters and the ethics of those trying to bar them from the campus, questions are asked whether the educational or service goals of an institution are furthered when the institution acts "in loco employment agency" to bring together potential employees with potential employers.

I see another dimension to goal clarification. Colleges and universities must muster the courage to admit that they cannot each excel in all fields of knowledge nor offer all kinds of cultural experiences nor participate in all kinds of community service, no matter how worthwhile. There must be a greater degree than now exists of a self-defined division of labor. Faculties and administrations must recognize their own strengths and weaknesses and dare to sacrifice some directions of development to the benefit of others. Some institutions have given up intercollegiate football; others have given up aspiring to high-energy physics. Some have a clear-cut mission to mingle work and study; others have a dedication to the arts. We need more forging of institutional characters. The way out of the grandiose verbiage that Mr. Eurich seeks may come when colleges and universities realize that they will gain from not trying to be pre-eminent in all phases of academic life.

As a second point, I agree with Dr. Eurich that we must explore all kinds of technological means to communicate knowledge and that teaching tools and techniques might increase individuality in learning rather than decrease it. However, we do not yet have a large body of superior materials to be used, even for primary schools. While we are experimenting with technological aids, we might also experiment with human aids. As part of their requirements, most students might teach someone else, possibly on a one-to-one basis, on the assumption that the best way to learn is to teach, and also on the assumption that learning from one's peers or near-peers can be the most stimulating and persuasive. Possibly more women might be attracted into part-time teaching. Possibly there might be more sharing of specialized talents among institutions on a regional basis.

It may be a good thing educationally to take information to the student rather than the student to the campus, but this may not be cheap. Where students lack study space at home, they will need satellite campuses, for example, in programs carried to the urban ghettos.

Third, more efficient management techniques can achieve cost reductions in university finances, but there are, of course, many other factors contributing to skyrocketing higher education expenses: inflation, the new level of aspirations, the capital expenditures required by the new technology, and the tight labor market which reflects the scarce number of qualified scholars in contrast with the constantly expanding needs of the university community.

Finally, the one point about which Mr. Eurich seems rigid is on the management of management. Possibly an Office of Planning and Development headed by an administrative vice-president who has no other responsibilities for budgeting or any other functions, is the solution to planned change in some institutions. But it might not be appropriate in others. For example, I can envision a council of deans and the president acting, with staff assistance, as the planning group.

Less than Utopia
MURRAY H. BLOCK

I READ Dr. Eurich's paper with the eagerness of one young enough to be vitally concerned with the future and with the apprehension of a college president who wonders if we will have the opportunity to "manage" the future—or even have a future. This mild schizophrenia, an affliction perhaps quite common in college presidents today, was somewhat abated by the forcefulness of Dr. Eurich's plan for the future. I did come away with one positive evaluation of the future: It can and must be managed or it may well manage us. Higher education has too frequently bent itself to meet the pressures of society, when it should have been actively pursuing a course that would have positively shaped those pressures, to make a happier world for all.

Dr. Eurich is quite correct in emphasizing the need for clarifying goals. Without goals, there is no future. Where there is no set purpose, pressure takes its place. Our author-critic is quite right—we administrators *do* tend to get completely bogged down in cleaning up the messes.

We *do* tend to treat the long-range future of our institutions on a piece-meal, *ad hoc* basis. We *do* cloud our own goals with "platitudes of the catalogues" that are often meaningless and rarely honest.

However, I must rush to the defense of the administrators who are caught up in this pressure. This defense is not an apology, nor an attempt to whitewash poor planning. Perhaps by noting the influences that tend to limit the vision of administrators, we can better see how to manage the future by overcoming these limitations.

Dr. Eurich is perfectly right when he says that "no college or university can set forth its goals in . . . windy and unexceptional generalities." True! But are we sure of the future? What do we use as a crystal ball to see what (or if) the world will be? We can easily set goals for our institutions to meet the needs of the future as we would like to see it. But can we be sure of setting goals for a nebulous future, a future buffeted by overpopulation, by the threat of nuclear war, by the great unknown of a fantastic technology, by the limitations of the nature of man that make the elimination of violence and prejudice so difficult? We cannot be sure and therefore find comfort in hiding behind the security of vagueness in setting goals for the unknown.

Dr. Eurich urges institutions to recognize their own limitations in setting goals. This, too, is easier said than done. It is an important warning that often is not heeded because of pressures from the power structure that both subtly and openly controls higher education. We live in an era of comparisons, an age of grants and special programs. It takes great courage to face a board, a public budget agency, a strong alumni group, or a public body which measures you by the number of grants or special programs you have developed and to refuse grants or programs that do not fit your view of the institution's goals.

These same publics must be accounted to when the goals require funds that are not readily available through grants or special programs. The academic community can well set goals that are "specific enough to indicate the action required and the programs needed." Master plans can be developed in great detail and with much academic foresight. They can even be planned to "change as rapidly and as fundamentally as do the needs of man and the society to which the institutions are supposedly responsive." But will the financial structure behind the institution be able to meet these goals? Often, administrators are forced to compromise goals and adjust master plans to accord with financial limitations rather than academic evaluations.

The proposal for a mechanism for discerning and expressing appropriate objectives is well stated. Dr. Eurich is right; if goals are to be realized, all important elements of the college must participate: trustees, administration, faculty, students, ancillary staff, constituents, alumni, community, and cooperating institutions. I am not sure, however, that his mechanism for bringing these elements together will create the kinds of goals he expects of the institution. An institutionwide committee on goals is fine in theory. It even exists at many institutions now. However, such committees have produced the high-sounding generalities we find in most college catalogues today, including my own. These committees have been subjected to the same uncertainties about the future, the same financial restrictions of the present, as have the presidents and administrators who set goals for their institutions. In the long run, the financial control of the institution (especially in public colleges) sets the goals and controls the future. Leadership is certainly needed to mobilize the academic forces in order to convince the financial control of the needs and goals of an institution, but that leadership will have to be forceful, direct, and perhaps even a bit dictatorial.

Dr. Eurich's discussion of "The Process of Instruction" was clearly put. He is shocked by college teaching as currently organized. He believes it to be inefficient and unimaginative. I agree! This point relates to one of our great weaknesses in planning for the future. We build for 1980 in 1968 with minds developed in the 1930s and 1940s under a system that goes back several centuries. Add to this a financial structure that is cumbersome, unrealistic, and obsolete. Is it any wonder we are having problems?

Despite the great technological advances in education, college teaching in general has been slow to adapt to new ways. As Eurich puts it: "our chief means of conveying information in college instruction is still the human larynx." This comment is true, but I hope we do not confuse the learning of facts with the development of attitudes and values. The former can best be done by the "new technology," leaving college professors free to concentrate on the latter. Students can learn facts by various means better than through our traditional patterns. Different students learn different things in different ways. The new technology provides means whereby each student may be helped and guided as an individual. However, values are not learned from a machine nor in a vacuum. Values must come from the interaction of young and old, students and professors, humans with other humans. We must insist, as Nevitt

Sanford has put it, that any discipline have a core that embodies a set of attitudes and values and not just an array of subject matter. This combination points to the true value of the new technology in the process of instruction—the freeing of the faculty to meet with the students on a high level of intellectual interaction, minus the drudgery of learning by rote. Dr. Eurich is quite right. Modern teaching tools *can* liberate the student and professor from conventional instruction, rather than dehumanize them. As administrators, we must assure both faculty and students that our acceptance of the new technology is made in this context only, not as another administrative ruse to save money or squeeze more students into our overcrowded campuses.

I part company with Dr. Eurich when he suggests that modern technology be used to bring education to the students rather than relying exclusively on bringing students to the campus. This, I fear, is going overboard. Again, I agree that "facts" can be learned this way. "Attitudes and values," however, cannot be learned in our own little cubicles or from an electronic monster at home. Attitudes and values develop only when the edge of one's intellect is honed against that of other human beings.

Perhaps "parting company" is too strong a term, because Dr. Eurich's point does make sense, despite my fear that it goes too far. I prefer a combination. Bring education to the students wherever they are, but bring the students to the campus, as well, for intellectual stimulation. Who says that a college education need be 128 credits of highly structured courses taken over a four-year (barring failures) period in residence at a physical facility known as a college campus? Why not include some home study to fortify the student with the vast accumulation of knowledge in this world? Why not include some residency at a campus to hone the edge of intellect so that the accumulation of knowledge can be viewed in the perspective of attitudes and values for the peaceful development of mankind? Why not include some travel to make us aware of what is going on in this world, to divert us from the parochialism that can lead to continuing world turmoil? Why not include some work experience to help apply the knowledge and attitudes to the economic well-being of both individual and society? Why not make higher education more like *life* or—to use the current vernacular—more like it is, man!

This blending of the new technology with the old student-professor relationships, plus a dash of broadening world travel and a portion of practical work-experience may seem a utopian view of the future direction of higher education. However, I would like to conclude with a prophetic statement made by John R. Platt in *The Step to Man:* "The world has become too dangerous for anything less than utopia."

Management, A Dirty Word

THEODORE M. HESBURGH, C.S.C.

Dr. Eurich's paper achieves the difficult blend of academic wisdom and practical ways and means that one has come to expect of its author over the years. There is a sense of quiet urgency about his theme of planning for the future, but it is urgent all the same. I almost expected him to say a few words about a circular philosophy of history that characterizes cultures other than our own: the view which holds that one just lives a life of reasonably calm frustration, day by day, expecting history to come full circle from age to age, without any hope of doing very much about it.

We in the West simply cannot live that way. We have accepted, as a style of life, that we make history every day, that we can control in some fashion almost everything except possibly the weather and young people. But too often our efforts have been characterized by "The Housewife's Principle." We spend all too much time immersed in the present, hopeful and vague about the future.

Part of the problem, I believe, is that so many academic administrators have come to their jobs with only the vaguest kind of preparation and, as a consequence, have spent all too many years learning how to administer the institution on a day-to-day basis, leaving little time to plan the march ahead.

I had been on the job eight years when, in 1960, James Armsey of the Ford Foundation's Special Program invited us to give him a ten-year projection of Notre Dame with dollar signs attached. Apart from the money that was forthcoming to project dreams into reality, that exercise in planning for the future was the most important factor in my education during all these years. For once, we had to take a *total* look at the university, to assess all of its strengths and weaknesses, to focus on verifiable facts as distinct from academic rhetoric, to say not only where we wanted to go, but also why, and in what measure, and with what means, and—most important—where the personnel and the financial resources would come from. We had to make hard choices, take real risks, and then sell the whole package to our whole constituency as well as to the Ford Foundation.

Looking back on that exercise now, and pondering what has happened since and, especially, what Alvin Eurich has specified as the inescapable present task for all of us, I can only say that the past was an elementary prelude to a much more demanding present and future.

As Dr. Eurich puts it so nicely toward the end of his paper: "At the root of the problem of Managing the Future is the management of *management* in American higher learning." And the stake is nothing less than survival. "Management" may be a dirty word to many faculty and students, but without it the whole educational enterprise becomes an exercise in growing frustration. A badly managed university is a monumental and shameful waste of human talent, not to mention other scarce resources.

I can only underline from my own experience a few of the most important points that Dr. Eurich has mentioned:

1. Good administration begins with good institutional goals, individualized for the particular institution by the total community involved. The president can exercise some leadership in achieving these goals, but they must be accepted and expressed by the total community; otherwise, the president is talking to himself. I believe also that these goals must represent real and attainable values, consonant with the tradition, resources, and valid hopes of the particular institution.

2. The functions of planning and development must be institutionalized *within* the university. All available assistance can be sought from outside resources, but ultimately each academic community must do its own planning, with its own staff, on its own terms. This enterprise requires a continual, competent, and intense effort; it must be headed by the most efficient team possible, with all the intellectual and creative resources of the institution behind them and with the president convinced that if they fail, he fails in his most important task.

3. Let there be no mistake about the intrinsic difficulty of planning, the complicated set of facts and circumstances surrounding it, not the least of which is the largely unknown future. Because of this difficulty, planning and development must be a total effort of the institution, geared always to the values and goals for which the institution professes to exist. Institutional structures are means to an end and can be continually revised to reach that end more effectively. Budgets, finances, computers, controls, information gathering and communications, chan-

nels for decisions, committees, and all the rest are means to an end. If the goals are fuzzy, if the personal human values are lost amid the planning paraphernalia, then all these become means leading nowhere, now or ever.

Impending and Profound Changes
THEODORE WALLER

DR. EURICH's suggestion that survival problems of the modern university be dealt with in part through the application of modern management and planning techniques and the full utilization of educational technology is timely and relevant. It seems clear that in searching for new patterns of leadership, one must not only define the qualities of the university administrator of the future but also give attention to the need for radical redefinition of the divisions of labor among administration, governing bodies, students, faculty, and other groups involved.

Dr. Eurich speaks of means of generating planning expertise. It might be appropriate here also to discuss the urgent need to develop a cadre of professional university administrators, partly through well-financed and thoroughly planned in-service training programs and partly by a concentrated, urgent effort to develop an interdisciplinary curriculum designed to train the university administrator. Clearly, we are beyond the point where we can afford to depend exclusively on other disciplines for leadership in higher education—any more than the Foreign Service could afford to depend wholly on political appointees for senior ambassadorial posts.

As Dr. Eurich suggests, making educational technology available to the college and university is the first small, relatively easy step. The larger and more difficult matter is to persuade and train the most productive members of the faculty to utilize the technology, to program the machines, to deal with the economics of this programming. The management of innovation in elementary and secondary schools has proved far more difficult than the innovators originally expected. The key, of course, in the elementary and secondary school is the classroom teacher and in the college and university it is the professor. The quality and character of the educational program will not improve any more surely because of the mere availability of technology than it improves when class size is reduced. The ablest professors will have to become committed and then discover how to utilize the technology fully and creatively. Above all, if the educational technologists rush forward to fill a vacuum created by the reluctance of the professors and if they acquire, even temporarily, an influence over the content of teaching out of proportion to their own intellectual skills and competence, deterioration is certain.

Dr. Eurich, in these connections, makes occasional mention of books. Surely he will agree that whatever increments of progress technology may produce, the efficiency and quality of education can be immediately and profoundly enhanced by fuller, more meaningful utilization of more adequate library resources.

Throughout, the highest priority in planning must be given to adjusting the policy and the character of the university to impending and profound changes in our society and our politics. The slogans of academic freedom need to be examined and modernized. The pressures and tensions will be such that the tradition of academic freedom alone cannot be expected to protect the scholarly community henceforth. No challenge would seem to be more important than the problem of finding how to protect and adapt the free university to the complex and tortuous times just ahead. In the 1970s, the old concepts of academic and intellectual freedom are unlikely to be any more serviceable than are the forms of liberalism developed in the 1930s. The university community must plan for freedom if freedom in the university and in the society is to survive.

Restructuring the Relationships

FRANKLIN PATTERSON

ALVIN EURICH reminds us that Whitehead said it is the business of the future to be dangerous. If the present—which Whitehead beautifully described as the vivid fringe of memory tinged with anticipation—provides us any reliable clues, the future seems likely to live up to its assigned business, at least in higher education. With hazards ahead, Mr. Eurich seeks to give us courage, in the sense defined by Plato as wisdom in the face of danger. At least that is how I read his "practical suggestions": wisdom operationally specified to help us meet and maybe even manage the future. One must be generally grateful for the imaginativeness and soundness of Mr. Eurich's suggestions, even while not being sanguine that they will wholly suffice to minimize the evil and increase the good in whatever lies ahead—no set of suggestions could do that.

My own comments will add a bit about the need for planning and development in admissions, scholarships, and financial aid. Mr. Eurich says that he sees little evidence of planning ahead "for the multitude of youngsters from the inner-city black communities who must and will be brought into the main stream of higher education in the next five years if we are to avoid social disaster." In this connection and in view of other developing changes in the students of the future, he makes several suggestions about upgrading plans and programs for admissions and scholarship aid, and I agree with these suggestions as far as they go. Unfortunately, I think his suggestions in this regard do not go far enough nor are they bold enough to give us a badly needed new stance from which creative management can proceed effectively, with the full social responsibility that the times increasingly demand of higher education.

Let me be specific about the line of action Hampshire College is pursuing in the responsibility we feel the present and future put upon us in responding to needs of potential students who are not now adequately reached by higher education. Possibly our line of action may have some attractive practicality for other institutions.

In planning the development and operation of Hampshire College, we are—among other things—concerned with the *very early* identification and encouragement of able but disadvantaged boys and girls who can benefit from higher education. Ordinarily, colleges seriously consider students for admission only when they are in their last years of high school, and are then dealing with middle-class youth whose families have encouraged (some, indeed, pushed) them toward college. The encouragement usually begins before the child is aware of it, and "preparation for college" is simply an implicit assumption of the family environment. The middle-class child realizes early both that he is expected to go to college and that, one way or another, it will be possible. In a real sense, the family *guarantees* college for him, culturally and financially.

Quite the opposite is true of many very able children in lower-income families. Young Negro boys in low-income families or urban and rural slums, for example, are likely to have no such expectation or encouragement, regardless of their ability. Often, as in the Boston schools, their academic performance falls steadily during elementary school, reflecting school, familial, and societal failure to support their intellectual growth.

Thomas Pettigrew of Harvard has commented to me in discussion of this that, by the age of ten, "most Negro boys know what the score is in school and know it's not for them." Professor Pettigrew means that Negro boys, by the end of the fifth grade or so, often have concluded that school really doesn't want them, and that they in turn do not want school.

The result at minimum is psychological withdrawal from any but apathetic involvement with school. In many cases apathy shifts to hostility, hostility is expressed in antisocial behavior, and the behavior leads to "dropping out" or being dropped out. This happens to many very bright Negro boys of low-income families, as well as many more who have less ability. The phenomenon is, of course, not limited to a single race, although in the case of Negro children of low-income background, the factor of poverty is complicated by that of racial discrimination. The upshot is that, by the time the last year of secondary school arrives, the boy is either not in school at all or, if he is still there, he is so ill-prepared and diffusely motivated that college is a poor bet for him if it is a bet at all.

Thus far, colleges for the most part have tried salvage operations with such youth only after the twelfth grade, or, at the earliest, a year or so before. Hampshire is certain that this type of operation can work for some disadvantaged students, but that it is far too late for many others.

We are, therefore, beginning now, as we move into the future, to identify a small number of high-potential, economically disadvantaged children in their tenth year of life, and we are guaranteeing their parents that their children will have full scholarships at Hampshire, *if* the children proceed through the remainder of their schooling at an acceptable level. In addition to the financial incentive, the college will also supply children so identified with voluntary tutorial help by Hampshire students and staff during the seven years before their high school graduation.

We believe that such a program of very early incentive and encouragement will demonstrate the utility of a totally new approach to admissions for children of poverty. To wait until the senior year of high school is certainly to wait too long. We think some way needs to be devised, in cooperation with the public schools, so that higher education can make an effective link with Head Start and with the early years of elementary school education.

This innovation means much more than strengthening the manpower and skill of admissions services. It means, indeed, reconceiving relationships between the college and the urban community and restructuring the relationships among the functions of admissions, student and faculty social service, and the instructional nature of the institution.

The reconstruction—briefly described here—does not have the dramatic impact of the instant talent search or the instant retraining program aimed at late-adolescent disadvantaged students who ought to be in college. Instead, it is a long-range commitment which, it is hoped, will produce long-range payoff. Part of our response to the future is to recognize that short-changing disadvantaged boys and girls begins early in their lives. If, then, the colleges are to respond effectively, it is necessary to plan and operate on a much more long-range basis than that to which we have been accustomed.

JOHN CAFFREY

Predictions for Higher Education in the 1970s

ORACLES OF EARLIER TIMES sought to forecast the future with a variety of occult aids to supplement wisdom. They examined the entrails of sacrificed animals, studied the flights of birds, examined the patterns of drifting smoke or of clouds, inhaled vapors of the earth, or peered into crystal orbs. Modern prophecy or conjecture uses more sophisticated approaches, such as statistical projections, computerized models, "probabilistically" hedged forecasts, and opinion polls.

Speculation about probable futures is more or less "idle" depending on how well informed are those whose opinions are solicited. If the general public is asked for opinions about who will be elected to office, it is assumed that responses to questions reflect voter preferences and intentions. However, in subject areas involving complex or special-interest factors and considerations, the opinions of experts and of those closely involved in the area are of greater significance than opinions of the general public.

In announcing "The Future Academic Community" as the theme for its 1968 Annual Meeting, the American Council on Education drew attention not only to the need for studies of the future environment to which higher education must relate but also to the need for the leadership of colleges and universities to engage in long-range planning. Our view of What Will Happen both influences and is expressed by the policies and objectives we formulate.

Barring catastrophes (thermonuclear war, extraterrestrial collision) and major social revolutions, we can make actuarially sound statements about population numbers and life expectancy of age groups, supply and demand factors affecting life support systems and natural resources, and the probable geographical distribution of the world's peoples.

For a larger class of variables we can make predictions that are less

261

reliable but with probabilities considerably greater than zero. It seems highly probable, for example, that by 2000 A.D. man will have reached the moon, will be mining and farming in the ocean, will have generated still higher mountains of information and questionnaires, will have conquered most major diseases except the common cold, and will probably have a still longer record of bloody wars of varying magnitude all over the globe.

We can safely predict that technology will continue to deliver its mixed bag of blessings and dilemmas, most of them on the positive side of balance; that drugs, alcohol, and narcotics will influence the lives and behavior of still larger numbers of people, sometimes as a matter of policy; that in affluent societies the former work of the lower-skilled and less-able will have been extensively automated; that the average man will live longer and spend less of his life working and more of his life learning and relearning—and in leisure; that the dividing lines between institutions of learning and the rest of society's systems and institutions will have been extensively eroded; that local and international transportation will be increasingly cheap, rapid, and widespread; that man's pollution of both the lithosphere and the atmosphere will have been controlled (if we are to survive); and that some of the children born in the 1960s will in the year 2000 be members of college faculties, with salaries too frightening even for speculation by the AAUP.

The very fact of a large class of variables about which prediction is extremely risky means that we will still have to educate the young to adapt, to think, to vanquish the unknown, to take care of themselves, and to invent new wonders. We cannot with any confidence predict birth rates, the dates of significant inventions and breakthroughs in science, the real usefulness of reaching the moon, the evolution of new benevolent or harmful forms of life, the endless aberrations of the human mind or soul, or the length of women's skirts, if any.

It is generally safer to predict problems than to predict their solutions. The struggle for survival, requiring both "Continuity and Change," will continue to be man's oldest and toughest problem, though it has taken on new forms in our time. The survival of life itself is threatened by civil disorder, overpopulation, air and water pollution, and the constant menace of thermonuclear extermination—a menace that since World War II has become a fixed condition of life. The quality of life itself is threatened by the boredom that unused leisure generates and by the menaces to sanity inherent in social strife, the collapse of once-comforting value systems, the pressures of overcrowding, speed, noise, and emotional strain, and the frustration of too much for most men to know, even about their own specialties and professions.

A major purpose of this year's annual conference is to sample presumably informed speculations about our future environment. We must try to see what higher education must or will probably contribute both to the struggle for survival and to the very quality of man's life which makes the struggle seem worthwhile.

In analyzing predictions, it is important to distinguish between what one thinks *will* happen and what one thinks *should* happen. This distinction is not always clear in opinion polls. Thus, if one asks me who I think will win an election, I may name X, but if I were asked who I think *ought* to win I might name Y. Both questions elicit "subjective" responses, but both responses reveal something of interest. The fact that one thinks an event *will* happen, with a specified degree of probability, presumably reflects his understanding of the factors which will determine the event. What one thinks *should* happen presumably reflects his value judgments or his objectives.

Predictions are only guesses. Informed guessing, however, elicits two useful kinds of information. It reveals something about the technical basis upon which both policy and management decisions may be made. After all, most policy decisions reflect estimates of their probable consequences. Second, predictions of probabilities and ratings of desirabilities may be either dissonant or consonant. Thus if a given event is generally believed to be highly probable *and* highly desirable, the implications for policy decisions are quite different from those arising from judgments that an event is highly probable and very undesirable.

Nature of the Survey

The present study, limited to the field of higher education in the United States, is concerned with the probability and desirability of a set of hypothetical events, conditions, or developments in the decade 1968–78. The opinions and ratings of five groups were solicited: Institutional members of the American Council on Education, other members of the Council (associations and organizations, for the most part), members of governing boards, and faculty and student leaders.

The 35 "events" were selected to reflect concerns with such issues or

HYPOTHETICAL EVENTS OR

P 1. The proportion of students enrolled in *private* institutions of higher education will decline at an even faster rate.

F 2. Significantly more Federal and state funds will go directly to students, as scholarships or loans.

S 3. State-wide coordinating councils will have increasing influence over public colleges and universities.

S 4. Separate colleges for men and women will, largely through merger, virtually disappear.

F 5. The Federal government will give more and larger general support grants to states as intermediaries for distribution to colleges and universities.

C 6. TV, computers, and other machines will significantly displace human instructors at the undergraduate level.

F 7. By 1978, the Federal government will meet upwards of 60 percent of the instructional costs of private and public higher education in the United States.

F 8. Use of the project-proposal, subject to panel reviews by peers, will increase as a means of allocating general Federal support to colleges and universities.

P 9. The great majority of high school graduates will take at least two years of instruction after high school.

C 10. Undergraduate curricula will undergo major revisions (e.g., along multidisciplinary lines).

O 11. Of all persons receiving earned doctorates in the 1970s, a steadily increasing proportion will be employed by business, industry, and government.

O 12. More than half of all four-year graduates will begin work on a graduate or professional degree.

F 13. The *proportion* of tax-dollar support of higher education will level off as a result of competitive demands from welfare and public improvement programs (e.g., health, air and water pollution).

C 14. Breakthroughs in understanding the human learning process will lead to major improvements in instructional methods at the college level.

S 15. New colleges and universities (or branches) will continue to be established at the current rate of about forty per year.

S 16. By 1978, higher education in general will be centrally planned and coordinated on some nationwide basis.

G 17. An increasing proportion of administrative personnel, other than business officers, will be recruited from nonacademic sources (e.g., business, government).

DEVELOPMENTS IN THE 1970S

P 18. Standards for admission and graduation will continue to rise in highly selective institutions.

F 19. Formulas will increasingly be used to determine levels of state and Federal support for various academic programs.

S 20. As a corollary of tax-dollar support, government agencies will have increasing influence over private colleges and universities.

F 21. Support from all sources for the humanities and social sciences will be as great as for the natural sciences.

C 22. The need to expand access to higher education for the economically disadvantaged will result in some lowering of standards in the higher education system as a whole.

G 23. Students will serve as voting members on most important academic committees on the typical campus.

C 24. In most undergraduate curricula, the number of required courses will decline to permit more electives and individualized programs.

G 25. Faculty participation in major aspects of academic governance will become a widely adopted practice.

E 26. Average faculty salaries will continue to increase somewhat faster than the general cost of living.

G 27. College students will on an even wider scale use direct-action methods to assert their demands for changed conditions.

E 28. The average total cost *to the student* of attending more expensive undergraduate institutions will at least double by 1978, assuming no increase in the *rate* of inflation.

G 29. The authority of top administrators in making broad policy decisions will be significantly eroded or diffused.

C 30. Academic credit will be given by most institutions for student experience (work, service) in the nonacademic community.

G 31. In most colleges and universities, faculty will have at least as much a part as the trustees in the process of selecting a president.

F 32. Most states will provide some tax support for private colleges and universities.

G 33. *In loco parentis* will be much less important than responsibility for self-regulation as a basis for codes of nonacademic student affairs and conduct.

G 34. Collective bargaining will become widely adopted as a method of determining faculty salaries and conditions of employment.

E 35. Colleges and universities will gradually allocate more of their resources to action programs designed to solve interracial and other social problems.

problems as the following: The nature and distribution of the student population (P), Federal and other financial support (F), curriculum and instruction (C), graduate output and its distribution (O), modes of internal governance (G), the general structure of higher education (S), and socioeconomic factors (E). In some cases, an event may fall in more than one of these categories. The events to which respondents were asked to assign ratings of "probability" and "desirability" are listed on pages 264–65. Each is coded to show its main classification in the above-mentioned list of substantive concerns.

Respondents were asked to make their ratings according to the "General Directions," shown below:

GENERAL DIRECTIONS

The accompanying questionnaire presents a list of hypothetical events or conditions. For each of these, you are asked to indicate how likely (or unlikely) you personally think it is that such an event *will occur* within the 1970s and then to indicate your attitude or feeling about the *desirability* of each event.

1. The "Probability" scale runs from "Almost Certain" to "Highly Improbable." To help define these terms, we have attached approximate probabilities, as shown below. These reactions should indicate your best guess about likelihoods, regardless of whether you approve or disagree with the event or development.
2. The "Desirability" scale, which implies varying degrees of necessity, benefit, or detriment, calls for your more subjective personal reactions. Note that there is no middle position; if you feel the event is *neither favorable nor unfavorable*, or that "desirability" is not relevant, *do not mark any of the four*.

"Probability" Scale	Approximate Probability	"Desirability" Scale
ALMOST CERTAIN =	95% or better	ESSENTIAL
VERY LIKELY =	65–95%	
APPROXIMATELY = EVEN CHANCE	35–65%	DESIRABLE
NOT VERY LIKELY =	5–35%	UNDESIRABLE
HIGHLY ≈ IMPROBABLE	5% or less	DETRIMENTAL

Note: For purposes of this survey, please make the arbitrary assumption that the war in Vietnam will have ended or be reduced in scale by 1970.

An optically processed answer sheet was used to facilitate tallying and analysis.

The survey forms were mailed May 8–9, 1968, to members of the Council, to American Association of University Professor chapter heads, to a list of National Student Association leaders, and to principal members of the Association of Governing Boards of Colleges and Universities. Respondents were asked to return the response sheets by May 24, 1968. Slow returns prompted a follow-up reminder mailing to two of these groups. The number of survey forms mailed, and the number and percentage of usable returns received by June 4, 1968 are shown in Table 1.

TABLE 1: *The Survey Population and the Response*

Respondent Group	Mailed	Usable Returns	
		Number	Percent
ACE Institutional members........	1,300	837	64.3
Other ACE members.............	200	117	58.5
AAUP.........................	1,129	636	56.3
NSA..........................	1,055	322	30.5
AGB..........................	330	128	38.7
Total......................	4,014	2,040	50.8

The survey forms were accompanied by a covering letter from the respective principal executive of each of the four organizations. The letter stressed that the results of the survey would not be used to determine the policies or programs of those organizations and that they would be used solely as a basis for discussion about probable trends in higher education.

Caution: The small proportion of returns from students and trustees, even after a follow-up note was mailed, makes it dangerous to draw any firm conclusions from the responses of these groups. The head of each governing board in the sample was sent two copies of the survey; he was requested to complete one himself and to ask the secretary of the board to complete the other. It may be, then, that the trustee sample, through small, is more representative than might at first appear. In any case, the reports from these two groups should be interpreted as statistically biased.

Ranking of Events

Table 2 shows, for each of the 35 events, the probability and desirability rankings given by each of the five groups of respondents.

TABLE 2: *Ranked Mean Ratings on Probability and Desirability by Five Respondent Groups*

Event No.	Group I Prob	Group I Desir	Group O Prob	Group O Desir	Group F Prob	Group F Desir	Group S Prob	Group S Desir	Group T Prob	Group T Desir
1	5	31	5	30	3	31	10	31	9	32
2	6	4	7	8.5	5	6	12	8	5	5
3	4	14	4	15	8	25	25	30	10	21
4	15	21	20	16	10	16	9	18	16	23
5	11	11	23	20	21	20	20	19	15	10
6	35	34	35	33	33	34	32	33	35	28
7	32	18	32	23	27	19	29	20	33	24
8	26	22	31	25	20	22	23	21	23	19
9	1	2	1	2	1	9	1	5	1	2
10	9	3	9	3	12	5	5	2	8	3
11	8	24	6	17	4	21	6	22	2	7
12	18	10	16.5	13	16	14	14	17	20	9
13	29	27	29	27	30	27	31	29	29	26
14	27	1	28	1	32	4	27	4	21	1
15	24	16	16.5	7	22	15	16	15	19	8
16	34	30	34	31.5	34	32	35	32	34	29
17	31	25	26	19	26	28	28	26	28	12
18	13	23	14	24	6	17.5	4	23	3	13
19	7	15	8	18	9	23	15	28	6	18
20	16	33	13	31.5	15	35	21	35	11	34
21	33	5	33	4	35	8	34	13	32	4
22	23	26	24	26	25	29	33	27	17	27
23	12	17	11.5	21	17	17.5	7	1	22	25
24	10	9	15	10	18	12	13	9	13	16
25	3	8	3	6	7	1	8	7	4	11
26	19	7	25	5	24	2	26	10	24	15
27	21	35	21	35	11	30	3	25	14	35
28	22	29	22	34	14	33	22	34	25	30
29	20	28	19	28	23	13	17	16	26	31
30	30	20	30	22	31	24	18	11	31	20
31	25	19	18	14	29	3	30	12	27	22
32	14	6	11.5	8.5	19	11	19	14	18	6
33	2	12	2	12	2	7	2	3	7	17
34	28	32	27	29	28	26	24	24	30	33
35	17	13	10	11	13	10	11	6	12	14

Key to Group Code:
I = ACE Institutional members
O = Other ACE members
F = AAUP
S = NSA
T = AGB

Note: See pages 264–65 for a list of "Events."

(*Reminder:* The number of responses obtained from the student and trustee samples is too small to warrant much confidence in the data. The rankings are included in this case because of the many striking agreements and disagreements with other groups.) For example, Group I (ACE Institutional member administrators) ranked Event #1 as fifth in probability (four other events were rated as more probable) and as thirty-first in desirability (only four other events were rated as less desirable).

The most interesting comparisons are among the top and bottom ten events on both scales. Table 3 shows the probability and desirability ranks for the ten events rated most probable and most desirable by the Institutional member respondents and then the rankings assigned by the other four groups. For example, all five groups ranked Event #9 ("The great majority of high school graduates will take at least two years of instruction after high school") as mostly highly probable. Institutional and other members of the Council and trustees agreed that Event #14 ("Breakthroughs in understanding the human learning

TABLE 3: *Events Ranked as the Top Ten in Probability or Desirability*
by Institutional Administrators,
Compared with Four Other Respondent Groups

Ranked Probability Ratings						Ranked Desirability Ratings					
		Groups						Groups			
Event [a]	I	O	F	S	T	Event [a]	I	O	F	S	T
9	1	1	1	1	1	14	1	1	4	4	1
33	2	2	2	2	7	9	2	2	9	5	2
25	3	3	7	8	4	10	3	3	5	2	3
3	4	4	8	25	10	2	4	8.5	6	8	5
1	5	5	3	10	9	21	5	4	8	13	4
2	6	7	5	12	5	32	6	8.5	11	14	6
19	7	8	9	15	6	26	7	5	2	10	15
11	8	6	4	6	2	25	8	6	1	7	11
10	9	9	12	5	8	24	9	10	12	9	16
24	10	15	18	13	13	12	10	13	14	17	9

[a] Average (mean) ratings were used to establish ranks.

Key to Group Code:
I = ACE Institutional members
O = Other ACE members
F = AAUP
S = NSA
T = AGB

Note: See p. 270 for a list of "Events."

"EVENTS" LISTED IN TABLE 3

Events Ranked as the Top Ten in Probability:

9. The great majority of high school graduates will take at least two years of instruction after high school.

33. *In loco parentis* will be much less important than responsibility for self-regulation as a basis for codes of nonacademic student affairs and conduct.

25. Faculty participation in major aspects of academic governance will become a widely adopted practice.

3. State-wide coordinating councils will have increasing influence over public colleges and universities.

1. The proportion of students enrolled in *private* institutions of higher education will decline at an even faster rate.

2. Significantly more Federal and state funds will go directly to students, as scholarships or loans.

19. Formulas will increasingly be used to determine levels of state and Federal support for various academic programs.

11. Of all persons receiving earned doctorates in the 1970s, a steadily increasing proportion will be employed by business, industry, and government.

10. Undergraduate curricula will undergo major revisions (e.g., along multidisciplinary lines).

24. In most undergraduate curricula, the number of required courses will decline to permit more electives and individualized programs.

Events Ranked as the Top Ten in Desirability:

14. Breakthroughs in understanding the human learning process will lead to major improvements in instructional methods at the college level.

9. The great majority of high school graduates will take at least two years of instruction after high school.

10. Undergraduate curricula will undergo major revisions (e.g., along multidisciplinary lines).

2. Significantly more Federal and state funds will go directly to students, as scholarships or loans.

21. Support from all sources for the humanities and social sciences will be as great as for the natural sciences.

32. Most states will provide some tax support for private colleges and universities.

26. Average faculty salaries will continue to increase somewhat faster than the general cost of living.

25. Faculty participation in major aspects of academic governance will become a widely adopted practice.

24. In most undergraduate curricula, the number of required courses will decline to permit more electives and individualized programs.

12. More than half of all four-year graduates will begin work on a graduate or professional degree.

process will lead to major improvements . . . . .") is most highly desirable, while faculty and student respondents agreed on assigning this event fourth rank. Faculty respondents assign the highest desirability to Event #25 (faculty participation in governance), while students do not assign desirability rank 1 to any of the events rated as the top ten by administrators!

Table 4 is similar to Table 3 but shows the bottom ten events as ranked on both probability and desirability by institutional member administrators, together with the ranks assigned by the other four groups. It does not require a correlation coefficient to show that all five groups are in much more substantial agreement about low probabilities and desirabilities than about high ones. Among the probability ratings, Event #30 (credit for experience) provokes the strongest disagreement (by student respondents). On the desirability side, Event #29 (erosion of administrative authority) provokes the only striking disagreement (on the part of faculty and students). On both probability and desirability, Event #13 (tax-dollar support) received strik-

TABLE 4: *Events Ranked as the Bottom Ten in Probability or Desirability by Institutional Administrators, Compared with Four Other Respondent Groups*

	Ranked Probability Ratings						Ranked Desirability Ratings				
		Groups						Groups			
Event ª	I	O	F	S	T	Event ª	I	O	F	S	T
8	26	31	20	23	23	22	26	26	29	27	27
14	27	28	32	27	21	13	27	27	27	29	26
34	28	27	28	24	30	29	28	28	13	16	31
13	29	29	30	31	29	28	29	34	33	34	30
30	30	30	31	18	31	16	30	31.5	32	32	29
17	31	26	26	28	28	1	31	30	31	31	32
7	32	32	27	29	33	34	32	29	26	24	33
21	33	33	35	34	32	20	33	31.5	35	35	34
16	34	34	34	35	34	6	34	33	34	33	28
6	35	35	33	32	35	27	35	35	30	25	35

ª Average (mean) ratings were used to establish ranks.

Key to Group Code:
I   = ACE Institutional members
O = Other ACE members
F = AAUP
S = NSA
T = AGB

Note: See p. 272 for a list of "Events."

"EVENTS" LISTED IN TABLE 4

Events Ranked as the Bottom Ten in Probability

8. Use of the project-proposal, subject to panel reviews by peers, will increase as a means of allocating general Federal support to colleges and universities.

14. Breakthroughs in understanding the human learning process will lead to major improvements in instructional methods at the college level.

34. Collective bargaining will become widely adopted as a method of determining faculty salaries and conditions of employment.

13. The *proportion* of tax-dollar support of higher education will level off as a result of competitive demands from welfare and public improvement programs (e.g., health, air and water pollution).

30. Academic credit will be given by most institutions for student experience (work, service) in the nonacademic community.

17. An increasing proportion of administrative personnel, other than business officers, will be recruited from nonacademic sources (e.g., business, government).

7. By 1978, the Federal government will meet upwards of 60 percent of the instructional costs of private and public higher education in the United States.

21. Support from all sources for the humanities and social sciences will be as great as for the natural sciences.

16. By 1978, higher education in general will be centrally planned and coordinated on some nationwide basis.

6. TV, computers, and other machines will significantly displace human instructors at the undergraduate level.

Events Ranked as the Bottom Ten in Desirability

22. The need to expand access to higher education for the economically disadvantaged will result in some lowering of standards in the higher education system as a whole.

13. The *proportion* of tax-dollar support of higher education will level off as a result of competitive demands from welfare and public improvement programs (e.g., health, air and water pollution).

29. The authority of top administrators in making broad policy decisions will be significantly eroded or diffused.

28. The average total cost *to the student* of attending more expensive undergraduate institutions will at least double by 1978, assuming no increase in the *rate* of inflation.

16. By 1978, higher education in general will be centrally planned and coordinated on some nationwide basis.

1. The proportion of students enrolled in *private* institutions of higher education will decline at an even faster rate.

34. Collective bargaining will become widely adopted as a method of determining faculty salaries and conditions of employment.

20. As a corollary of tax-dollar support, government agencies will have increasing influence over private colleges and universities.

6. TV, computers, and other machines will significantly displace human instructors at the undergraduate level.

27. College students will on an even wider scale use direct-action methods to assert their demands for changed conditions.

ingly similar ratings by all five groups, and Event #1 (proportion of students in private institutions), rated among the top ten in probability by all groups, receives very low and almost identical ranking in desirability.

Event #21 (support for the humanities), rated almost at the bottom by all groups as to probability, is rated among the top ten in desirability by all groups except students. Event #16 (central planning, nationwide), rated almost identically low in probability by all five groups, is also rated low, with almost equal agreement, in desirability.

Sampling the striking disagreements in Table 2, one notes the low probability given to Event #3 (influence of state coordinating councils) by students and guesses that this rating reflects lack of knowledge about the growth of coordinating councils.

Institutional administrators rank four events (9, 10, 24, 25) as among the top ten in both probability and desirability and another four events (6, 13, 16, 34) as among the bottom ten on both scales.

Though many items ranked low in desirability are (perhaps optimistically) also rated low in probability, this tendency to match expectation to evaluation is not uniform throughout the 35 events. *Rank-order correlations* between rankings of probability and desirability for all five groups are as follows:

I	(ACE Institutional members)	.40
O	(Other ACE members)	.37
F	(Faculty)	.14
S	(Students)	.43
T	(Trustees)	.36

Intergroup agreement about desirability is more interesting than agreement about probability. *Rank-order correlations* between all ten possible pairs of groups, on the desirability ratings only, are given here:

	O	F	S	T
I	.94	.84	.78	.86
O		.87	.78	.88
F			.87	.70
S				.63

One might infer (cautiously) from these figures that academic administrators and officers of other ACE members are in substantial agreement about what is desirable and undesirable. Indeed, the amount of agreement is surprisingly great. Faculty and students are in greater agreement with each other than either is with trustees. It may also be that the 35 events rated in this study did not touch on "controversial" matters sufficiently often to disclose any extensive disagreements.

The very high correlation (.94) between Institutional and other members of ACE may be interpreted as meaning that association heads are in close agreement with Institutional officers on the questions advanced in this survey. It is moderately surprising to see that both groups are also in substantial agreement with trustees *and* faculty, even though faculty and trustee responses are less highly correlated (.70) with each other.

The tables which follow indicate the percentage of persons in each of the respondent groups (excluding students and trustees) who rated each event both as to probability and as to desirability. From the tables, it is possible to see both the general ratings (marginal totals) and the joint ratings (the number of respondents who feel an event is highly probable *and* desirable, highly probable but not desirable, etc.). Thus in Table 5, line 1, column 1, among Institutional member respondents, 11 percent feel that Event #17 is almost certain or very likely *and* that it is undesirable; 29 percent give the same probability rating but feel the event is desirable or essential; in all, 40 percent of this group rated the event as almost certain or very likely.

The following discussion is intended to spotlight the high points of the tables and certainly does not exhaust the possibilities for analysis, comparison, or interpretation. The 35 events or developments are grouped by major subject or content emphasis rather than in the order in which they were presented in the survey instrument.

Governance

Eight of the events touched on aspects of governance. Some were more "controversial" than others, in the sense that the respondent groups differed in their ratings. There was often more disagreement about desirability than about likelihood. See Table 5 (pages 276–77).

Institutional member administrators, other ACE members, and faculty—even students—are in almost complete agreement about the probability that the authority of top administrators in policy decisions will be eroded (Event #29). Over half feel it is almost certain or very likely, and somewhat less than a third feel there is an even chance. However, this trend is regarded as undesirable or detrimental by more than eight out of ten administrators, whereas three out of four faculty respondents believe this is desirable or essential. About half of the administrators who feel this development is undesirable also feel it is almost certain or very likely to happen.

The possibility that more administrators will be recruited from non-academic sources (Event #17) is taken seriously by about four out of five respondents from all groups, and the agreement for each level of probability is extremely close, but there is considerable disagreement about desirability. Administrators disagree among themselves about this development. About one out of four feels that this development is both undesirable and unlikely, while about the same proportion feels exactly the opposite. About seven out of ten faculty respondents feel this development is undesirable or detrimental, while two out of three constituent and associated ("other") Council members feel it is desirable or essential. Administrators (like students) are roughly evenly split in their desirability ratings. (Trustees appear to feel very strongly that this development is desirable or essential.)

Regarding the increased participation of faculty in academic governance (Event #25), the respondent groups are very close in their agreement on the high desirability of the development. Faculty feel more strongly (99 percent) that it is highly desirable or essential, while more than eight out of ten administrative respondents agree. There is considerable disagreement amoung groups about probability, however. Fewer than half of the administrators who think it is very desirable think it is very likely to happen. Three out of four faculty (and students) feel this development is almost certain or very likely, and other ACE members feel even more certain, but no more than one out of three administrators agrees. Half the administrators give this development an "even chance" rating.

Understandably, faculty respondents are almost unanimous (96 percent) in rating as desirable or essential their greater participation in the selection of presidents (Event #31). Administrators are not so enthusiastic—about three out of five agree (and trustees are even cooler on this development). When it comes to probability, however, the respondent groups are in considerable agreement (even with students and trustees). About one out of four respondents in all groups feels that this development is unlikely or highly improbable, and a slightly larger number give it only an even chance. (With regard to many events in this study, respondents tended to regard highly probable events as quite desirable, and vice versa, but in this case fewer

MATERIALS RELATED TO TABLE 5

"Events" Related to Governance

17. An increasing proportion of administrative personnel, other than business officers, will be recruited from nonacademic sources (e.g., business, government).

23. Students will serve as voting members on most important academic committees on the typical campus.

25. Faculty participation in major aspects of academic governance will become a widely adopted practice.

27. College students will on an even wider scale use direct-action methods to assert their demands for changed conditions.

29. The authority of top administrators in making broad policy decisions will be significantly eroded or diffused.

31. In most colleges and universities, faculty will have at least as much a part as the trustees in the process of selecting a president.

33. *In loco parentis* will be much less important than responsibility for self-regulation as a basis for codes of nonacademic student affairs and conduct.

34. Collective bargaining will become widely adopted as a method of determining faculty salaries and conditions of employment.

Key to Desirability Code:
U = Undesirable or detrimental
D = Desirable or essential
T = Total probability rating

Key to Group Code:
I = ACE Institutional members
O = Other ACE members
F = AAUP

Note: Numbers in *italics* indicate how many respondents made a rating for the event on both probability *and* desirability.

TABLE 5: *Joint Responses to Items Concerning Governance*

(Percentage of Each Group Rating Each Event on Both Probability and Desirability)

Desirability Ratings for Each Numbered Event

Probability	Group	17 U	17 D	17 T	23 U	23 D	23 T	25 U	25 D	25 T	27 U	27 D	27 T	29 U	29 D	29 T	31 U	31 D	31 T	33 U	33 D	33 T	34 U	34 D	34 T
Almost Certain or Very Likely	I	11	29	40	9	54	63	2	35	37	49	4	53	42	15	57	7	40	47	17	71	88	32	7	39
	O	11	43	54	11	41	58	3	81	84	48	7	55	32	25	57	6	50	56	9	79	88	20	22	42
	F	27	21	48	7	51	58	1	74	75	15	50	65	7	48	55	0	42	42	5	82	87	12	27	39
Even Chance	I	18	14	32	16	11	27	7	42	49	34	1	35	27	2	29	13	15	28	6	4	10	39	2	41
	O	9	19	28	17	14	31	3	11	14	18	6	24	21	9	30	11	16	27	3	6	9	35	4	39
	F	23	7	30	11	13	24	0	18	18	9	17	26	7	17	24	1	28	29	3	8	11	23	13	36
Not Very Likely or Highly Improbable	I	25	3	28	9	1	10	6	8	14	12	0	12	14	0	14	19	6	25	1	1	2	20	0	20
	O	15	3	18	7	4	11	2	0	2	21	0	21	12	1	13	10	7	17	1	2	3	18	1	19
	F	19	3	22	12	6	18	0	7	7	4	5	9	9	12	21	3	26	29	1	1	2	21	4	25
Total Desirability Rating	I	54	46	767	34	66	797	15	85	799	95	5	801	83	17	795	39	61	788	24	76	798	91	9	803
	O	35	65	102	37	65	104	8	92	106	87	13	107	65	35	108	27	73	107	13	87	103	73	27	106
	F	69	31	570	30	70	597	1	99	609	28	72	568	23	77	569	4	96	612	9	91	592	56	44	571

than half of most respondent groups who feel that Development #31 is desirable feel it is very likely or almost certain.)

With regard to collective bargaining about faculty salaries (Event #34), there is high agreement among probabilities but considerable difference of opinion about desirabilities. About two out of five respondents in the administrative group, the other ACE members, and the faculty feel such bargaining is almost certain or very likely. About the same proportion of respondents in each group give this development an even chance. However, more than nine out of ten administrators feel this trend is undesirable or detrimental, about seven out of ten other ACE members agree, and more than half of the faculty agree. (Students are more approving of this development than are faculty, while trustees overwhelmingly disapprove.) Almost eight out of ten administrators who feel this development is undesirable also give it an even chance or better. There is a strong tendency for faculty respondents who feel collective bargaining is desirable to feel that it has an even chance or better, while a low probability is assigned by those faculty who make low desirability ratings.

That students will serve as voting members on important academic committees (Event #23) seems almost certain or very likely to about three out of five administrators, other members of the Council, and faculty. It may surprise some students to know that two out of three administrators—and a slightly higher proportion of faculty—believe this development is desirable or essential. (Over half of the trustee respondents disagree, while students, not surprisingly, almost unanimously approve.) Over half of both administrators and faculty feel this development is both highly desirable and highly probable.

The gradual substitution of responsibility for self-regulation instead of *in loco parentis* as a basis for codes of nonacademic student conduct (Event #33) seems highly probable to more than four out of five respondents in all five groups. More than nine out of ten faculty (and students) regard this as desirable or essential, while one out of four administrators disagrees.

The increased use by students of direct-action methods to assert their demands for changes in higher education (Event #27) is regarded as almost certain or very likely by a little more than half of administrators and other Council members and by two out of three faculty respondents. More than nine out of ten administrators, however, regard this possiblity as undesirable or detrimental, whereas seven out of ten faculty respondents take the opposite view. (Faculty are even more approving than are students!) About half of the administrators who feel this trend is undesirable or detrimental also feel, nonetheless, that it is highly likely to continue.

Curriculum and Educational Program

Seven of the events (6, 10, 14, 22, 24, 30, 35) touch on aspects of instructional and educational programs and objectives of higher education. See Table 6. Almost all respondents feel that the displacement of human instructors by TV, computers, or other devices (Event #6) is undesirable or detrimental, though 40 percent of faculty respondents feel that, no matter how undesirable this development is, it has an even chance or better of happening. It is interesting to note that more administrators (77 percent) give this development a low probability rating than do faculty respondents (60 percent).

The overwhelming majority of all three major groups feel that it is highly desirable or essential that undergraduate curricula should undergo major revisions (Event #10). About two out of three in all three groups also feel that this has a high probability of happening. One out of ten faculty respondents look upon this possibility as undesirable.

With regard to the possibility that major improvements in instruction will follow breakthroughs in understanding the learning process (Event #14), 98 or 99 percent of all three groups see this development as highly desirable. Faculty (43 percent) are more discouraged about the probability, however, than are administrators (25 percent) and other ACE members (27 percent).

The old question about the balance between required and elective courses does not provoke much difference of opinion among administrators of member institutions, other ACE members, and faculty. About four out of five respondents feel that it is highly desirable if the number of required courses declines in favor of more electives (Event #24). Those who see this as undesirable are about evenly split in their opinions about probabilities, while about two-thirds of all those who feel that this change is desirable also give it a high probability.

The idea of giving academic credit for nonacademic student experience (Event #30) provokes a mixed reaction. More than half of those who see this as undesirable also give the idea a low

MATERIALS RELATED TO TABLE 6

"Events" Related to Curriculum and the Educational Program:

6. TV, computers, and other machines will significantly displace human instructors at the undergraduate level.

10. Undergraduate curricula will undergo major revisions (e.g., along multidisciplinary lines).

14. Breakthroughs in understanding the human learning process will lead to major improvements in instructional methods at the college level.

22. The need to expand access to higher education for the economically disadvantaged will result in some lowering of standards in the higher education system as a whole.

24. In most undergraduate curricula, the number of required courses will decline to permit more electives and individualized programs.

30. Academic credit will be given by most institutions for student experience (work, service) in the nonacademic community.

35. Colleges and universities will gradually allocate more of their resources to action programs designed to solve interracial and other social problems.

Key to Desirability Code:
U = Undesirable or detrimental
D = Desirable or essential
T = Total probability rating

Key to Group Code:
I = ACE Institutional members
O = Other ACE members
F = AAUP

Note: Numbers in *italics* indicate how many respondents made a rating for the event on both probability *and* desirability.

TABLE 6: *Joint Responses to Items Concerning Curriculum and Educational Program*

(Percentage of Each Group Rating Each Event on Both Probability and Desirability)

Desirability Ratings for Each Numbered Event

Probability	Group	6 U	6 D	6 T	10 U	10 D	10 T	14 U	14 D	14 T	22 U	22 D	22 T	24 U	24 D	24 T	30 U	30 D	30 T	35 U	35 D	35 T
Almost Certain or Very Likely	I	5	3	8	1	69	70	0	43	43	28	23	51	5	63	68	3	36	39	9	54	63
	O	4	6	10	0	68	68	0	39	39	25	30	55	4	61	65	4	33	37	7	57	64
	F	11	6	17	2	62	64	0	29	29	32	15	47	7	50	57	8	26	34	7	57	64
Even Chance	I	13	2	15	2	21	23	0	32	32	24	6	30	8	15	23	15	20	35	14	13	27
	O	13	4	17	0	20	20	0	34	34	16	3	19	4	19	23	13	25	38	9	18	27
	F	19	4	23	3	19	22	0	28	28	22	7	29	8	20	28	14	19	33	7	20	27
Not Very Likely or Highly Improbable	I	73	4	77	2	5	7	1	24	25	17	2	19	4	5	9	21	5	26	9	1	10
	O	68	5	73	2	10	12	1	26	27	23	3	26	5	7	12	21	4	25	7	2	9
	F	58	2	60	5	9	14	2	41	43	20	4	24	6	9	15	25	8	33	5	4	9
Total Desirability Rating	I	91	9	*810*	5	95	*807*	1	99	*808*	69	31	*776*	17	83	*807*	39	61	*791*	32	68	*787*
	O	85	15	*107*	2	98	*106*	1	99	*105*	64	36	*98*	13	87	*104*	38	62	*106*	23	77	*105*
	F	88	12	*594*	10	90	*583*	2	98	*569*	74	26	*563*	21	79	*588*	47	53	*572*	19	81	*584*

281

probability rating, while half or more of those who rate this practice as highly desirable also give it an optimistic probability rating. Faculty are about evenly divided in their desirability ratings, while three out of five administrators and other ACE members favor the idea. Overall opinions about probabilities are about evenly divided from high to low, and the three groups differ very little in their opinions on this aspect.

The relationship between higher education and social problems of great current interest is the subject of two events. The thought that there may be some lowering of standards in higher education systems as a whole as a result of attempts to expand educational opportunities for the disadvantaged (Event #22) is rated as undesirable or detrimental by about three out of four faculty respondents and by about two out of three administrators and others. About half or more of all three groups, however, see this development as highly likely. Almost three out of four of those administrators who see this as undesirable also give it an even chance or better of happening, as does about the same proportion of faculty respondents.

Nine out of ten of all three groups feel that there is an even chance or better that action programs designed to solve interracial and other social problems will receive increased attention and resource allocation by colleges and universities (Event #35). The agreement among the three groups is striking as to probabilities, but there is some disagreement about desirability. About one out of three administrators sees this as undesirable, while only about one out of five faculty respondents agrees.

Student Population

Five events (1, 9, 11, 12, 18) involve the nature of the student population and the student output of higher education. See Table 7. There is almost uniform gloom about the probable decline of the *proportion* of students enrolled in private institutions (Event #1). In all three groups, almost three out of four respondents feel that this decline is both very undesirable and highly probable. About nine out of ten feel it is very undesirable, regardless of probability, and about the same number feel that this development has an even chance or better, regardless of desirability. There is almost no difference of opinion among the three groups on either aspect.

TABLE 7: *Joint Responses to Items Concerning Student Population*

(Percentage of Each Group Rating Each Event on Both Probability and Desirability)

Probability	Group	Desirability Ratings for Each Numbered Event														
		1			9			11			12			18		
		U	D	T	U	D	T	U	D	T	U	D	T	U	D	T
Almost Certain or Very Likely	I	73	8	81	2	88	90	30	45	75	4	56	60	20	46	66
	O	72	11	83	2	87	89	25	63	88	5	56	61	20	42	62
	F	74	9	83	6	82	88	25	54	79	9	51	60	14	62	76
Even Chance	I	13	1	14	1	7	8	14	7	21	6	24	30	11	6	17
	O	9	0	9	0	7	7	3	3	6	7	22	29	13	5	18
	F	10	1	11	1	8	9	10	7	17	8	19	27	8	5	13
Not Very Likely or Highly Improbable	I	5	0	5	1	2	2	4	0	4	5	5	10	16	1	17
	O	8	0	8	1	3	4	4	2	6	2	8	10	18	2	20
	F	5	1	6	1	2	3	3	1	4	8	5	13	9	2	11
Total Desirability Rating	I	91	9	*708*	3	97	*818*	48	52	*750*	15	85	*783*	47	53	*787*
	O	89	11	*102*	3	97	*107*	32	68	*100*	14	86	*106*	51	49	*101*
	F	89	11	*571*	8	92	*588*	38	62	*509*	25	75	*547*	31	69	*567*

"Events" Related to Student Population:

1. The proportion of students enrolled in *private* institutions of higher education will decline at an even faster rate.

9. The great majority of high school graduates will take at least two years of instruction after high school.

11. Of all persons receiving earned doctorates in the 1970s, a steadily increasing proportion will be employed by business, industry, and government.

12. More than half of all four-year graduates will begin work on a graduate or professional degree.

18. Standards for admission and graduation will continue to rise in highly selective institutions.

Key to Desirability Code:
U = Undesirable or detrimental
D = Desirable or essential
T = Total probability rating

Key to Group Code:
I = ACE Institutional members
O = Other ACE members
F = AAUP

Note: Numbers in *italics* indicate how many respondents made a rating for the event on both probability *and* desirability.

283

There seems little question that there is overwhelming approval of the possibility that most high school graduates will take at least two years of further instruction (Event #9), though faculty respondents are a little less favorable in this attitude. More than four out of five respondents feel that this development is both highly probable and highly desirable. Almost nine out of ten of all three respondent groups give this development a very high probability rating.

Among administrators, opinion is about evenly divided about the desirability of a continuing rise in admission and graduation standards in highly selective institutions (Event #18). More than two out of three faculty respondents, however, give this development a high desirability rating, and nine out of ten who feel this way also think the trend is highly probable. About two out of five who see this as undesirable also rate it high in probability.

That an increasing proportion of persons receiving earned doctorates will find nonacademic employment (Event #11) seems highly probable to most respondents in all three groups. With regard to most events, both Institutional and other ACE members are usually in close agreement, but on this point the "other" members rate this development higher in probability than do the administrators. Administrators are about evenly divided about the desirability of this trend, but "other" members and faculty tend more strongly to rate it as desirable.

Although a smaller proportion of faculty respondents than of ACE members feel that it is desirable if more than half of all four-year graduates undertake a graduate or professional degree program (Event #12), there is striking agreement about probabilities; three out of five in all three groups see this as highly likely. More than half of all three groups feel this possibility is both very desirable and very probable.

Structural Matters

Five events (3, 4, 15, 16, 20) involve opinions about the general structure of higher education. See Table 8. The virtual disappearance of separate colleges for men and women (Event #4) is regarded as very desirable by more than three out of four faculty respondents, while more than two out of five administrators feel this is undesirable, and other ACE members fall between the two extremes. About four out of five faculty respondents who give this development a high desirability rating also rate it high on probability, while more than

TABLE 8: Joint Responses to Items Concerning Structural Matters

(Percentage of Each Group Rating Each Event on Both Probability and Desirability)

Probability	Group	Desirability Ratings for Each Numbered Event														
		3			4			15			16			20		
		U	D	T	U	D	T	U	D	T	U	D	T	U	D	T
Almost Certain or Very Likely	I	26	57	83	15	47	62	9	40	49	8	7	15	53	7	60
	O	20	66	86	6	51	57	8	57	65	5	7	12	51	14	65
	F	30	44	74	8	63	71	6	46	52	7	7	14	54	7	61
Even Chance	I	7	7	14	14	9	23	14	15	29	19	6	25	25	2	27
	O	2	8	10	11	15	26	4	18	22	20	7	27	17	3	20
	F	13	7	20	7	11	18	11	16	27	13	5	18	21	2	23
Not Very Likely or Highly Improbable	I	2	1	3	13	2	15	17	5	22	56	4	60	13	0	13
	O	4	0	4	14	3	17	7	6	13	54	7	61	15	0	15
	F	4	2	6	8	3	11	16	5	21	61	7	68	15	1	16
Total Desirability Rating	I	35	65	*789*	42	58	*775*	40	60	*760*	83	17	*808*	91	9	*807*
	O	26	74	*107*	31	69	*101*	19	81	*102*	79	21	*108*	83	17	*107*
	F	47	53	*566*	23	77	*549*	33	67	*540*	81	19	*602*	90	10	*592*

"*Events*" *Related to Structural Matters:*

3. State-wide coordinating councils will have increasing influences over public colleges and universities.

4. Separate colleges for men and women will, largely through merger, virtually disappear.

15. New colleges and universities (or branches) will continue to be established at the current rate of about forty per year.

16. By 1978, higher education in general will be centrally planned and coordinated on some nationwide basis.

20. As a corollary of tax-dollar support, government agencies will have increasing influence over private colleges and universities.

Key to Desirability Code:
  U = Undesirable or detrimental
  D = Desirable or essential
  T = Total probability rating

Key to Group Code:
  I = ACE Institutional members
  O = Other ACE members
  F = AAUP

Note: Numbers in *italics* indicate how many respondents made a rating for the event on both probability *and* desirability.

285

one out of four administrators gives both a low desirability rating and sees this development as having an even chance or better,

The possibility that new institutions (or branches) will continue to appear at the rate of about forty per year (Event #15) again provokes a rare disagreement between Institutional and other ACE members. Three out of five administrators rate this possibility high in desirability, while four out of five "other" ACE members make a similar rating. Two out of three faculty respondents agree, and, of these, about nine out of ten give this development an even chance or better. Of those administrators who feel this trend is desirable, two out of three also feel it is highly likely to continue.

There is striking agreement among all three groups about both the undesirability and the probability of the increasing influence of government agencies over private institutions, as a corollary of tax-dollar support (Event #20). About nine out of ten administrators and faculty see this as undesirable or worse, and three out of five of all three groups feel this development is highly likely, regardless of desirability. Administrators and faculty are in closer agreement on this point than either is with "other" ACE members.

The possibility of increasing influence to be exerted over public colleges and universities by state-wide coordinating councils (Event #3) is given an even chance or better by more than nine out of ten respondents in all three groups, but opinions are more sharply divided on the matter of desirability. About two out of three administrators see this trend as very desirable, while three out of four other ACE members agree. Faculty respondents are about evenly divided. The great majority of all those in the three groups who give this trend a low desirability rating nevertheless give it an even chance or better of continuing.

All three groups are in substantial agreement about both probability and desirability with respect to the future development of nationwide planning and coordination of all higher education (Event #16). Three out of five (or more) in all three groups give this development a low probability rating, and about four out of five make a low desirability rating as well. In fact, more than half of respondents in all three groups rate this possibility as both undesirable and improbable.

Federal Funds

Five of the ten events involve questions of finance related to Federal sources (2, 5, 7, 8, 19). See Table 9. Some of these items provoked sharper reactions than did others. The possibility that more funds will go directly to students in the form of scholarships or loans (Event #2) is regarded as highly desirable by about nine out of ten respondents in all three groups, "other" ACE members lagging a little in enthusiasm. The great majority of all three groups rate this trend highly probable. More than two out of three respondents, in all three groups, regard this as both desirable and very likely.

The possibility of giving more and larger general support grants to states as intermediary distribution agents (Event #5) is regarded as very desirable by almost three out of four administrators, while other ACE members and faculty are less enthusiastic. With respect to both desirability and probability, "other" ACE members and faculty agree more with each other than either does with administrators. While two out of three administrators see this trend as very likely, only half of the other two groups agree. Just over half of the administrators feel that this practice is both desirable and highly likely, while only about two out of five other ACE members and faculty agree.

Opinion is about evenly divided, among all three groups, concerning the probability that by 1978 upwards of 60 percent of the instructional costs of both public and private colleges and universities will be met out of Federal sources (Event #7). The majority of all three groups feels this to be desirable or essential, faculty members feeling even more positively about this aspect. There is a small but noticeable tendency for those who regard this development as desirable to regard it as more probable, and vice versa.

There is a moderately sharp difference of opinion among the three groups about the increased use of the project proposal, to be reviewed by panels of peers, as a means of allocating general support to academic institutions (Event #8). Faculty are notably more enthusiastic about this practice than are "other" ACE members, and the probability ratings of both groups follow the same pattern. More than half of the "other" ACE members feel this trend is undesirable, and more than half of those making this low rating also rate it low on probability.

There is somewhat more agreement among the three groups about

TABLE 9: *Joint Responses to Items Concerning Federal Funds*

(Percentage of Each Group Rating Each Event on Both Probability and Desirability)

Probability	Group	Desirability Ratings for Each Numbered Event														
		2			5			7			8			19		
		U	D	T	U	D	T	U	D	T	U	D	T	U	D	T
Almost Certain or Very Likely	I	7	78	85	13	53	66	8	25	33	9	36	45	25	58	83
	O	8	68	76	11	39	50	8	28	36	10	25	35	22	56	78
	F	4	74	78	11	39	50	10	33	43	15	41	56	34	44	78
Even Chance	I	4	10	14	9	17	26	14	19	33	16	18	34	9	6	15
	O	5	14	19	21	13	34	11	15	26	17	15	32	13	3	16
	F	2	14	16	17	17	34	11	20	31	13	19	32	11	7	18
Not Very Likely or Highly Improbable	I	0	1	1	5	3	8	24	10	34	17	4	21	1	1	2
	O	3	2	5	11	5	16	23	15	38	30	3	33	6	0	6
	F	2	4	6	12	4	16	15	11	26	19	3	22	3	1	4
Total Desirability Rating	I	11	89	810	27	73	802	46	54	784	42	58	773	35	65	762
	O	16	84	108	43	57	105	42	58	100	57	43	104	41	59	100
	F	8	92	605	40	60	558	36	64	561	37	63	522	48	52	499

"Events" Related to Federal Funds:

2. Significantly more Federal and state funds will go directly to students, as scholarships or loans.
5. The Federal government will give more and larger general support grants to states as intermediaries for distribution to colleges and universities.
7. By 1978, the Federal government will meet upwards of 60 per cent of the instructional costs of private and public higher education in the United States.
8. Use of the project-proposal, subject to panel reviews by peers, will increase as a means of allocating general Federal support to colleges and universities.
19. Formulas will increasingly be used to determine levels of state and Federal support for various academic programs.

Key to Desirability Code:
U = Undesirable or detrimental
D = Desirable or essential
T = Total probability rating

Key to Group Code:
I = ACE Institutional members
O = Other ACE members
F = AAUP

the increasing use of formulas to determine levels of financial support from government sources (Event #19). This development is regarded as highly likely by more than three out of four in all three groups. On the desirability of this practice, faculty are about evenly divided, while about two out of three administrators give a high desirability rating. One out of three faculty respondents rate this practice low on desirability but high on probability.

Other Money Matters

The remaining five items (13, 21, 26, 28, 32) deal with various aspects of financial support and costs. See Table 10. The possibility of competition for funds from whatever sources between higher education and welfare and public improvement programs (e.g., health, air and water pollution) and a proportionate levelling-off of tax-dollar support for higher education (Event #13) may be said to be taken seriously by the majority of respondents. Administrators are the most discouraged —four out of five give this possibility an even chance or better. Faculty are a little more optimistic. About three out of four administrators rate this development low on desirability, but only about three out of five faculty respondents agree. About one out of five respondents in all three groups rate this possibility as both very likely and very undesirable.

The possibility that support for the social sciences and humanities will equal that for the natural sciences (Event #21) is regarded as highly desirable, with striking unanimity, by all three groups. However, the great majority, even of those who give high desirability ratings, see this development as not very probable. All respondents who rate this high on probability also rate it as highly desirable.

Though faculty differs somewhat from the other groups about probabilities, all three are almost identical in their approval of some provision of tax support at the state level for private institutions (Event #32). About four out of five rate this possibility as highly desirable. Almost one out of five faculty respondents, however, are not sanguine about the probability aspect.

It is not surprising that 97 percent of faculty respondents regard it as very desirable if average faculty salaries continue to rise a little faster than the general cost of living (Event #26), but it is surprising that most administrators agree. Half or more of all three groups see

TABLE 10: *Joint Responses to Items Concerning Other Money Matters*

(Percentage of Each Group Rating Each Event on Both Probability and Desirability)

Desirability Ratings for Each Numbered Event

Probability	Group	13 U	13 D	13 T	21 U	21 D	21 T	26 U	26 D	26 T	28 U	28 D	28 T	32 U	32 D	32 T
Almost Certain or Very Likely	I	23	17	40	0	18	18	6	52	58	44	6	50	7	56	63
	O	19	17	36	0	16	16	1	51	52	50	6	56	14	50	64
	F	18	22	40	0	12	12	0	50	50	52	5	57	5	48	53
Even Chance	I	31	8	39	1	22	23	4	25	29	29	2	31	10	18	28
	O	27	12	39	1	18	19	4	26	30	23	1	24	4	18	22
	F	18	13	31	1	16	17	1	32	33	26	0	26	7	22	29
Not Very Likely or Highly Improbable	I	20	1	21	10	49	59	4	9	13	19	0	19	4	5	9
	O	22	3	25	7	58	65	1	17	18	20	0	20	5	11	14
	F	25	4	29	11	60	71	2	15	17	17	0	17	8	10	18
Total Desirability Rating	I	74	26	*773*	11	89	*805*	14	86	*792*	92	8	*783*	21	79	*802*
	O	68	32	*102*	8	92	*109*	6	94	*104*	93	7	*107*	21	79	*107*
	F	61	39	*521*	11	88	*595*	3	97	*599*	95	5	*560*	20	80	*590*

"Events" Related to Other Money Matters:

13. The *proportion* of tax-dollar support of higher education will level off as a result of competitive demands from welfare and public improvement programs (e.g., health, air and water pollution).
21. Support from all sources for the humanities and social sciences will be as great as for the natural sciences.
26. Average faculty salaries will continue to increase somewhat faster than the general cost of living.
28. The average total cost to *the student* of attending more expensive undergraduate institutions will at least double by 1978, assuming no increase in the *rate* of inflation.
32. Most states will provide some tax support for private colleges and universities.

Key to Desirability Code:
U = Undesirable or detrimental
D = Desirable or essential
T = Total probability rating

Key to Group Code:
I = ACE Institutional members
O = Other ACE members
F = AAUP

Note: Numbers in *italics* indicate how many respondents made a rating for the event on both probability *and* desirability.

this trend as both desirable and very likely. Oddly enough, more administrators than faculty rate this development as highly probable.

The possibility that average total cost *to the student* of attending more expensive undergraduate institutions will double by 1978 (Event #28) is regarded as very undesirable by more than nine out of ten respondents in all three groups. But it is also regarded as highly probable by half or more of all respondents. No one who thinks it is desirable (there are a few) thinks it is unlikely. About four out of five respondents in all three groups give this possibility an even chance or better.

(Technical note: Correlations between desirability and probability ratings for all 35 events were computed. The data are of little general interest—though the writer will provide a brief report to anyone interested enough to write. The general conclusion reached was that there was little tendency, in any of the five respondent groups, to let ratings as to probability affect ratings of desirability. A factor analysis simply confirmed that the subjectively "logical" groupings of events under various subject headings were, in general, valid.)

General Comments

It is difficult to make sweeping generalizations about the results of this survey as a whole. What is most surprising is the amount of agreement on some fairly controversial items. Most of the differences between respondent groups are fairly predictable from the view of their own interests and responsibilities and the amount of information available to them. Most of the "conservative" responses, especially concerning desirabilities, are not surprising, but some of the more "liberal" or reform-minded responses are somewhat surprising. The paucity of responses from student leaders and trustees, and therefore the unreliability of any detailed analyses, is disappointing. The responses of the three major groups do, however, provide some starting point for discussion of issues and alternatives for higher education in the next decade.

It is perhaps useful to reflect especially on the differences between "desirables" and "probables." Why don't we proceed at once to implement what we see as desirable? Probability estimates are not blind: they also reflect what we want, but they take the realities into account.

If one believes that there is "no alternative" to a certain event or course of action, no decision seems possible. But there is always an alternative—if only disaster. We must, to avert disaster, make the bad alternatives as credible as the good ones. If we see "no alternative," we have probably not thought the matter through. Peter Drucker tells an apt story about a meeting of the board of General Motors, presided over by Alfred Sloan. An idea was presented and discussed. Every member of the board was asked by Sloan, "Do you see anything wrong with this idea?" Everyone said, "No," and was very enthusiastic. "I agree with you," said Sloan. "I see nothing wrong with it either. Therefore we will put it off for a while, until someone can think of a possible difficulty."

If we extrapolate many present trends, we become nervous because so many are "bad." Perhaps the most important use of both subjective and extrapolative predictions is the prevention of what we don't want to happen if we can avoid it. Thus credibility is as important as ultimate accuracy. There is also a difference between the values of short- and long-term predictions. A longer time span permits periodic revision and provides an interval to question data or estimates.

One must also distinguish between active and passive predictions. If I say, "I am going to New York tomorrow," I am predicting that I will unless something prevents me. In all predictions there are overtones of "unless" or of "only if" conditions. Some of these are subject to control or intention, and some are not. "Our enrollment will increase next year" is both a prediction and an implied policy.

In a sense, planning and informed speculation should always have as one objective bringing desirability and probability into the same rank order. If we look at the dissonances, we must ask, "Why does what we desire seem so improbable?" What is often called "wishful thinking" may not be all bad, at least if it is based on some reality. For even the most "objective" speculation or surmise shows the color of what we think *should* happen.

COMMENTARIES ON

Predictions for Higher Education in the 1970s

ROBERT H. KROEPSCH, WILLIAM H. SEWELL,

JOSEPH E. SLATER

A More Active Humanism

ROBERT H. KROEPSCH

THE BACKDROP here is the "Caffrey Predictions." I chose to call them thus because they are certain to be referred to in that fashion as they are read, probed, argued over, and even, in some instances, acted upon. And they should be called the Caffrey Predictions, not because John Caffrey made them—the respondents, more than 2,000, made them—but because his concept and planning made them possible. This approach, derived from a systematic analysis of higher education as a whole, can provide us with a very useful technique for self-evaluation.

The technique is ingenious, but I suggest that the predictions themselves are ingenuous. They are ingenuous because they do not map out 1978 as much as 1968. If one looks at them as a means of understanding the present, they are revealing indeed. Traditionally, whenever higher education undertakes the task of projecting its own future, it has manifested a high degree of self-centeredness. Mature, respected elder statesmen are asked to draw on their experience and wisdom and suggest guidelines for the future. The recent book edited by Alvin Eurich, *Campus 1980*, is an excellent example. (My investigation indicates that the median age of the seventeen contributors is about fifty-seven.) And now Caffrey has given us the opportunity to estimate the probability and desirability of 35 possible "events."

Contemporary American society, in its search for direction and purpose, appears at times to be tottering on the brink of paralysis and de-

293

spair. And efforts to shake free of this paralysis and despair may well result in revolutionary restructuring of our national political institutions. (Some are now talking about the Second American Republic.) Meanwhile, higher education, one of the American institutions that must bear awesome responsibility for leadership in this time of troubles, predicts its own future almost as if the agonizing adjustments taking place outside our campuses would not unleash forces that will reshape our future within.

Like others, I am impressed with the degree of apparent unanimity among the several groups within the academic community concerning these current internal trends and problems. But I must suggest that some of these "now" problems and trends will so quickly merge into the milieu of higher education, losing their uniqueness within the next decade, that by 1978 we shall wonder why we bothered to predict anything about them at all.

It could well be that the real significance of most current predictions lies, not in the answers collected, but in the questions that are not asked. And those questions must deal with the ways in which human conflicts, problems, trends, and solutions are going to affect the shape and destiny of higher education as an institution within the next ten years and beyond.

Based on this distinction between external and internal influences on the future of higher education, I offer a suggestion: The American Council on Education should commission a variety of creative thinkers in our society, composed primarily of those now outside academia, with a median age under forty and who are not exclusively white males. The charge to this commission would be to tell us what they think our society and our planet will be like in twenty to twenty-five years. Then there should be compiled another set of events related to this human picture —to this new model—including, as it would, the vast and predictable technological changes; biomedical changes; changes in ethics and law; and changes in our political, economic, and social philosophies and systems.

Then, with this instrument, let us again conduct a survey to give us a reassessment of what we see as the future of higher education. The results of this systematic approach might help us find ways for higher education to lead the inhabitants of this planet into the twenty-first century—instead of being pushed into it by them.

Considering the substance of my remarks thus far, perhaps I should illustrate by using a few of the predictions we already have before us.

The item we ranked number one in desirability we ranked to become number twenty-seven in probability. It was stated as follows: "Breakthroughs in understanding the human learning process will lead to major improvements in instructional methods at the college level." First in desirability; twenty-seventh in probability!

This, I suggest, illustrates our inability to look beyond higher education to recognize our power to cause change. While we in higher education resign ourselves to the improbability of such a desirable breakthrough, and the major changes that would result, our colleagues at the elementary and secondary levels are not sitting on their hands. Instead, they are acting constructively on solid, though not sensational, progress in understanding the human learning process. Their actions are kindling a revolution in learning stretching from nursery school through high school. Old concepts of the relationship of age to learning ability are rapidly being discarded, and concern with pupil-teacher interaction is giving way to a concern with the learner's interaction with his environment. These trends, along with an effort to increase the independence of pupils in the laboratory, may well give us high school graduates who possess new levels of sophistication and confidence concerning the acquisition and the application of knowledge.

Assuming higher education does not change much, what will happen when teenagers who were learning scientific classification as first-graders, Spanish as second-graders, calculus at age ten, who were working with cybernetics in the ninth grade and writing and producing their own plays in the twelfth grade—what will happen when these teenagers reach our campuses and find that their independent interaction with the world environment has ended for four years? What will happen when they realize that its resumption depends upon their admission to a narrow and rigidly specialized graduate department?

Let us hope that before that time, we in higher education will find the will to improve instructional methods despite the lack of a major breakthrough. Perhaps the new magazine *Change in Higher Education* will help—a mock-up of the first issue was impressive and I commend it to you.

Another of the gaps between desirability and probability occurs with the event concerning support for the humanities and social sciences. We indicated on the survey that support for these disciplines at the level currently enjoyed by the natural sciences was highly desirable; yet at the same time we indicated that such an event was highly improbable. But another related item whose probability and desirability gained no noticeable positive or negative reaction was: "Colleges and universities will gradually allocate more of their resources to action programs designed to solve interracial and other social problems."

Is there not reason to believe that financial support for the social sciences and humanities would increase if these disciplines were committed to action programs designed to solve human problems? Is there not reason to believe that society and government will demand a more active humanism from our colleges and universities, just as they have demanded, supported, and received a more active scientism? And if such humanistic action programs were carried out, at least in part, by undergraduates, would this not in itself help lead the way to the instructional breakthroughs we find so desirable, yet so improbable?

It was at the fortieth annual gathering of the American Council on Education, eleven years ago, that one of my most memorable experiences took place—some of you here today shared it with me. During that meeting, it was announced to the world and to us that the Soviet Union had launched the first man-made satellite to orbit the earth. That news gripped and electrified everyone present. After all, weren't we educators who shared a major responsibility for staying at the vanguard of the search for knowledge?

At the final session, we met to hear our chairman, Franklin Murphy, deliver the closing remarks. He put aside his original text and spoke instead from notes he had made during the night. He told us briefly and clearly that Sputnik beamed a message that would persistently penetrate superficial interpretations. He told us that the meaning of the satellite was that it had provided a dramatic glimpse into the depth and violence of the great scientific revolution which was altering our lives. He said,

> This then is the message that the satellite is beeping down to those who will listen. . . . It is trying to say that time is already short and unprecedented effort is needed to reach unprecedented educational goals.

Today, we stand eleven years into the future as Franklin Murphy saw it then. We can now say that we did listen, and we did act, and we have given to this country a scientific capability beyond the wildest dreams of most of us who gathered at that meeting.

Today we are gathered to the beat of another signal, but it is not a mechanical "beep, beep, beep," shooting through cold, lifeless regions. It is instead an impassioned human cry from the throats of men, "Why? Why? Why?"

The cry persists. It has already penetrated all of the superficial answers thrown before it. The real meaning of that cry, to paraphrase the statement made eleven years ago, is that it provides a dramatic glimpse into the depth and violence of the great revolution of the human spirit in which we are all caught up, and which daily alters all aspects of our personal and national lives—a revolution which may manifest itself in large-scale destruction of and reconstruction of national political, social, and economic systems throughout the world.

And though that cry is often fearful, frustrated, angry, and even dangerous, never before have so many genuinely given voice to it in the hope of finding, not "The Answer," but at most a better answer. And never before have the humanities and the social sciences had such an opportunity to lead the evolution of human thought and action up another step or two.

This, then, brings me back to the Caffrey Predictions.

T. S. Eliot has written, "Between the Idea and the Reality falls the Shadow." In our survey, we have written, "Between the Desirability and the Probability falls the Shadow." Who, we must ask ourselves, is casting that shadow?

Involving Trustees

WILLIAM H. SEWELL

ONE COMES AWAY from John Caffrey's survey of the probability and desirability of certain developments in higher education with a feeling that we need more analyses of these and other data before we can make accurate predictions about trends on campuses during the next decade. As with all surveys, one wishes other emphases had been selected. For instance, I wish that more questions had dealt directly with major student concerns, particularly with such issues as student power, undergraduate teaching and curricular reform, and the sociopolitical context of the university. These are the areas likely to give us our greatest problems, both within the university community and in our relations with the general public. The survey does, however, include some items bearing on these issues and thus provides some basis for speculations about them.

In examining the results of the survey, I find the probability ratings less interesting than the desirability ratings because the developments that are deemed most probable (the degree of agreement among the several categories of respondents on this is remarkable) are mainly extensions of trends already apparent in higher education. The possible exceptions are the two items (#10, #14) dealing with the likelihood of undergraduate curriculum reform. Even though activity in this area has thus far been limited except for the usual tinkering that results from the labors of standing committees on curriculum, it is students who will exert the greatest and most continuous pressure for reform in the instruction and curriculum area. This area of concern is the one most relevant to the purposes of the university, the one with which the students, faculty, and administration have the greatest competency to deal, the one that is of greatest enduring importance to the present and future lives of students, and the one that almost everyone agrees is in need of considerable reform.

By far the most interesting data relate to the desirability of the events predicted. As the correlations show, the general trend was for a rather high degree of agreement on the desirability of most items between groups of respondents, particularly administrators and trustees, administrators and faculty, and faculty and students. The lesser degree of agreement between faculty and trustees and especially the markedly lower level of agreement between students and trustees is perhaps the most significant finding of the study.

Dr. Caffrey was properly cautious in not analyzing the data on students and trustees because of their low response rates; yet a further look is worthwhile, even though conclusions must be quite tentative.

In examining the desirability rankings, one is impressed to find that on those potential developments having the closest bearing on the distribution of power within the university (items #23, #25, #27, #29, #31, and #33), students and faculty are in greater accord than are students and administrators, and students are in much closer agreement with both faculty and administrators than with trustees. This pattern is particularly true of items #23, #27, and #33, the three items most directly related to student power demands and tactics. No group other than students is enthusiastic about students serving on important academic committees (#23), although faculty and administration are mildly tolerant of the prospect, while trustees have little sympathy with this development. And whereas students welcome the decline of *in loco parentis* (#33), and faculty members seem to favor it, and administrators find it acceptable but less desirable, the trustees—although not strongly opposed—view this development with the least enthusiasm. No group, including students, really favors the wider use of direct-action techniques to achieve student demands (#27), but students are the most tolerant of this possibility, followed by faculty, while administrators and trustees both rank it the least desirable of all the potential developments covered in the survey.

On the items dealing with increased faculty power, or decreased administrative power (#25, #29, #31), where in each case the faculty considers the prospect as most desirable, students are in closer agreement with faculty opinion than with the opinions of administrators or trustees. The trustees are the least favorable of all groups to erosion of top administrative authority (#29), to increased faculty participation in academic government (#25), and to increased faculty participation in the selection of a president (#31).

If we turn to more purely academic concerns—items that deal mainly either with changes in undergraduate instruction or curriculum (items #6, #10, #14, #24, #30) or with what might be thought of as the academic context (items #11, #12, #17, #18, #21, #35)—the same general trend holds, although not without exception; students and faculty, and even students and administration, are much closer in their judgment of the desirability of possible changes than are students and trustees. These patterns are less true for those items having to do with instructional and curricular reform than for those dealing with the academic context of the university. Every group is highly in favor of undergraduate curricular reform along interdepartmental lines (#10), all would welcome breakthroughs in the learning process that would lead to improvements in instruction (#14), but students and faculty are a little less favorable to this prospect than are administrators and trustees. No group would favor machines to replace instructors (#6), but trustees find this possibility more tolerable than others. Only students support the idea of giving academic credit for work and service experiences (#30). All groups favor a decrease in required undergraduate courses, but trustees are least enthusiastic about the prospect (#24).

The largest discrepancies between students and trustees are to be found in the items dealing with what may be called the academic context—the kind of a social and intellectual climate the campus should maintain, its relationship with the manpower market, and its orientation to the problems of society. Thus, the students look with disapproval on any trend which suggests the channeling of more students into government, business, or the professions (#11, #12)—read "the military-industrial complex"—but trustees strongly endorse this prospect; faculty and administration are closer to the students' position on these items. Faculty, students, and administration are all opposed to recruiting an increasing proportion of administrative personnel from nonacademic sources (#17), but trustees find this prospect quite acceptable. Students are much less favorable to the possible trend toward higher standards for admission and graduation (#18) than are trustees, and again faculty and administration are closer to the students' position. And students are more in favor of allocating increased proportions of university resources to action programs (#35) than are trustees, with faculty in closest agreement with students.

The evidence from the survey that student views are in greatest opposition to those of trustees must be considered tentative. But it is at least suggestive and squares with the experience and observations of administrators on many troubled campuses. I believe that if the survey had contained more questions directed at major student concerns, the differences between the two groups would have been much sharper. But even the evidence of the present survey supports the assertion that the greatest source of conflict within the university community will come from the gulf in interests, values, and behavioral norms which separates students from trustees (and the public they represent). This is not to say that student-administration or student-faculty disputes will disappear or that the traditional sources of tension between administration and faculty, or faculty and trustees, or administration and trustees will diminish. (Actually they all may be heightened as students focus their action more on academic power and curricular reform.) But it is to assert that the student-trustee conflict will be more direct and difficult to cope with because these groups have not developed means of communication or modes of response that are generally mutually acceptable. Consequently, it is difficult for them to resolve their conflicts of interest. I would argue that other major groups in the academic community have developed ways of communication and modes of action which usually make it possible for them to express, discuss, and resolve their differences without a great deal of overt conflict—even though this has been much less true in the past few years since the increase in student demands for power and their use of direct-action techniques. But even in the recent and current situations, faculty and administration have been much more able to understand, if not accept, both the rhetoric and the behavior of student activists than have trustees and the general public.

One of the univerity's greatest needs in the next few years will be to develop organizational mechanisms by which student interests, needs, and demands can be heard, debated, and accepted, revised, or denied in a fashion befitting an academic community—and, it is to be hoped, without exacerbating public opinion. To accomplish this end, a good deal of thought must be given to involving trustees more directly in university affairs, especially in those matters concerning students. It may even be necessary to have trustees serve as fully participating members on selected academic committees, together with students, faculty, and administration. The risk may be great, but I doubt that we can continue to follow the practice of using trustees as "rubber stamps" for policies that the administration and faculty recommend. And if student participation in administrative and academic affairs becomes more common, the greater participation of the trustees also becomes the more necessary.

If this alternative is not feasible, we owe it to our governing boards— if they are to act as buffers rather than conduits for public pressures in times of crisis—to provide much more background on both general and specific considerations involved in short-term and long-term policy decisions regarding students. I am not advocating that trustees or regents make detailed academic policy decisions. Rather, I am saying that governing boards must, at the least, be enabled to understand more fully than in the past the deliberations and reasoning that underlie these decisions if they are to interpret and defend the university in times of crisis.

An Educational Common Market

JOSEPH E. SLATER

THAT MANY NEW TYPES of institutional arrangements in the field of higher education will be required to meet or live with the problems and challenges of the 1970s is clear. That a number of persons under forty will play a substantial role in helping to tailor new national and international educational ideas and institutions which permit rapid if not radical change within a sound framework—this is important.

Following are some obvious conceptual and institutional innovations that must come to being in the teaching-learning process:

1. Substantial subsidies should be given to support research on the human learning processes and capacities, with particular attention to the very early years. This field should involve, among others, neurophysiologists, psychologists, and educators.

2. Quasi-private corporations (such as General Dynamics) should be set up to develop and construct more effective and cheaper educational buildings and facilities—at all levels.

3. In addition to direct Federal grants to education, a public foundation should be established to support extensive innovative educational projects throughout the country. The organization might take the form of a National Education Foundation, with both public and private representatives on its board of trustees. This public foundation (operating on funds made available without strings by the Congress) should be flexible, experimental, and substantially larger than the Ford Foundation's Educational and Research Program. It could help bring about changes in existing governmental programs and set the stage for new programs in both the public and the private sectors.

4. The United States should support joint and integrated educational exchanges and projects involving other regions of the world. The rapid and full implementation of the International Education Act would give us a start in this direction. We might think along the lines of an Educational Common Market.

Educational institutions and practices that would work as an integral part of a plan to provide a more satisfactory urban life should be devised. The concerns should include material matters as well as the quality of life and the integrity of the individual. I believe Vice-President Humphrey's proposal of a Marshall Plan for the cities is on the right track in that it represents a fundamental attack on the problem, using the best resources of the country mobilized to do the job.

We must promote significantly greater mobility within our own society: we must encourage a larger number of persons to move more freely between the intellectual and educational worlds on the one hand, and government and business, on the other. Some system of transferred benefits (for example, through TIAA-CREF) might facilitate such mobility.

We should have continuing and fuller public discussion of scientific and other developments which will directly affect men's lives and for which society needs "lead time" if it is to deal with them wisely and democratically. Such developments include, for example, advances in the life sciences, especially genetic engineering, artificial or machine intelligence, and improvement in our understanding of the mind. The educational community should take an active lead in promoting such public discussion.

We should develop and support international educational activities. The United States, working in the first instance with the Western European countries, should engage them at once in the long and arduous process of establishing an "Educational Common Market," involving transnational agreements with all of Europe on educational norms and standards, in a fashion that will ultimately make it possible to internationalize the educational process. The unimpeded flow of students and faculty across national borders without prejudice to the formal educational accreditation of the student or to the professional career of the faculty should be the goal. To the extent the East Europeans and Soviets feel able to do so, they should participate in this effort.

Among short-term undertakings, I believe that the United States must pursue all steps necessary to encourage the flow of American students and faculty abroad and also the flow of European students and faculty to this country. Joint institutional research and other projects are essential to this process, as is a frontal attack on the language problem. The Fulbright program, which has served well, should immediately be revitalized and broadened. The United States should encourage the formation of international professional associations, with a view to making possible continuous professional careers in more than one country. Such a course, if wisely pursued, far from reducing the benefits of cultural diversity, will enhance these benefits.

I also believe that an international foundation should be created to develop and make grants internationally. Such a foundation would operate much as do private philanthropic foundations within the United States. It would be multinational in its support, its staff, and its direction; it would address itself, by means of grants and contracts, to the process of institution building on an international scale. The highly successful CERN (European Center for Nuclear Research), though it operates within a very limited field, constitutes a model for activities over the entire range of education and technology, as well as of social, political, and industrial management.

In brief, when we use the word "community," we must now think in international as well as national terms. We should recognize also that the educational field is the most productive area for "common approaches to common problems" in building bridges to other societies, including the Communist world.

Finally, the educational world, in planning for the 1970s, must keep in mind a few central facts:

1. Societies generally are turning to *man* as opposed to *things*. This movement is reinforced by the fact that biology will have the impact in the '70s and '80s that the physical sciences (particularly physics) had in the '30s, '40s, and '50s.

2. All developed societies face multiple crises which can be approached effectively only if the university community takes a broad, activist role.

3. Both the university and individual institutes must work at breaking down the compartments which separate knowledge, ideas, and people. In particular, knowledge of the life sciences needs to be more closely synthesized with ideas and programs involving education, environment, and population, as well as with those involving the social sciences generally.

*All cities are mad, but the madness
is gallant. All cities are beautiful, but the
beauty is grim.*

Christopher Morley, *Where the Blue Begins*

CONSTANTINOS A. DOXIADIS

Cities in Crisis and the University

MY SUBJECT IS: "Cities in Crisis and the University," or "The Whole
That Suffered and the Part That Suffers." We will look at the city as a
whole system, and the university as a subsystem. We could call the
subsystem the center of knowledge, or the center of "inter-thinking,"
in the word of George Gaylord Simpon,[1] which defines the cultural
evolution as interbreeding defines the organic evolution.

In undertaking this responsibility, I must define my limitations. First,
I know one part of my subject better than the other: I am supposed to
know something about the city. Second, my training was wrong. When
I was in the university, people thought that we could understand cities
by studying their anatomy. But medicine has shown over the last hundred years that anatomy does not teach, that only physiology does. We
are in the process of understanding the physiology of the city. My third
limitation is that we can contribute to the solution of problems only by
measuring. There are many physical and metaphysical ways whereby we
can explain our life in the city. Personally, I have been convinced, after
thirty-five years of experience, that only if we have the ability to measure

[1] *The Meaning of Evolution* (New Haven: Yale University Press, 1949), p. 337.

Editor's note: This paper is a revision of a speech originally illustrated by
colored lantern slides. These illustrations were not only helpful but were
also an integral part of the presentation.

Since it proved impractical to scatter them throughout the text, the most
essential slides are included as plates in this volume. They are gathered
together, in the sequence of reference to them, beginning on page 309.—J.C.

the phenomena can we contribute to the solution of problems. This is definitely a limitation.

I will develop four points and reach four conclusions:

First, the cities are already in a severe crisis.

Second, a crisis also exists in the relationship between the city and the university.

Third, we can already see the city of the future.

Fourth, we can already begin to understand the university in relation to the city of the future.

The crisis, I believe, is a crisis of the *whole* system (which we often overlook because we speak about man in crisis, society in crisis, or the university in crisis), and our city is a confused system. We can see how confused it is in the paintings of Jackson Pollock.

Man is in danger; man is confused. We struggle for survival against all the enemies of the system which we have built around us. Thinking in these terms, I was interested to see the signs written by French students during the May (1968) riots: "It is not man but the world that has become abnormal." These words by a French playwright were seen on many walls in Paris and in other cities.

The City Comes to Crisis

If we really believe that the world is abnormal, that the city of man is abnormal, we must try to understand why. Our city is really like a molecule, consisting of the five elements: Nature, Man, Society, Shells (buildings), and Networks (see Plate 1). If we break this molecule, if we fail in solving the problems of one of its elements, the system cannot work.

Humanity has been facing continual crises, as individuals and as society. I believe that for the first time in human history we are facing a crisis of the whole system. For the first time, the structure of the city does not help to solve some of the problems of Man and Society. For the first time, the structure of the city spoils the first and basic element, Nature. This is why we must strive to understand the structure and the operation of the whole system as we understand the human body's anatomical and physiological processes. There are many serious problems because so many fail to see the whole molecule and instead concentrate on one aspect, on one atom, at a time. Specialization has added to the problems of the city.

In order to understand the city better, we must consider the cities which have existed for thousands of years. We can contrast Athens of the classical era (see Plate 2) with the picture of Athens in the frame of the big city of the present (see Plate 3). What was for many thousands of years a basic unit of social life has now become an unimportant small spot within the frame of the average big city of two and a half million people.

It is thus completely wrong to speak about the cities of the past and try to apply all the findings about them to the cities of the present. We still teach our young people to think mostly on the basis of the cities of the past; but the cities which have been created since the seventeenth century are systems which suffer enormously.

Plate 4 shows a city of two and a half million people, expressed as a large and expanding system of basic structure and forces, linked by and growing around the basic transportation networks. Plate 5 shows how the large urban systems suffer from great stresses. The areas which suffer most are the central areas, the inner cities, and the main lines of transportation. People are isolated by buildings and cannot move across the transportation lines. The city is ugly and they draw their curtains in order not to participate in the ugly city's life. We have contaminated the air, polluted the water; we have eliminated human values completely (Plate 5).

For example, in thirty-four years, between 1929 and 1963, the areas covered by motor vehicles in the city shown in Plate 6 have become three times larger. You cannot have safety and security in this area of the city; it can no longer be inspected by only a few policemen. In this way we have created conditions that, especially in the central city, have reached the stage of crisis.

In the period 1940 to 1960, while the American, European, and even African societies, were enjoying higher incomes, the people who lived in the inner city were losing in incomes. A very critical area has been created here, one that can be understood even better if we examine a cross-section as in Plate 7, which shows that incomes drop in the central areas while they rise in the outskirts.

The outward movement of the rich in the average big city is now two yards a day. This movement suggests both the unprecedented size of the system and the speed of the increase. But we still insist on dealing with parts. We do not know the anatomy of the very big city, much less its physiology.

The real maps of the physiology of the city are maps of motor vehicles, because we have been overcome by their influx into the cities. By now, we can be sure that—barring catastrophe—even if we change the policies today, the trends will continue for five to ten years. The large urban systems shown in Plate 4 will suffer much more from stresses; the areas in crisis will multiply and expand.

We can ask ourselves whether we are making a wrong assumption in saying that this phenomenon will get worse. Plate 8 is drawn from a study of the urban Detroit area in 1900 and in 1959. It shows how the urban forces spread into the countryside, how the whole area from Detroit to Bay City, Michigan, has been turned into urban land. Urban decisions which will determine our life for the next generation have already been taken. Even if we look at this phenomenon in a different time scale, from 1950 to 1959 (see Plate 9), we will see that the urban forces were much smaller in 1950 than in 1959, and by now they have spread much more.

Plates 10 and 11 show the Great Lakes area exhibiting the same phenomenon. Between 1920 and 1959 the farming area has been squeezed to less than half its original size some forty years earlier. We are now sure that urban systems grow and turn into huge systems which determine the quality of life for decades to come.

My first conclusion: We are in the midst of a crisis of the whole system of the city. Many of the forces that will define our future are already in full operation.

The Physiology of the Urban University

Second, there is also a crisis in the relationship between the university and the city. This crisis could not be avoided. If the whole system is in a crisis, the relationship with subsystems must, by necessity, also be in crisis. There are several types of relationships between the university and the city. The university both influences and is influenced. But there are most confusing moments in this crisis, as in the student uprisings. Again I refer to what was written on the walls of Paris. "Politics take place in the streets" was one extreme expression of students who wanted to demonstrate. There were also students who wrote on the walls that "the city whose prince is the student" is the city we need to build.

The impact of the university on the city in the large scale of space is beneficial. We have a university or a college in our city. Excellent! But

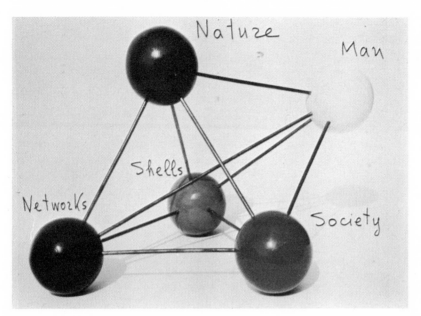

PLATE 1

ATHENS IN THE 5th CENTURY BC

PLATE 2

309

PLATE 3

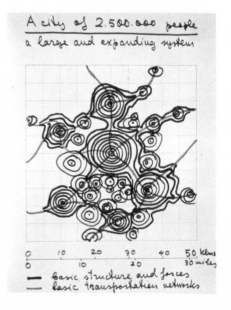

PLATE 4

310

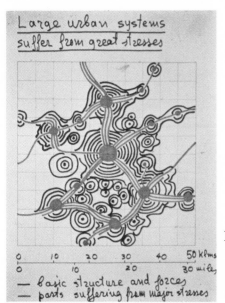

Large urban systems
suffer from great stresses

0   10   20   30   40   50 klms
0   10   20   30 miles

— basic structure and forces
— parts suffering from major stresses

PLATE 5

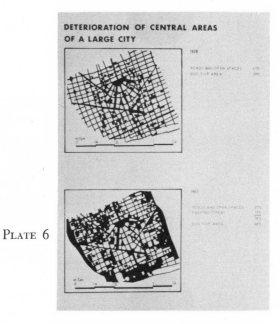

DETERIORATION OF CENTRAL AREAS
OF A LARGE CITY

1929

ROADS AND OPEN SPACES
BUILT-UP AREA

1963

ROADS AND OPEN SPACES
PARKING (OPEN)
BUILT-UP AREA

PLATE 6

311

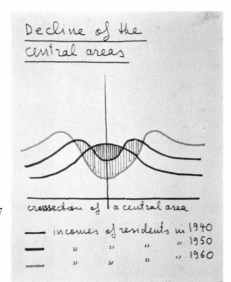

PLATE 7

PLATE 8

312

PLATE 9

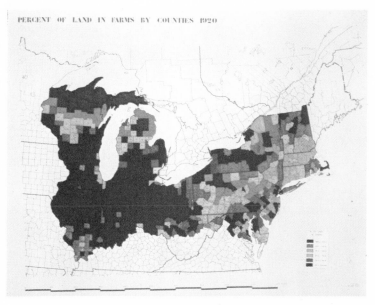

PLATE 10

313

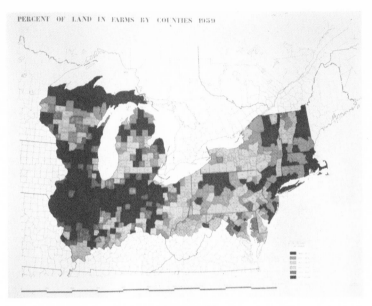

PERCENT OF LAND IN FARMS BY COUNTIES 1959

PLATE 11

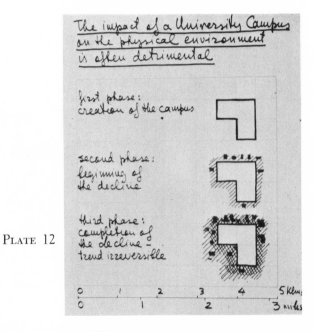

The impact of a University Campus
on the physical environment
is often detrimental

first phase:
creation of the campus

second phase:
beginning of
the decline

third phase:
completion of
the decline —
trend irreversible

PLATE 12

314

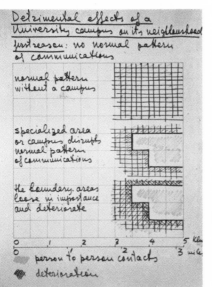

PLATE 13

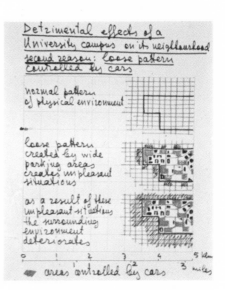

PLATE 14

315

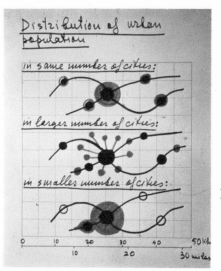

PLATE 15

PLATE 16

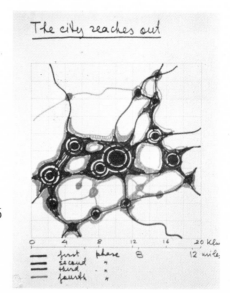

316

PLATE 17

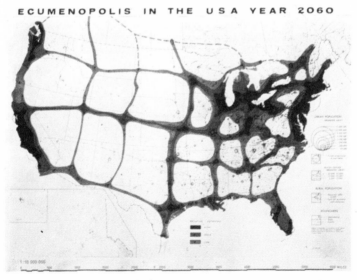

PLATE 18

317

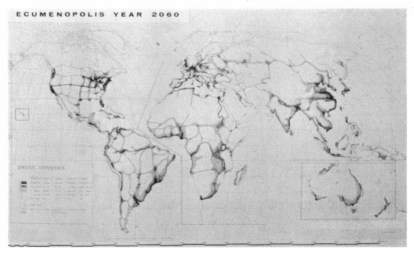

PLATE 19

PLATE 20

318

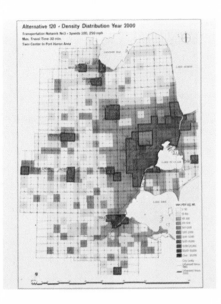

PLATE 21

PLATE 22

319

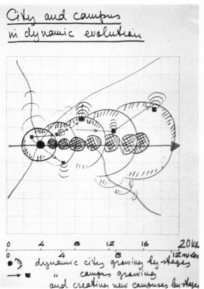

PLATE 23

PLATE 24

320

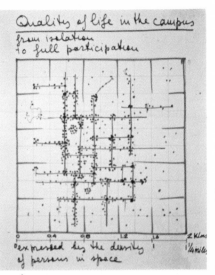

Plate 25

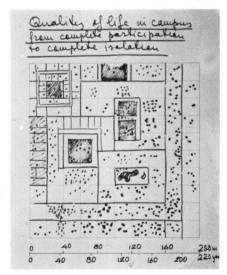

Plate 26

321

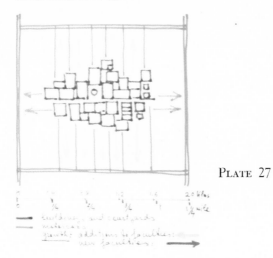

PLATE 27

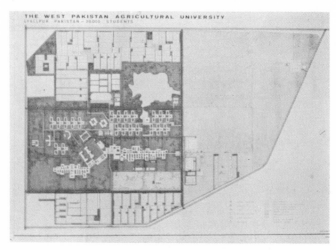

PLATE 28

we should add, excellent, for the large scale of the city. The qualification is needed because if we turn to the physical aspects and look at the small scale, as in Plate 12, we see that the impact of a campus on the physical environment can be detrimental.

When we first create a campus, it has a normal relationship with the city. Later, the surrounding area begins to decline and even later the completion of the decline is an irreversible trend.

Why does this happen? Look at Plate 13. We see first a normal city pattern with communications among people throughout the pattern. But if we insert a specialized area, such as a university, the normal pattern of communications is broken, both the physical pattern and the social pattern. The boundary areas, therefore, lose in importance and deteriorate. There are problems in planning a campus (see Plate 14). In the normal pattern, streets pass through the campus area. But, next, we usually create very strange patterns of isolated buildings, with big areas for parking all around the campus and in its center. In this way, we break the continuity of the urban system, and, as a result, the whole area around deteriorates. Normal patterns are broken again.

The third cause is the dynamic character of the university. In a normal condition, if we knew that the university would not grow, the people around should be happy. But because of the dynamic growth of the university we begin to have a decline in the areas which are in the line of growth. Thus the whole area around the university, including the area where a university may *not* grow, declines.

My second conclusion: The crisis is also in the subsystems and in their relationship with the whole system.

The City in the Future

We must look at the future now because it is too late to look at the present. Any decisions taken today for the city will have an impact five or ten years from now at the earliest. This is why we must both think of the future and change the future.

The first question is about the size of the city. I am asked very often, "Are we going back to the Williamsburgs and the very small cities?"

We have to be realistic. The future population of the world in billions a century from now can be somewhere between 12 billion and 50 billion (minimum and maximum projections). We don't know where we are going, but we do know that we cannot stay at the present level. Biologists tell us we cannot successfully decrease our population unless nuclear weapons help us. But even if we think that this growth is our problem, we make a very grave mistake. What matters is the urban population. The rural population, which today is around 2 billion, will decline slightly. Even in a world of 12 billion people, we will not have four times as many urban problems: we will have ten times as many urban problems. The urban population in a century from now will be ten times larger.

How will this population be distributed? In the same number of cities, in larger numbers of cities, in smaller numbers of cities? Different people, different solutions (Plate 15).

However, certain laws have already dictated what is going to happen. Plate 16 shows that the city (for biological, physiological, and economic reasons) can be seen as an energy system which is constantly reaching out. The expanding cities will be gradually interconnected into the system we call megalopolis, which will become part of an even larger system. I will not attempt here an analysis of the energy system in mathematical terms, but there is no doubt that the system grows as a system of energy.

In 2018, you will celebrate the one hundredth anniversary of the American Council on Education. Then the United States will have a population on the order of 550 million people, of which 93 percent will be urban, versus 205 million today, with 79 percent urban. If you think this is crazy, note that the growth from 1918, when the American Council on Education was established, was even larger, for then the density of the urban population was only 50 percent. By the year 2000 we believe that in the United States the urban population will look as in Plate 17. The system is mostly an eastern-western megalopolis, with the California and Florida portions interconnected by urban branches and areas of higher density.

Plate 18 shows the probable map of the United States in the year 2060, given present trends. Plate 19 shows the probable map of the world. If anyone says, "How abnormal!" I will answer, "How abnormal that Theseus created the City of Athens and humanity moved to the cities." There is nothing to prove that broader systems of society are more abnormal than those of the present time.

These greater systems will remain inevitable as long as humanity believes in two very basic principles—the freedom of an individual in a democracy to move where he likes, and the belief in human development and in the right of people to be near the centers of education, which will become even more important in the future. Our country already consists of major urban systems, each spreading 80 to 100 miles, comprising almost 99 percent of the American population. These are the areas within which people will commute in the next ten years. In this system we must have an interchange of services.

Granted that these are the forces, are we going to fold our hands and do nothing? Whatever we do, we cannot alter these forces; but we can develop something, and this something is the quality of the city that will be created. We cannot reasonably think that we can escape from the big city; analysis proves we cannot escape. But there is no reason why the big city should be inhuman, as it is now. We must now move in a realistic direction, recognize the forces that humanity has created, and try to guide them for the formation of a much more human surrounding, one that could enrich the city and make it more beautiful than the Florence of Michelangelo and more human than ancient democratic Athens.

How can this be done? The answer lies in creating systems which will consist of cells, each cell representing the values of the old cities that humanity has learned to build by trial and error over thousands of years, and the whole system operating as one. In Plate 20, nature has been infiltrated into the larger system of the city of the future. It is a real challenge to organize this broad system; our task is to find the corresponding structure.

After a study of the urban Detroit area, the 49 million alternatives which exist for the year 2000 were considered, and by elimination of the weakest and the unacceptable ones, we came to the conclusion what type of urban system would serve man best. Plate 21 shows Detroit and the Twin City that modern analysis led us to. This is the solution which will operate in the best possible way mechanically, as a whole system, and humanly in the small unit.

This kind of system can guarantee both continuity and change. The effort to create new small towns or cities, an effort which is so fashionable now, is an effort of escape. But the escape, even if it leads to temporary success and causes people to abandon the big city, will lead to disaster for the whole system. We should not escape from our system; we should develop a system guaranteeing this continuity and change.

Every square of the new city of Islamabad, Pakistan, corresponds to Paris, London, Jerusalem, or Athens within their ancient walls. These famous cities of the past define the unit we have to respect. If we do so, we will gradually develop the ability to create great cities.

Plate 22 shows a square of the size of Athens or of Florence which is a new sector in Islamabad. The cars are limited to large specialized areas, and the children and the people are free to walk in between. Children can go to school without crossing the street. People can walk to their office or to their shopping center. The city can have squares which are beautiful, with no parking on the surface.

My third conclusion: We are by now convinced that we can build the human city within a frame which is extrahuman in dimensions.

The University in the City of the Future

The challenge is a dynamic city and a dynamic university. The dynamic city is growing (Plate 23). We think of the university as growing in several directions and spreading into new campuses so that it can serve the dynamic system. If we think of the university as the system of the "learning mechanism," we can see that in the future it will play a role that will become gradually more important than the system of commerce and trade.

Today our cities are still organized on the basis of the system of commerce and trade where we have most of the employment. Gradually we can develop education more systematically; in the long run it will employ many more people, it will take many more hours of our life than commerce and trade today.

Can one organism operate on the basis of two systems? Look at our body, at the difference between the digestive and the nervous system. There is no reason why inorganic life cannot have organisms operating on the basis of two or more systems. With such considerations in mind we can answer, from the organizational point of view, the question of the correct location of the centers of the learning mechanism by saying we need them everywhere, but they must be properly organized and properly connected by lines of transportation (Plate 24).

I cannot yet accept the campus which operates with a car connecting its parts. If the pedestrian is to develop all of his capacities, he must not have to worry about the green and red lights, but be able to think while walking. Thus we have a maximum dimension for a campus—one and a quarter miles by one and a quarter miles so that the inner part of the campus can be controlled completely by the pedestrian, who will walk at most three-quarters of a mile (or ten minutes) between classes. This was the condition which defined the dimensions of all the cities of man which we admire, until the seventeenth century.

Within such a campus I think we are obliged to create a quality which will guarantee isolation as well as full participation. Plate 25 shows a campus with places of high density and places of low density. We have overlooked, I think, the isolated garden. We should not forget the importance of isolating ourselves in small gardens. In Plate 26, in a smaller scale now, one-tenth of the previous one, we see the interplay of long corridors, halls, buildings, and smaller green places, with varying densities—a point of very great importance to increase the quality of life.

We must begin to understand what kind of boundaries we need between the city and the campus. Plate 27 shows the dynamic growth of a university campus in two dimensions: growing within its surrounding transportation system and adding new learning resources in one direction and new facilities for existing functions in the other. Plate 28 is an example of a dynamic university.

My fourth conclusion: We can build, in spite of all the difficulties, a university for continuity and change.

The question now is how to proceed. We must have final goals in a proper frame of space and time. We have to be realistic about the city, and we can be realistic about the university. We need a new science, which we call "Ekistics," and we need to learn the relationship of the subsystems to the system.

Again, it is encouraging to quote the Paris students: "The revolution must occur within men before it can be achieved in action." At this very great moment of anarchy (this was a big sign scrawled at the Sorbonne), people were thinking about the need to change our mental attitude before we start revolutionary action.

Another of these signs said: "The action should not be a reaction but a creation," and this was written on a wall in the middle of Paris. We must create not only the city where the prince is the student, but also the city where the prince is every citizen, where every citizen feels like a prince because we have provided him with an organized structure guaranteeing him the maximum of freedom; where the artist can express in his way the harmony of life in the city and where the philosopher and the scientist contribute in the same way as the artist to freedom for all.

AMERICAN COUNCIL ON EDUCATION

LOGAN WILSON, *President*

The American Council on Education, founded in 1918, is a *council* of educational organizations and institutions. Its purpose is to advance education and educational methods through comprehensive voluntary and cooperative action on the part of American educational associations, organizations, and institutions.

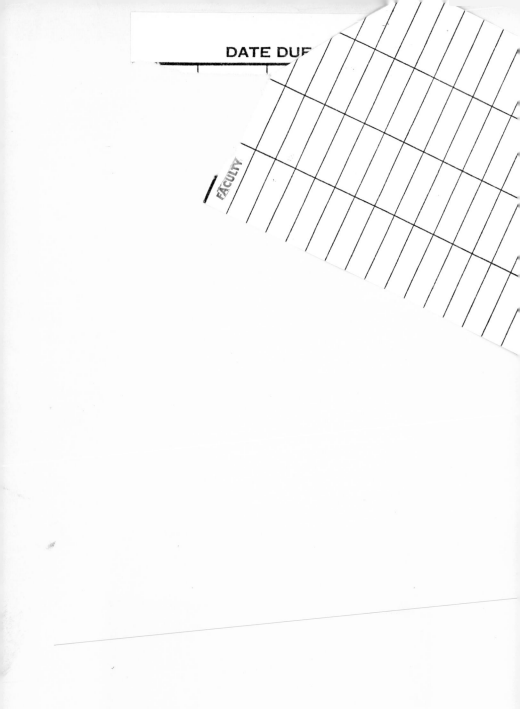

DATE DUE

FACULTY